2019-2020 Edition

SAT Guide
Reading Strategy

PREPVANTAGE

ISBN-13: 978-1731085214

Visit us at **PrepVantageTutoring.com**

SAT Guide: Reading Strategy, 2019-2020 Edition
Copyright © 2019 PrepVantage Publishing

ISBN-13: 978-1731085214

Table of Contents

Introduction: Reading Fundamentals

Initial Assessment: Testing, Skills, and Scoring

Part 1: Major Issue Questions

Continues on the next page

Part 2: Passage Detail Questions

Part 3: Command of Evidence

Part 4: Word in Context

Part 5: Paired Passages

Introduction

SAT Reading
Test Overview

Introduction
Reading Test Overview

Test Fundamentals

With the 2016 re-design of the entire SAT, test-takers were presented with a Reading section that follows a highly predictable structure. Each SAT Reading test features the same five passage types and the same question areas, all in combinations that have experienced only minimal changes in three years since the first re-designed full tests appeared.

SAT Reading: Full Structure

Timing	Test Length	Passage Types	Question Areas	Special Features
65 Minutes	52 Questions 3250 Words for ALL Passages	One Fiction (10 Questions)	Major Issue	Always ONE Paired Passage Set (either Science or History Documents)
		One Social Studies (10-11 Questions)	Passage Detail	
		One Historical Document (10-11 Questions)	Command of Evidence	Always TWO Passages with Visuals (Social Studies and ONE Science)
		Two Science (10-11 Questions EACH)	Word in Context	
			Passage Comparison	
			Graphics and Visuals	

Introduction: SAT Reading Overview

Although the test displays considerable range in terms of passage types and question types, taking the test itself can become supremely predictable with the right amount of practice. As you will soon see, passages occur in a mostly fixed order, and questions occur in mostly fixed proportions. Moreover, the testing task itself is designed to test the same mindset on every single SAT administered.

> ## The Reading Section will ALWAYS test comprehension, logic, and attention to detail.

The primary goal, with most passages, is to retain useful information on an initial read-through—and then to work with precise textual details and mostly straightforward logic in order to answer the questions. Although strengthening your vocabulary can definitely help with some passage types, the test is PRIMARILY evidence-based. Other types of analysis and background are of almost no use at all.

> ## Personal assessment, creative interpretation, and outside knowledge are NEVER tested.

If you are accustomed to actively evaluating what you have read or to ingeniously "reading between the lines" as part of your normal coursework, you must learn to abandon these habits for the sake of the SAT Reading section. On occasion, though, having strong opinions about a passage can help you to remember it more effectively. Something similar can be said regarding outside knowledge: if you know about a topic that appears on the SAT, you may automatically find it more accessible. Using assessments and outside knowledge in this manner—to aid basic comprehension—is the ONLY effective use of these skills here, since any other use may cause you to deviate from the EXACT evidence that a passage requires you to consider.

Passage Types

Each SAT Reading test will consist of the same five passage types, as designated by topic. The order in which these appear is open to only a single and fairly minor variation, as shown below.

1. Fiction

2. Social Studies or History

3. Science

4. Social Studies or History

5. Science

Keep in mind that each test will have one Social Studies and one History passage; while the earliest College Board tests always placed Social Studies as the second passage and History as the fourth, this order was flipped with some regularity on the 2017-2018 administered tests. Just be aware of these facts if you do eventually determine a preferred order for completing the passages.

Regardless of topic, all passages will run between 500 and 750 words. All passages will also feature the same few question types, and each type should be approached in roughly the same way regardless of a passage's subject and difficulty.

Question Types

Major Issue

Questions about the overarching issues in a passage—purpose, main points, themes, structure—are typically the first few questions that follow the passage itself. Since you have 65 minutes for a total of 52 questions, you should DEFINITELY have enough time to read all of the passages in full if you pace yourself properly. Use such reading to figure out some of the main issues BEFORE you are directly asked about them, and to determine whether there are any shifts in topic, position, or writing strategy that are worth noting.

Major Issue questions are, in at least one way, topic sensitive. The types of details that you should read for and the passage structures that you should be familiar with do vary from one passage type to another. For instance, while History passages often call upon readers to understand the repercussions and counter-arguments that surround socio-political issues, Science passages will in many cases rely on statistical information. However, the necessity of finding and logically analyzing evidence NEVER varies, for this or any other question area.

Passage Detail

Passage Detail questions cover a range of issues—tone, characterization, inference, how a writing device functions, how a paragraph is structured. These questions are nonetheless connected by format (since they call attention to precise line references, or to details that are highly localized) and by strategy (logical prediction based on passage content, then process of elimination). It will not always be easy to see at first glance how a passage detail—which may feature dozens of lines or require considerable reading around—is meant to be understood. However, careful work with evidence can help you to focus and to work step-by-step towards the only appropriate answer.

Command of Evidence

The questions classified under Command of Evidence are something of a special feature of the current SAT: neither the pre-2016 SAT nor the current ACT features a consistent equivalent. Some of these (Single Command of Evidence) will be consolidated questions that begin with a phrase such as "Which line reference . . . " and require you to decide which line reference best supports a specific idea or inference. The remainder (Paired Command of Evidence) will consist of linked questions: an initial question that reads like a Passage Detail question, and a second question introduced by the sentence "Which choice provides the best evidence for the answer to the previous question?" and accompanied by four line references for answers. These two questions MUST be solved together for the sake of clarity and precision.

Introduction: SAT Reading Overview

You can always expect roughly 15-20 Command of Evidence questions, some single and some paired. Of these, 10 will feature answer choices that are nothing but line references, while the rest will be initial questions that are linked to line reference choices.

Word in Context

Any question that opens with the phrasing "As used in line [#], [WORD/PHRASE] most nearly means . . ." should be automatically understood as a Word in Context question. Your task with this topic area is to analyze a word that takes on multiple possible meanings or contexts in standard English—all in order to determine which meaning the passage is utilizing. Although the words themselves are not always strange or obscure, these questions can challenge your ability to work through multiple possibilities and conscientiously eliminate those that are not supported by a close reading.

You can expect to see 10 Word in Context questions on a typical SAT Reading section, yet there have been exceptions to this formatting. On some College Board tests, there are fewer than 10 questions that take the classic "As used in line . . ." form described above—and there are additional Passage Details questions that focus on individual words or phrases. Do not be disoriented by such disparities. Simply solve each question type on its own terms.

Paired Passage Questions

Every SAT Reading test will feature ONE Paired Passage (either History or one of the Science readings). These linked passages may agree with or build upon one another, though with some regularity they present contrasting or conflicting perspectives on a single issue. Your task is NEVER to side with one author or the other (even though some of the authors in the SAT History readings do put forward outdated and unappealing opinions). Instead, you must understand how the passages relate to one another, and may need to draw logical conclusions about how one author would respond to the other on the basis of the available evidence.

Like questions about visuals, questions that ask about both passages will normally occur near the end of a question set. Note that it IS possible for a Paired Passage to be accompanied by visuals; in such a case, you will need to coordinate a considerable amount of information when you reach the final questions.

Visuals Questions

On any given SAT Reading test, TWO passages (Social Studies and one of the Science readings) will be accompanied by visuals or graphics. These visuals can be tables, graphs, charts, maps, or some combination. You will need to deal with two or three Visuals questions per passage, and the questions will ask you to either 1) analyze visual information on its own terms or 2) analyze visual information while taking into account information from the passage. Normally, questions about visuals will be the last items to accompany a passage.

Next Step: Diagnostic Test

Now that you know exactly what will appear on the SAT Reading section, put your skills to the test with the fully-formatted Diagnostic section that begins on the next page. The best way to run this section is as follows.

- Complete the section under the official 65-minute timing.

- If you do not finish at the 65-minute mark, note how far you got, then complete your remaining questions.

- Check your work using the Answer Key

- Complete the Self-Evaluation Checklists

- Consult the Answer Explanations that accompany the Answer Key

Of special importance here are the Self-Evaluation checklists. Even if you are working with a tutor, you should be subjecting each SAT Reading section to rigorous examination to determine BOTH your strengths and weaknesses. The checklists will help you to decide what areas of your approach should be preserved as effective, and which ones require refinement or re-thinking.

- Passage Types
- Question Types
- Vocabulary

- Pacing and Timing
- Annotating the Passages
- Notes and Elimination for Questions

Additional copies of the checklists—which should be used well into your practice—are available online at prepvantagetutoring.com/reading. Yet for the time being, see what the Diagnostic Test and a conscientious self-analysis can teach you.

Reading Test

65 MINUTES, 52 QUESTIONS

Turn to Section 1 of your answer sheet to answer the questions in this section.

Questions 1-10 are based on the following passage.

This passage is adapted from Anton Chekhov, "The Grasshopper." Published in 1892 and translated from the original Russian in this version by Constance Garnett.

Olga Ivanovna was twenty-two; Dymov was thirty-one. They got on splendidly together when they were married. Olga Ivanovna hung

Line all her drawing-room walls with her own and
5 other people's sketches, in frames and without frames, and near the piano and furniture arranged picturesque corners with Japanese parasols, easels, daggers, busts, photographs, and rags of many colours . . . In the dining-room she papered the
10 walls with peasant woodcuts, hung up bark shoes and sickles, stood in a corner a scythe and a rake, and so achieved a dining-room in the Russian style. In her bedroom she draped the ceiling and the walls with dark cloths to make it like a cavern,
15 hung a Venetian lantern over the beds, and at the door set a figure with a halberd. And every one thought that the young people had a very charming little home.

When she got up at eleven o'clock every
20 morning, Olga Ivanovna played the piano or, if it were sunny, painted something in oils. Then between twelve and one she drove to her dressmaker's. As Dymov and she had very little money, only just enough, she and her dressmaker
25 were often put to clever shifts to enable her to appear constantly in new dresses and make a sensation with them. Very often out of an old dyed dress, out of bits of tulle, lace, plush, and silk, costing nothing, perfect marvels were created,
30 something bewitching—not a dress, but a dream . . . She sang, she played the piano, she painted in oils, she carved, she took part in amateur performances; and all this not just anyhow, but all with talent, whether she made lanterns for an
35 illumination or dressed up or tied somebody's cravat—everything she did was exceptionally graceful, artistic, and charming. But her talents showed themselves in nothing so clearly as in her faculty for quickly becoming acquainted and on
40 intimate terms with celebrated people. No sooner did any one become ever so little celebrated, and set people talking about him, than she made his acquaintance, got on friendly terms the same day, and invited him to her house. Every new

CONTINUE

45 acquaintance she made was a veritable fête* for
    her. She adored celebrated people, was proud of
    them, dreamed of them every night. She craved
    for them, and never could satisfy her craving. The
    old ones departed and were forgotten, new ones
50 came to replace them, but to these, too, she soon
    grew accustomed or was disappointed in them,
    and began eagerly seeking for fresh great men,
    finding them and seeking for them again. What
    for?

55   Between four and five she dined at home with
    her husband. His simplicity, good sense, and
    kind-heartedness touched her and moved her up
    to enthusiasm. She was constantly jumping up,
    impulsively hugging his head and showering
60 kisses on it.

        "You are a clever, generous man, Dymov," she
    used to say, "but you have one very serious defect.
    You take absolutely no interest in art. You don't
    believe in music or painting."

65   "I don't understand them," he would say
    mildly. "I have spent all my life in working at
    natural science and medicine, and I have never
    had time to take an interest in the arts."

        "But, you know, that's awful, Dymov!"

70   "Why so? Your friends don't know anything
    of science or medicine, but you don't reproach
    them with it. Every one has his own line. I don't
    understand landscapes and operas, but the way
    I look at it is that if one set of sensible people
75 devote their whole lives to them, and other
    sensible people pay immense sums for them, they
    must be of use. I don't understand them, but not
    understanding does not imply disbelieving in
    them."

80   "Let me shake your honest hand!"

        After dinner Olga Ivanovna would drive off to
    see her friends, then to a theatre or to a concert,
    and she returned home after midnight. So it was
    every day.

---

*A pleasant occasion; a celebration or festivity

1

One of the important themes present in the passage
is that

A) pleasing conditions may nonetheless be
   accompanied by desires that are impossible to
   satisfy.

B) excessive wealth has a tendency to distort a
   person's priorities in ways that are difficult to
   foresee.

C) people who frequently misunderstand one another
   may still form close bonds.

D) the appearance of happiness can mask a craving
   for fundamental changes.

2

The passage as a whole characterizes Olga as

A) earnest and inexperienced.

B) affectionate and extravagant.

C) sociable and energetic.

D) thoughtful and meek.

3

The first paragraph serves mainly to describe how

A) one character altered her surroundings in a
   manner that met with approval.

B) one character assigned a series of meaningful
   decisions to a second character.

C) one character reinvented a setting as an
   expression of her unique personality.

D) two characters developed a collaborative method
   for making improvements to their household.

CONTINUE

4

As used in line 25, "clever shifts" most nearly means

A) practiced movements.

B) resourceful decisions.

C) wise evasions.

D) unexpected transitions.

5

As used in line 52, "fresh" most nearly means

A) lively.

B) forthright.

C) different.

D) sudden.

6

As described in the passage, Olga often reacts to Dymov in a manner that can best be described as

A) quietly sarcastic.

B) intensely admiring.

C) playfully uncomprehending.

D) instinctively loyal.

7

Which choice provides the best evidence for the answer to the previous question?

A) Lines 23-27 ("As Dymov . . . them")

B) Lines 56-58 ("His . . . enthusiasm")

C) Lines 58-60 ("She was . . . on it")

D) Line 80 ("Let me . . . hand!")

8

Dymov's statement in line 72 ("Everyone . . . line") mainly functions as

A) an elaboration of Dymov's viewpoint.

B) a reference to Olga's past experience.

C) an admission of a flaw in Dymov's reasoning.

D) a criticism of Olga's friends.

9

Which choice best supports the idea that Dymov values pursuits that he does not fully comprehend?

A) Lines 66-68 ("I have . . . the arts")

B) Lines 70-72 ("Your . . . with it")

C) Lines 72-77 ("I don't . . . use")

D) Lines 77-79 ("I don't . . . them")

10

The final sentence of the passage serves primarily to indicate that

A) Olga is eager to make changes in her way of living.

B) the reader is meant to see the passage's characters as unwilling to change.

C) Dymov and Olga are not fully aware of the psychological effects of their marriage.

D) the passage as a whole describes a predictable lifestyle.

CONTINUE

Questions 11-20 are based on the following passage and supplementary material.

This passage is adapted from Deanne Dunbar, "Country Food Sharing in the Canadian Arctic: Does It Feed the Neediest?" Originally published* in 2018 in *Worth a Thousand Words*.

About 750 Inuit call Kangiqsujuaq (Nunavik, Canada) on Quebec's Ungava Peninsula their remote, arctic home. Because there are no roads
Line to their community, the Kangiqsujuarmiuts hunt,
5 fish, and forage for most of their food. Arctic char, caribou, and seal account for about 58% of total meat intake in the village and are considered "country foods." The sale of country foods is prohibited by the land claim agreement in the
10 region. Therefore, a Kangiqsujuarmiut must be able to harvest these foods individually or access them through a food-sharing network.

Historically, indigenous populations in the difficult subsistence environments of the
15 Arctic have had strong social norms around the sharing of food. However, exactly how food sharing networks facilitate the flow of resources throughout the community has not been well studied. Over the next 30 years, climate models
20 suggest that coastal erosion and melting sea ice will have major impacts on food security in this region by disrupting the availability of and access to the traditional Inuit dietary staples. Therefore, it is important to understand how food sharing
25 buffers modern hunter-gatherer populations like the Kangiqsujuarmiut from climate change risk.

To shed light on these questions, anthropologist Elspeth Ready from the University of Nebraska-Lincoln spent a year in Kangiqsujuaq examining
30 the size, quality, and density of the food sharing networks of 109 households in the village. She asked each to list its most important food sharing partners, measured household harvest production over the year (in kilocalories), and
35 calculated household wealth by counting the number of all-terrain vehicles, snowmobiles, cars/

trucks, fishing boats, and freighter canoes owned by the household.

From the data collected, Ready was able to
40 construct a food sharing network model for the community, composed of 500 unique ties among 109 households of varying harvest levels. She found a mean of 4.54 ties per household for both giving and receiving, although ties per household
45 ranged from 0 to 32 ties for giving and 0 to 16 ties for receiving. Interestingly, households that had more out-going food sharing ties also had more incoming ties. In fact, giving away food was the strongest predictor of a large network size.

50 The ability of Inuit households to participate in food harvesting activities is highly dependent upon access to land, cash, and equipment as well as individual harvesting knowledge, interest, and ability. Villagers who cannot access land or do not
55 harvest food on their own—such as single women with dependents and elders—had the largest food sharing networks in the village. However, single women's networks were of slightly lower quality, and were comprised of fewer ties to high harvest
60 households. Surprisingly, the main driver of food sharing behavior in Kangiqsujuaq was not "trickle-down" sharing, whereby those with lower wealth or harvest production receive food from higher harvest households. Instead, Ready found
65 that reciprocity and kinship ties between high harvest households were the principal driver for food-sharing. The study results therefore suggest that households with lower wealth and harvest production may also be less able to access country
70 foods through sharing networks.

Ready's important research sheds light on how, why, and when food sharing networks buffer households from resource shocks. If food resources do not "trickle-down" through
75 sharing networks to households in need, this may mean that low resource households will be more vulnerable to changes in food availability associated with climate change. In 2013-2014, 41% of Kangiqsujuarmiut had low or very low
80 food security. Poverty and food insecurity are serious social problems in Kangiqsujuaq that may only be partially addressed by traditional food

*See Page 36 for the citation for this text.

CONTINUE

sharing institutions. In the coming years, this remote northern community will see additional
85 challenges that promise to impact the dynamics of food sharing networks—climate change, population growth, health transitions, and further integration with the cash economy. Ready's study offers a critically important lesson: traditional
90 food sharing institutions may not buffer the most vulnerable members of indigenous communities against climate-based challenges to subsistence resources, despite a strong regional ethic of mutual aid.

11

The main purpose of the passage is to

A) propose a new method for addressing a problem faced by a traditional community.

B) survey the advantages and drawbacks of the methods utilized by an important researcher.

C) offer an overview of an anthropological study and present a few implications of the research.

D) examine how research involving one community can yield broad insights about traditional food sharing.

12

Which choice best indicates that Ready's work on food networks in Kangiqsujuaq had few effective or meaningful precedents?

A) Lines 16-19 ("However . . . studied")

B) Lines 23-26 ("Therefore . . . risk")

C) Lines 39-41 ("From . . . community")

D) Lines 71-73 ("Ready's . . . shocks")

13

One important phase of Ready's study relied upon

A) open-ended interviews with Kangiqsujuarmiut community leaders.

B) data directly recorded and provided by various households in Kangiqsujuaq.

C) comparison of worldwide climate change models and statistics from Kangiqsujuaq.

D) investigation of dietary changes in the most prominent Kangiqsujuaq households.

Number of Individuals Per Group, Four Food-Sharing Tiers

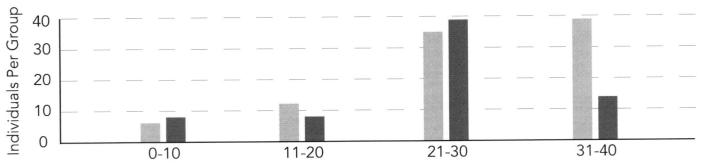

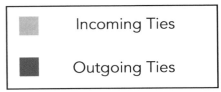

CONTINUE

14

As used in line 53, "individual" most nearly means

A) liberated.

B) eccentric.

C) isolated.

D) personal.

15

On the basis of the passage, a Kangiqsujuarmiut with a vast food-sharing network is most likely to

A) withhold assistance from the community's most prosperous households.

B) treat food-sharing as a charitable rather than a pragmatic activity.

C) store excess food in anticipation of hardship.

D) donate food to other households on a regular basis.

16

Which choice provides the best evidence for the answer to the previous question?

A) Lines 48-49 ("In fact . . . size")

B) Lines 54-57 ("Villagers . . . village")

C) Lines 60-64 ("Surprisingly . . . households")

D) Lines 73-78 ("If food . . . change")

17

As used in line 82, "addressed" most nearly means

A) denounced.

B) acknowledged.

C) lessened in severity.

D) described in detail.

18

The final paragraph of the passage mainly describes

A) a series of additional research possibilities suggested by Ready's completed work.

B) a presumed weakness in Ready's methods that has since proven to be one of her study's strengths.

C) a social arrangement that has proven valuable but that does not guarantee prosperity or stability.

D) a series of conversations related to current economic practices in Kangiqsujuaq.

19

According to the chart, which of the following groups would represent the largest number of individuals?

A) 0-20 Incoming Ties

B) 0-20 Outgoing Ties

C) 21-30 Incoming Ties

D) 21-30 Outgoing Ties

20

One of the factors that is explicitly addressed in Ready's study as described the passage but NOT in the accompanying graph is

A) a given household's incoming ties.

B) a given household's outgoing ties.

C) the role of gender in food-sharing networks.

D) the role of local political influence in food sharing networks.

CONTINUE

Questions 21-30 are based on the following passage.

This passage is adapted from "Bigger human brain prioritizes thinking hub—at a cost." Published by the National Institutes of Health* in May 2018.

Some human brains are nearly twice the size of others—but how might that matter? Researchers at the National Institute of Mental Health (NIMH)
Line and their NIH grant-funded colleagues have
5 discovered that these differences in size are related to the brain's shape and the way it is organized. The bigger the brain, the more its additional area is accounted for by growth in thinking areas of the cortex, or outer mantle—at the expense of
10 relatively slower growth in lower order emotional, sensory, and motor areas.

This mirrors the pattern of brain changes seen in evolution and individual development—with higher-order areas showing greatest expansion.
15 The researchers also found evidence linking the high-expanding regions to higher connectivity between neurons and higher energy consumption.

"Just as different parts are required to scale-up a garden shed to the size of a mansion, it seems
20 that big primate brains have to be built to different proportions," explained Armin Raznahan, M.D., Ph.D., of the NIMH Intramural Research Program (IRP). "An extra investment has to be made in the part that integrates information—but that's not
25 to say that it's better to have a bigger brain. Our findings speak more to the different organizational needs of larger vs. smaller brains."

Raznahan, P.K. Reardon, Jakob Seidlitz, and colleagues at more than six collaborating research
30 centers report on their study incorporating brain scan data from more than 3,000 people in *Science*. Reardon and Seidlitz are students in the NIH Oxford-Cambridge Scholars Program.

To pinpoint how the human brain's
35 organization varies in relation to how big it is, the researchers—including teams from the University of Pennsylvania, Philadelphia, and Yale University, New Haven, Connecticut, as

well as the Douglas Mental Health University
40 Institute, Verdun, Québec—analyzed magnetic resonance imaging brain scans of youth from the Philadelphia Neurodevelopmental Cohort, a NIMH IRP sample, and the Human Connectome Project.
45 Cortex areas showing relatively more expansion in larger brains sit at the top of a network hierarchy and are specialized functionally, microstructurally, and molecularly at integrating information from lower order systems.
50 Since this theme holds up across evolution, development, and inter-individual variation, it appears to be a deeply ingrained biological signature, Raznahan suggested.

"Not all cortex regions are created equal. The
55 high-expanding regions seem to exact a higher biological cost," explained Raznahan. "There's biological 'money' being spent to grow that extra tissue. These regions seem to be greedier in consuming energy; they use relatively more
60 oxygenated blood than low-expanding regions. Gene expression related to energy metabolism is also higher in these regions. It's expensive, and nature is unlikely to spend unless it's getting a return on its investment."
65 Since people with certain mental disorders show alterations in brain size related to genetic influences, the new cortex maps may improve understanding of altered brain organization in disorders. The higher expanding regions are also
70 implicated across diverse neurodevelopmental disorders, so the new insights may hold clues to understanding how genetic and environmental changes can impact higher mental functions.

"Our study shows there are consistent
75 organizational changes between large brains and small brains," said Raznahan. "Observing that the brain needs to consistently configure itself differently as a function of its size is important for understanding how the brain functions in health
80 and disease states."

"Notably, we saw the same patterns for scaled-up brains across three large independent datasets," noted Seidlitz.

---

*See Page 36 for the citation for this text.

CONTINUE ➡

21

The passage as a whole describes a study that

A) overturned a scientifically plausible yet ultimately flawed approach to classifying brains based on size.

B) uncovered data that will help to correct popular misconceptions intellect, memory, and brain size.

C) used psychological research to arrive at a new set of procedures for treating neurological disorders.

D) established connections between factors such as brain size, energy expenditure, and cognitive ability.

22

On the basis of the passage, the research pursued by Raznahan and his colleagues is premised on the idea that

A) the structure of the human brain is radically different from the structure of the brain of any other animal.

B) large brain size correlates to both higher cognitive ability and shorter lifespan.

C) organisms of the same species can exhibit significant differences in brain size.

D) animal species that don't rely on physical strength for survival normally develop relatively large brains.

23

As used in line 7, "additional" most nearly means

A) substitute.

B) sequenced.

C) superfluous.

D) supplementary.

24

In describing his research, Raznahan makes use of

A) emphatic language that hints that earlier researchers were misguided.

B) anecdotes and recollections that make his ideas more accessible to a large audience.

C) an analogy that helps to explain a neurological process central to his inquiry.

D) general statements that are meant to spur meaningful debate.

25

Which choice provides the best evidence for the answer to the previous question?

A) Lines 23-25 ("An extra . . . brain")

B) Line 54 ("Not all . . . equal")

C) Lines 56-58 ("There's . . . tissue")

D) Lines 74-76 ("Our study . . . brains")

26

The main purpose of lines 28-44 ("Raznahan . . . project") is to

A) suggest that specialized research such as Raznahan's is nonetheless easy to comprehend.

B) underscore the wide-ranging and cooperative nature of Raznahan's project.

C) show the ways in which the project led by Raznahan built upon earlier efforts.

D) explain the benefits of a multi-disciplinary approach to neurological science.

CONTINUE

27

What does the passage indicate about the "Cortex areas" mentioned in line 45?

A) Their size as a proportion of body mass is fairly consistent across species that have successfully adapted to changes in environmental conditions.

B) Their size can be indirectly measured by administering intelligence exams to test subjects.

C) They are less dense and more fragile than are other areas of the brain.

D) They exhibit higher energy consumption than do other areas of the brain.

28

Which choice provides the best evidence for the answer to the previous question?

A) Lines 50-53 ("Since . . . suggested")

B) Lines 58-60 ("These regions . . . regions")

C) Lines 69-71 ("The higher . . . disorders")

D) Lines 81-83 ("Notably . . . Seidlitz")

29

As used in line 70, "implicated" most nearly means

A) secondary.

B) significant.

C) suggestive.

D) submissive.

30

Which of the following findings would most clearly CONTRADICT the primary findings of the study described in the passage?

A) The quickest-growing areas of the brain can take over functions often assigned to slower-growing areas.

B) The typical neurodevelopmental disease renders the brain completely incapable of growing or changing.

C) The regions of the brain that govern higher-order thinking can experience unusually high growth rates in the brains of subjects who have psychological disorders.

D) The growth of brain regions related to analysis and problem solving can lead to impaired physical coordination.

CONTINUE

Questions 31-41 are based on the following passages.

Passage 1 is adapted from a speech on the Compromise of 1850 delivered by Senator Henry Clay of Kentucky; Passage 2 is from a speech on the same issue delivered by Senator John C. Calhoun of South Carolina. The Compromise itself was designed to deal with a series of nationwide tensions involving slavery. Under the terms of this measure, some of which were perceived as placing the states of the American South at a disadvantage, California was allowed to enter the Union as a free state.

Passage 1

In all such measures of compromise, one party would be very glad to get what he wants, and reject what he does not desire but which the
Line other party wants. But when he comes to reflect
5 that, from the nature of the government and its operations, and from those with whom he is dealing, it is necessary upon his part, in order to secure what he wants, to grant something to the other side, he should be reconciled to the
10 concession which he has made in consequence of the concession which he is to receive, if there is no great principle involved, such as a violation of the Constitution of the United States. I admit that such a compromise as that ought never to
15 be sanctioned or adopted. But I now call upon any senator in his place to point out from the beginning to the end, from California to New Mexico, a solitary provision in this bill which is violative of the Constitution of the United States.
20 The responsibility of this great measure passes from the hands of the committee, and from my hands. They know, and I know, that it is an awful and tremendous responsibility. I hope that you will meet it with a just conception and a true
25 appreciation of its magnitude, and the magnitude of the consequences that may ensue from your decision one way or the other. The alternatives, I fear, which the measure presents, are concord and increased discord . . . I believe from the
30 bottom of my soul that the measure is the reunion of this Union. I believe it is the dove of peace, which, taking its aerial flight from the dome of the Capitol, carries the glad tidings of assured peace and restored harmony to all the remotest
35 extremities of this distracted land. I believe that it will be attended with all these beneficent effects. And now let us discard all resentment, all passions, all petty jealousies, all personal desires, all love of place, all hankerings after the gilded
40 crumbs which fall from the table of power. Let us forget popular fears, from whatever quarter they may spring. Let us go to the limpid fountain of unadulterated patriotism, and, performing a solemn lustration, return divested of all selfish,
45 sinister, and sordid impurities, and think alone of our God, our country, our consciences, and our glorious Union—that Union without which we shall be torn into hostile fragments, and sooner or later become the victims of military despotism or
50 foreign domination . . .

Passage 2

It is time, senators, that there should be an open and manly avowal on all sides as to what is intended to be done. If the question is not now settled, it is uncertain whether it ever can hereafter
55 be; and we, as the representatives of the States of this Union regarded as governments, should come to a distinct understanding as to our respective views, in order to ascertain whether the great questions at issue can be settled or not. If you who
60 represent the stronger portion, can not agree to settle them on the broad principle of justice and duty, say so; and let the States we both represent agree to separate and part in peace.

If you are unwilling we should part in peace,
65 tell us so; and we shall know what to do when you reduce the question to submission or resistance. If you remain silent, you will compel us to infer by your acts what you intend. In that case California will become the test question. If you
70 admit her under all the difficulties that oppose her admission, you compel us to infer that you intend to exclude us from the whole of the acquired Territories, with the intention of destroying

CONTINUE

irretrievably the equilibrium between the two
75 sections. We should be blind not to perceive
in that case that your real objects are power
and aggrandizement, and infatuated, not to act
accordingly.
    I have now, senators, done my duty in
80 expressing my opinions fully, freely, and candidly
on this solemn occasion. In doing so I have been
governed by the motives which have governed
me in all the stages of the agitation of the slavery
question since its commencement. I have exerted
85 myself during the whole period to arrest it, with
the intention of saving the Union if it could be
done; and if it could not, to save the section where
it has pleased providence to cast my lot.

31

In Passage 1, Clay explains that the Constitution is

A) the first and most important manifestation of an American radiation of cooperation and negotiation.

B) a feature of national life that should be respected in the formulation of political compromises.

C) a document that was once thought divisive but has come to be held in universally high regard.

D) a source of guidance that may be modified as a result of ongoing deliberations.

32

Which choice provides the best evidence for the answer to the previous question?

A) Lines 1-4 ("In all . . . wants")

B) Lines 13-15 ("I admit . . . adopted")

C) Lines 15-19 ("But I . . . United States")

D) Lines 31-37 ("I believe . . . effects")

33

Clay's reference to the "limpid fountain" (line 42) serves primarily to

A) introduce an allusion to language contained in the Constitution.

B) emphasize Clay's willingness to take a principled yet unpopular stance.

C) signify virtues that Clay urges his audience to prioritize.

D) return to and extend a metaphorical reference presented earlier.

34

As used in line 48, "fragments" most nearly means

A) flakings.

B) features.

C) factions.

D) figments.

35

As used in line 57, "distinct" most nearly means

A) incompatible.

B) proudly-expressed.

C) unconnected.

D) well-defined.

CONTINUE

36

Calhoun explains that California serves as a "test question" (line 69) because

A) the people of California have embraced a viewpoint similar to Calhoun's but have been slighted by the federal government.

B) responses to the situation in California will prove useful in distinguishing ideological systems that had once seemed to overlap.

C) events in California are the most dramatic manifestation of a political conflict that has appeared in more subtle forms.

D) how the case of California is handled will allow him to gauge whether his interests face goodwill or hostility.

37

The final paragraph of Passage 2 indicates that Calhoun's priority has been to

A) promote the interests of his state even if such interests harm the Union.

B) preserve the Union if such a goal is feasible.

C) re-define the idea of the Union in a manner more acceptable to the South.

D) warn that crisis over the Union seems inevitable.

38

Passage 1 and Passage 2 both serve the purpose of

A) encouraging decisive action during a time of potential conflict.

B) convincing an audience that is believed to be indecisive.

C) critiquing misguided ideas about the Union.

D) prompting debate on whether individual states should remain within the Union.

39

On the basis of Passage 1, Clay would argue that the option described by Calhoun in lines 59-63 ("If you . . . peace") is

A) motivated by a cynical stance on national politics.

B) currently impossible though previously viable.

C) unrealistic given the options that face the Union.

D) bizarre given what Clay sees as a universal attempt at reconciliation.

40

Which choice provides the best evidence for the answer to the previous question?

A) Lines 20-22 ("The responsibility . . hands")

B) Lines 23-25 ("I hope . . . magnitude")

C) Lines 27-29 ("The alternatives . . . discord")

D) Lines 37-40 ("And now . . . power")

41

One of the important rhetorical differences between Clay's discussion in Passage 1 and Calhoun's discussion in Passage 2 is that

A) Clay uses collective references to promote cooperation, while Calhoun directly addresses a group that may not be in sympathy with him.

B) Clay explains his own expertise to lend credibility to his argument, while Calhoun professes faith in the judgment of his audience.

C) Clay does not consider possible arguments against his position, while Calhoun carefully analyzes the most popular cases against his stance.

D) Clay assumes that his ideas represent the will of the nation, while Calhoun explains that his ideas are intentionally provocative.

CONTINUE

Questions 42-52 are based on the following passage and supplementary material.

This passage is adapted from "Red Nuggets Are Galactic Gold for Astronomers," an article posted by NASA.gov* in July of 2018.

About a decade ago, astronomers discovered a population of small but massive galaxies called "red nuggets." A new study using NASA's
Line Chandra X-ray Observatory indicates that
5 black holes have squelched star formation in these galaxies and may have used some of the untapped stellar fuel to grow to unusually massive proportions.

Red nuggets were first discovered by the
10 Hubble Space Telescope at great distances from Earth, corresponding to times only about three or four billion years after the Big Bang. They are relics of the first massive galaxies that formed within only one billion years after the Big Bang.
15 Astronomers think they are the ancestors of the giant elliptical galaxies seen in the local Universe. The masses of red nuggets are similar to those of giant elliptical galaxies, but they are only about a fifth of their size.
20 While most red nuggets merged with other galaxies over billions of years, a small number managed to slip through the long history of the cosmos untouched. These unscathed red nuggets represent a golden opportunity to study how the
25 galaxies, and the supermassive black hole at their centers, act over billions of years of isolation.

For the first time, Chandra has been used to study the hot gas in two of these isolated red nuggets, MRK 1216, and PGC 032873. They are
30 located only 295 million and 344 million light years from Earth, respectively, rather than billions of light years for the first known red nuggets. This X-ray emitting hot gas contains the imprint of activity generated by the supermassive black holes
35 in each of the two galaxies.

"These galaxies have existed for 13 billion years without ever interacting with another of its kind," said Norbert Werner of MTA-Eötvös University Lendület Hot Universe and
40 Astrophysics Research Group in Budapest, Hungary, who led the study. "We are finding that the black holes in these galaxies take over and the result is not good for new stars trying to form."

Astronomers have long known that the material
45 falling towards black holes can be redirected outward at high speeds due to intense gravitational and magnetic fields. These high-speed jets can tamp down the formation of stars. This happens because the blasts from the vicinity of the black
50 hole provide a powerful source of heat, preventing the galaxy's hot interstellar gas from cooling enough to allow large numbers of stars to form.

The temperature of the hot gas is higher in the center of the MRK 1216 galaxy compared to
55 its surroundings, showing the effects of recent heating by the black hole. Also, radio emission is observed from the center of the galaxy, a signature of jets from black holes. Finally, the X-ray emission from the vicinity of the black
60 hole is about a hundred million times lower than a theoretical limit on how fast a black hole can grow—called the "Eddington limit"—where the outward pressure of radiation is balanced by the inward pull of gravity. This low level of X-ray
65 emission is typical for black holes producing jets. All these factors provide strong evidence that activity generated by the central supermassive black holes in these red nugget galaxies is suppressing the formation of new stars.
70 The black holes and the hot gas may have another connection. The authors suggest that much of the black hole mass may have accumulated from the hot gas surrounding both galaxies. The black holes in both MRK 1216 and
75 PGC 032873 are among the most massive known, with estimated masses of about five billion times that of the Sun, based on optical observations of the speeds of stars near the galaxies' centers. Furthermore, the masses of the MRK 1216 black
80 hole and possibly the one in PGC 032873 are estimated to be a few percent of the combined masses of all the stars in the central regions of the galaxies, whereas in most galaxies, the ratio is about ten times less.

*See Page 36 for the citation for this text.

CONTINUE

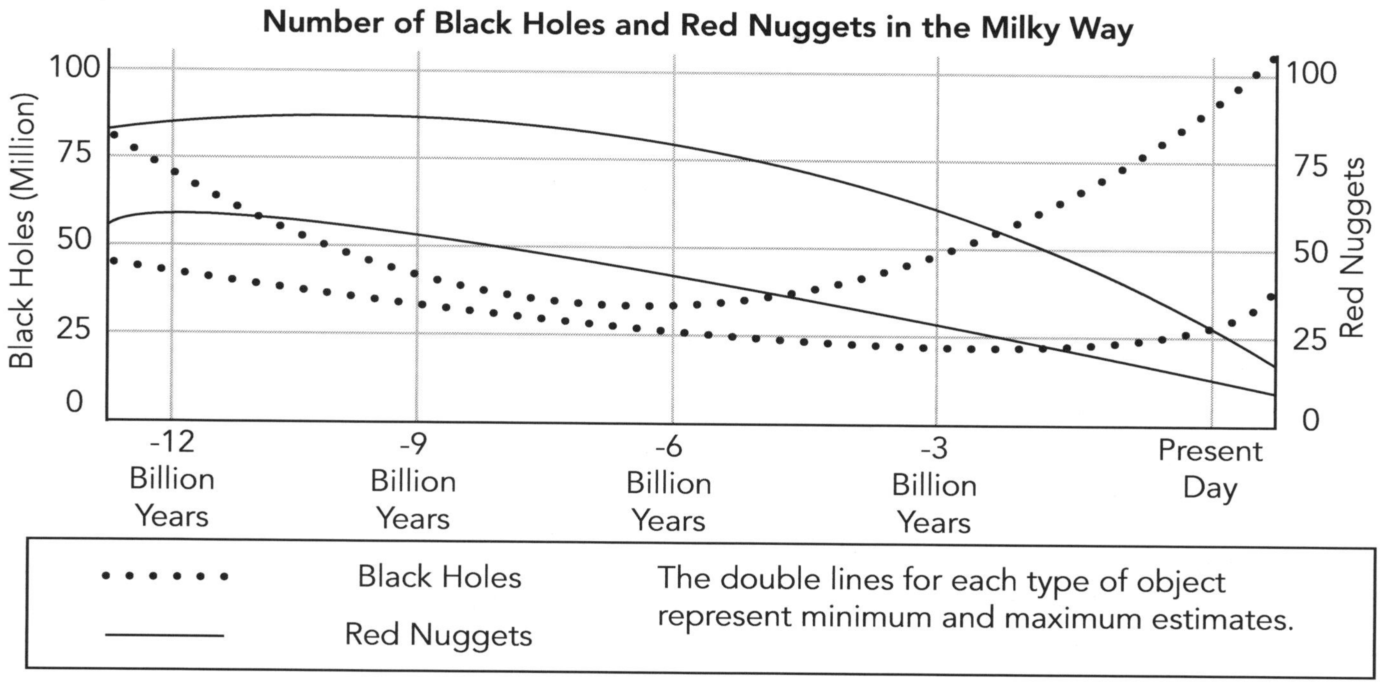
Number of Black Holes and Red Nuggets in the Milky Way
Black Holes (Million)
100
75
50
25
0
Red Nuggets
100
75
50
25
0
-12 Billion Years
-9 Billion Years
-6 Billion Years
-3 Billion Years
Present Day
Black Holes
Red Nuggets
The double lines for each type of object represent minimum and maximum estimates.

42

Over the course of the passage, the author's focus shifts from

A) a point of puzzlement regarding the formation of red nuggets to the resolution of this uncertainty.

B) different perspectives on the relationship between black holes and red nuggets to an extended discussion of red nuggets.

C) an account of outer space exploration to new protocols for black hole detection.

D) the basic properties of red nuggets to a series of observations regarding black holes.

43

As used in line 5, "formation" most nearly means

A) alignment.

B) institution.

C) generation.

D) patterning.

44

As used in line 23, "unscathed" most nearly means

A) uncorrupted.

B) intact.

C) unquestioned.

D) safe.

45

According to the passage, "hot gas" is significant to researchers because

A) it is one of the few forms of matter that can escape a black hole.

B) its presence can be understood as a sign of black hole activity.

C) it has been instrumental in the formation of several identified red nuggets.

D) its emission can help a black hole to overcome the "Eddington Limit" under some circumstances.

CONTINUE

46

Which choice provides the best evidence for the answer to the previous question?

A) Lines 27-29 ("For the . . . PGC 032873")

B) Lines 32-35 ("This . . . galaxies")

C) Lines 41-43 ("We are . . . form")

D) Lines 58-62 ("Finally . . . grow")

47

According to the passage, which of the following was NOT one of the main findings of the study led by Norbert Werner?

A) An individual black hole can grow larger by siphoning energy or material that could otherwise generate stars.

B) Star formation can be impeded by the presence of a black hole.

C) The massiveness of some black holes may be traced directly to interactions involving hot gas.

D) A magnetic field can deflect matter away from a black hole.

48

Which choice provides the best evidence for the answer to the previous question?

A) Lines 36-38 ("These . . . kind")

B) Lines 44-47 ("Astronomers . . . fields")

C) Lines 56-58 ("Also . . . black holes")

D) Lines 74-78 ("The black holes . . . centers")

49

The ideas about "black holes and hot gas" that are outlined in the final paragraph of the passage are best understood as

A) plausible but not entirely verified.

B) simultaneously imaginative and practical.

C) widely-accepted yet deeply problematic.

D) completely proven though still disputed.

CONTINUE

50

According to the graph, at what point is there the greatest difference between the minimum estimate and the maximum estimate for the number of black holes in the Milky Way?

A) 9 billion years ago

B) 6 billion years ago

C) 3 billion years ago

D) the present day

51

On the basis of the passage, one possible cause for the decrease in the number of red nuggets over time, as indicated in the graph, could be

A) the transformation of individual red nuggets into multiple black holes.

B) the complete disintegration of red nuggets into hot gas.

C) the combination of red nuggets with other galaxies.

D) the detonation of red nuggets that are drawn into black holes.

52

Does the graph provide support for the trend indicated by the "new study" (line 3) as described in the first paragraph of the passage?

A) Yes, because the graph provides persuasive evidence that red nuggets often disintegrate to become black holes.

B) Yes, because the graph supports the author's point that red nuggets are relatively difficult to detect and study.

C) No, because the graph does not provide any direct or relevant information about the sizes of individual black holes.

D) No, because the graph suggests that the number of black holes has expanded because black holes have grown less massive over time.

STOP
If you finish before time is called, you may check your work on this section only.
Do not turn to any other section.

Answer Key: Diagnostic

Passage 1	Passage 2	Passage 3	Passage 4	Passage 5
1. A	11. C	21. D	31. B	42. D
2. C	12. A	22. C	32. B	43. C
3. A	13. B	23. D	33. C	44. B
4. B	14. D	24. C	34. C	45. B
5. C	15. D	25. C	35. D	46. B
6. B	16. A	26. B	36. D	47. D
7. B	17. C	27. D	37. B	48. B
8. A	18. C	28. B	38. A	49. A
9. C	19. D	29. B	39. C	50. D
10. D	20. C	30. B	40. C	51. C
			41. A	52. C

Question Types

Major Issue
1-2, 11, 13, 21-22, 42

Passage Details
3, 8, 10, 18, 26, 30, 33, 36-37, 49

Command of Evidence
6-7, 9, 12, 15-16, 24-25, 27-28, 31-32, 45-48

Word in Context
5-6, 14, 17, 23, 29, 34-35, 43-44

Graphics and Visuals
19-20, 50-52

Passage Comparison
38-41

Self-Evaluation
Checklist for the Diagnostic Test

Passage Types

- Hardest Readings _____ ; _____
- Easiest Readings _____ ; _____

Sources of Difficulty
(Check all that apply.)

_____ Comprehending Main Idea (Passages ___ , ___ , ___)

_____ Remembering Passage Details (Passages ___ , ___ , ___)

_____ Working with Style and Vocabulary (Passages ___ , ___ , ___)

Question Types

- Major Issue: Incorrect _____   Tossup _____   Challenges: _____
- Passage Details: Incorrect _____   Tossup _____   Challenges: _____
- CoE: Incorrect _____   Tossup _____   Challenges: _____
- Word in Context: Incorrect _____   Tossup _____   Challenges: _____

Sources of Difficulty
(Check all that apply.)

_____ Understanding the Question   _____ Locating or Analyzing Evidence

_____ Predicting the Answers   _____ Eliminating False Answers

Vocabulary

- New Words: _____
- Total Questions with Advanced Vocabulary _____   Number Right _____   Number Wrong _____

Overall Strategy

- Time Per Passage (Estimate): 1 _____ 2 _____ 3 _____ 4 _____ 5 _____
- Total Time for the Test _____   Time Left Over _____   OR Time Needed Beyond 65 Minutes _____
- Passages with Note-Taking _____   Questions Right for These _____   Questions Wrong for These _____
- Passages with NO Notes _____   Questions Right for These _____   Questions Wrong for These _____

Sources of Difficulty
(Check all that apply.)

_____ Slow Reading or Rereading   _____ Complicated or Time-Consuming Notes

_____ Inaccurate Annotations   _____ Rushed Through Passages or Questions

Answer Explanations
Diagnostic, Pages 8-23

Passage 1, Pages 8-10

1. <u>A</u> is the correct answer.

The passage describes how Olga leads a pleasant and enjoyable life, but the narrator also states that "She craved for [well-known people], and never could satisfy her craving" (47-48). This content best supports A. B can be eliminated as illogical, since Olga and her husband are not wealthy, while C can be eliminated since the passage indicates that Olga and her husband do misunderstand each other on one occasion but NOT that they frequently misunderstand each other. Be careful not to choose D, since Olga does seem both happy on the surface and dissatisfied underneath; HOWEVER, the passage does not indicate that she seeks fundamental change, just constant variety.

2. <u>C</u> is the correct answer.

The passage focuses on how Olga leads a busy life that revolves around many different social interactions. This content best supports C. Be careful not to choose B, since while the passage does describe how Olga is very affectionate with her husband, it does NOT depict her as extravagant; rather, Olga is described as carefully stretching a limited budget for her clothing. A (which presents a faulty negative) and D (which goes against the depiction of Olga as outgoing) can both be eliminated since they present descriptions at odds with Olga's representation as skilled, sociable, bubbly, and playful.

3. <u>A</u> is the correct answer.

The first paragraph describes how Olga sets up her household, and concludes with the statement that "every one thought that the young people had a very charming little home" (16-18). This content best supports A. B and D can be eliminated since the passage does NOT focus on Dymov specifically assigning the decorating decisions to Olga, or on the two of them making these decisions together. C is a trap answer, since the passage focuses on Olga but does NOT specify that Olga's decorating decisions specifically reflect her personality.

4. <u>B</u> is the correct answer.

In line 29, "clever shifts" refers to how Olga and her dressmaker are able to create beautiful clothes even though they have few resources to work with. Choose B to reflect this content. Do not choose A, since it does not capture the meaning of their decisions being a response to scarcity; C can also be eliminated, since Olga's primary purpose is not avoidance or evasion. Do not choose D, since Olga and her dressmaker are accustomed to these strategies, and do not have to formulate them unexpectedly.

5. <u>C</u> is the correct answer.

In line 52, "fresh" refers to "great men" desired by Olga and thus means new or distinct from the individuals Olga already knows as part of her social circle. B can be eliminated, since Olga is interested in meeting individuals whom she does not know, not in the specific personalities of those individuals; this answer choice also raises the context of directness or honesty, NOT of novelty. A (indicating energy) and D (indicating something that is rapid or surprising) can be eliminated as introducing similarly inappropriate contexts.

6. <u>B</u> is the correct answer.

In lines 56-58, the passage describes how Dymov's "simplicity, good sense, and kind-heartedness touched [Olga] and moved her up to enthusiasm." She also tells him that he is "a clever, generous man" (61). This content best supports answer B. A and C can both be eliminated as illogical, since Olga (whose characterization is often positive) does NOT demonstrate sarcastic or uncomprehending behavior in the passage. Be careful not to choose D, since she displays affection for but NOT necessarily loyalty to her husband.

7. <u>B</u> is the correct answer.

See the previous answer explanation for analysis of the correct line reference. A focuses on how and why Olga and her dressmaker must be resourceful with the clothing budget, while C describes the physical affection that Olga shows towards her husband. D involves a playful comment that Olga makes to him. None of these other answers reflect the admiration she shows towards him, and all should be rejected.

8. <u>A</u> is the correct answer.

In line 72, Dymov explains why he is not bothered by the fact that he is not knowledgeable about the arts. He rationalizes that people have different interests and areas of specialization. This comment functions as an extension of his viewpoint; choose A. Both C and D can be dismissed, since the comment shows that Dymov is calm and accepting in his viewpoint, not critical or admitting fault. B can be dismissed since Dymov is mainly interested in explaining a present opinion, NOT in any direct reference to past experience.

9. <u>C</u> is the correct answer.

In lines 72-77, Dymov explains that he personally does not understand or value artistic pursuits, but that he recognizes that other people devote their lives to these pursuits, and therefore he assumes that such endeavors have value. This comment shows him demonstrating respect for activities that he does not understand; choose C. A explains why he has not had time to learn about the arts, and what he spends his time on instead; in B, he explains how he does not hold the ignorance of other people against them when they are not knowledgeable about the areas which interest him. D focuses on the distinction between failing to understand something and failing to respect it. None of these other answers show that Dymov values activities that he does not understand, and all should be rejected.

10. <u>D</u> is the correct answer.

The passage ends with a sentence showing that the couple's routine takes a predictable form every day; choose D to support this idea. Be careful not to choose B, since the passage does NOT clarify whether the couple is resistant to change, or just has no reason to make lifestyle alterations. A directly contradicts the positive and mostly accepting tone that is applied to Olga's lifestyle throughout the passage; C would require a critique of the main characters or an extensive depiction of Dymov's thought processes, and neither feature is present in the passage.

Passage 2, Pages 11-13

11. <u>C</u> is the correct answer.

The passage focuses on contextualizing the anthropological research conducted by Elspeth Ready, and then describes the methodology and findings of this research. The final portion of the passage discusses some implications from the research. Choose C to support this content. Be careful not to choose B, since Ready is NOT explicitly positioned as an important researcher, nor does the passage focus on evaluating the merits of her research (as opposed to simply presenting findings). A and D can also be dismissed, since the research aims to explore existing practices, NOT to articulate a solution, or to generate widely applicable insights (since a single community remains the focus).

12. <u>A</u> is the correct answer.

Lines 16-19 state that "exactly how food sharing networks facilitate the flow of resources throughout the community has not been well studied." These lines make it clear that Ready's research was not preceded by significant studies on the same topic; choose A. B focuses on the value of the insights to be gained from conducting this type of research, while C focuses on how Ready conducted her research. D also describes the insights generated by Ready's research. None of these other answers explicitly discuss the lack of prior existing research, and all should be rejected.

13. <u>B</u> is the correct answer.

Lines 31-33 describe how "[Ready] asked each [household] to list its most important food sharing partners," indicating that she used a research model in which data was directly provided by households in Kangiqsujuaq. Choose B to reflect this content. A can be rejected since there is no mention of interviewing in Ready's research methodology, while C is illogical since no climate change statistics were collected in this community. D represents an area of investigation (dietary changes, NOT changes in food exchange networks) that Ready did not explore, and should be dismissed.

14. <u>D</u> is the correct answer.

In line 53, "individual" refers to the resources and knowledge held by a specific person. Choose D to reflect this meaning. A (inappropriately implying a belief or attitude), B (inappropriately referring to personality), and D (implying lack of connection rather than individual possession) all introduce improper contexts and should thus be eliminated.

15. <u>D</u> is the correct answer.

Lines 48-49 state that the giving away of food was an indicator of large network size; this situation indicates that someone with a large network would be likely to give away food on a regular basis, and that D is the correct answer. A, B, and C can all be rejected, since there is no discussion in the passage of food donation being correlated to household wealth or treated as a form of charity, nor is there mention of storing excess food; instead, Ready's research primarily links food sharing to social connections and family ties.

16. <u>A</u> is the correct answer.

See the previous answer explanation for analysis of the correct line reference. B describes the categories of people who held the largest food sharing networks, while C suggests a plausible hypothesis which the research ultimately did not support. D describes a possible implication from the findings of the research. None of these answers directly describe a typical behavior for someone who possesses a large food-sharing network.

17. <u>C</u> is the correct answer.

In line 82, "addressed" refers to the action of institutions that set out to solve problems, and thus means improved or ameliorated by; choose C to support this meaning. A (inappropriately implying condemnation), B (implying only recognition but not improvement), and D (implying description rather than improvement) all introduce improper contexts and should thus be eliminated.

18. <u>C</u> is the correct answer.

The passage concludes with a paragraph describing how traditional food sharing networks may not be sufficient to counter increasing sources of strain and food instability, especially for low-income individuals. Choose C to support this content. A and B can both be dismissed, since the conclusion does NOT focus on weaknesses in the research or on future research possibilities. D can also be dismissed since it characterizes the final paragraph as presenting conversation, which should NOT be confused with analysis of different groups from the author's own perspective.

19. <u>D</u> is the correct answer.

The chart indicates that close to 40 individuals have between 21-30 outgoing food ties, and that this is the largest of all the groups. Choose D to reflect this content. A, B, and C can all be dismissed since the numbers of individuals who possess either 0-20 incoming or outgoing food ties and the number of individuals who possess 21-30 incoming food ties are all lower in comparison.

20. <u>C</u> is the correct answer.

Ready's research determined that gender, as demonstrated by the role of "single women" (line 55), is a factor in food-sharing networks; however, this factor is NOT documented in the graph. Choose C to reflect this configuration of content. A and B can both be dismissed since they describe factors which ARE documented in the graph, while D describes a factor that is not directly present in the passage: "political influence" is not necessarily identical to the community factors that Ready does address, such as kinship and social ties.

Passage 3, Pages 14-16

21. <u>D</u> is the correct answer.

The passage focuses on describing how brain size is connected to factors like energy expenditure and cognitive ability. Choose D to reflect this content. Be careful not to choose A or B, since the passage does NOT focus on countering or correcting prior beliefs about the implications of brain size. C can be dismissed since neurological disorders, though a secondary topic, are not the primary focus of the passage.

22. <u>C</u> is the correct answer.

As the first lines of the passage state, humans exhibit a wide range of different brain sizes. This premise creates an opportunity to conduct research in order to explore the significance of those different ranges. Choose C to reflect this content. B can be rejected since it represents a perspective explicitly rejected by the researchers quoted in the passage. A can also be eliminated, since the discussion of human brains is contextualized within wider discussions about primate brains, implying that human brains are comparable to these other brains. D can also be dismissed as being outside the scope of the passage, since brain structure itself (NOT the relationship between brain size and physical strength) is the author's focus.

23. <u>D</u> is the correct answer.

In line 7, "additional" refers to area taken up by a "bigger" brain and thus means "extra" or "more". Choose D to reflect this meaning. A (inappropriately implying an alternative), B (inappropriately implying a particular order), and C (implying a lack of value) all introduce improper contexts and should thus be eliminated.

24. <u>C</u> is the correct answer.

In lines 56-58, Raznahan uses an analogy in which he compares the extra biological resources necessary to develop high-growth brain regions to money. This analogy is important because it allows Raznahan to effectively explain a process that is central to his research study; choose C to reflect this content. Be careful not to choose B, since this analogy is more specific than the general inclusion of anecdotes and recollections. A and D can also be dismissed, since the passage is NOT clearly negative towards earlier researchers in a manner that indicates the necessity of debate or criticism.

25. <u>C</u> is the correct answer.

See the previous answer explanation for analysis of the correct line reference. A focuses on preventing a reader from making an incorrect inference, while B offers a distinction between different parts of the brain by using straightforward language. D concisely summarizes the key findings of the study. Since none of these other answers includes an analogy, they can all be dismissed.

26. <u>B</u> is the correct answer.

Lines 28-44 describe the scope of the study, the collaborators involved, and where the findings were published. This content emphasizes that the study involved a large sample size and collaborators from different institutions and locations; choose B to reflect this information. Be careful not to choose D, since the project is described as collaborative but NOT necessarily multi-disciplinary. A and C can also be dismissed since these lines do NOT discuss either the connection between this work and previous studies or the accessibility of the findings.

27. <u>D</u> is the correct answer.

Lines 58-60 indicate that cortex regions require high levels of energy, provided in the form of oxygenated blood. Choose D to reflect this content. B and C are both outside the scope of the passage, since neither the relative fragility of different regions nor the use of intelligence exams are discussed directly. A can also be dismissed since there is no discussion of correlating cortex size to body size in the passage.

28. <u>B</u> is the correct answer.

See the previous answer explanation for analysis of the correct line reference. A explains how certain traits of cortex regions remain consistent, while C describes a connection between high-expanding cortex regions and some neurological disorders. D focuses on an important factor that supports the validity of the findings. Since none of these answers discuss how cortex regions consume more energy, they can all be dismissed.

29. <u>B</u> is the correct answer.

In line 70, "implicated" refers to brain regions linked to disorders and thus means "involved in" or "associated with". Choose B to reflect this meaning. A (implying inferiority), C (inappropriately implying a subtle, indirect connection), and D (implying subordination) all introduce improper contexts and should thus be eliminated.

30. <u>B</u> is the correct answer.

The study described in the passage found that larger and smaller brains showed consistent patterns in how the available brain space was organized, and that high-growth brain regions are often implicated in neurodevelopmental disorders. Findings that neurodevelopmental diseases rendered brains incapable of changing or growing would contradict these implications; choose B as the correct answer. C does not contradict the study's findings, since it would be expected for individuals experiencing brain disorders to show unusually high rates of growth. It would also be plausible for fast-growing regions to take over functions from slower-growing regions, and for the growth of some regions to lead to impairment in areas governed by other regions; therefore, neither A nor D contradicts the primary findings.

Passage 4, Pages 17-19

31. <u>B</u> is the correct answer.

In lines 13-15, Clay states that he does not believe that any compromise that violates the Constitution should ever be adopted. This idea suggests that he believes that the Constitution is something to be respected and accounted for whenever political compromises are proposed; choose B to support this content. Be careful not to choose A because Clay does NOT represent the Constitution as the first example of a more extensive tradition; C can also be eliminated, since Clay does NOT discuss whether views of the Constitution have changed over time. D can be dismissed as an explicit contradiction of the point that Clay makes in his speech.

32. <u>B</u> is the correct answer.

See the previous answer explanation for analysis of the correct line reference. A describes the goals and aspirations of each party during negotiations for a compromise, while C asserts Clay's confidence that the proposed bill does not violate the Constitution. D describes the hope that he has for the positive consequences of the bill. None of these other answers describe how Clay regards the Constitution.

33. <u>C</u> is the correct answer.

In line 42, Clay uses the metaphor of individuals washing in a fountain to describe his hope that his audience will focus on the virtues of patriotism and set aside their conflicting desires to pursue compromise; choose C to support this content. Be careful not to choose D, since the metaphor of a fountain is first introduced here, NOT reintroduced from an earlier point. A can be dismissed since nothing signals that this language is intended to echo the Constitution (despite the positive tone in both cases), while B can be rejected as requiring inference outside the scope of the passage, since nothing signals that Clay's point of view is unpopular.

34. <u>C</u> is the correct answer.

In line 48, "fragments" refers to divided or disconnected groups of individuals. Choose C to reflect this meaning. A (inappropriately implying a physical substance), B (inappropriately referring to elements or aspects), and D (implying something imagined or unreal) all introduce improper contexts and should thus be eliminated.

35. <u>D</u> is the correct answer.

In line 57, "distinct" refers to "respective" views that Calhoun aims to distinguish and thus means specified or clear. Choose D to reflect this meaning. A (inappropriately implying conflict or discord), B (inappropriately referring to how something is described or represented), and C (implying something unrelated) all introduce improper contexts and should thus be eliminated.

36. <u>D</u> is the correct answer.

Calhoun explains that he sees actions around how the situation with California is handled as determining whether or not he and his allies are being treated fairly and transparently. Choose D to reflect this content. Be careful not to choose C, since Calhoun does NOT position California as the most dramatic example of an ongoing conflict. A can be dismissed since no mention is made of the perspective of the Californian people in this debate, while B contradicts the passage's content suggesting that existing ideological systems are distinctive and conflicting, NOT overlapping.

37. <u>B</u> is the correct answer.

In the final paragraph, Calhoun states that "I have exerted myself during the whole period to arrest it, with the intention of saving the Union if it could be done" (84-87), a statement which suggests that he hoped to preserve the Union. Choose B to support this content. Dismiss A as contradicting what Calhoun explicitly states as his intention, while C can be dismissed as unsupported by evidence, since Calhoun does NOT discuss renegotiating the terms of Union. D can be eliminated since the passage is intended to describe a crisis that is already occurring, NOT to warn of an impending one.

38. <u>A</u> is the correct answer.

In Passage 1, Clay urges his audience to render the Compromise legally binding, thereby securing peace and stability; in Passage 2, Calhoun urges an explicit rejection of the Compromise in order to clarify positions on the questions of slavery and slave-owning. Both of these passages encourage decisive action; choose A to support this content. Be careful not to choose B, since the rhetoric of persuasion does NOT necessarily assume that the audience is indecisive. C and D can both be rejected as answers that contradict Clay's positive ideas about the Union in Passage 1: his primary goal is to call attention to the importance of preserving the Union, not to delve into the perspectives of his antagonists in a manner that spurs debate.

39. <u>C</u> is the correct answer.

In lines 27-29, Clay argues that the proposed compromise will prevent further antagonism from dividing those who support and those who challenge slavery. This position suggests that he believes that animosity and conflict are inevitable unless a compromise is reached, and would not believe Calhoun's suggestion of a peaceful separation to be feasible. Choose C to support this content. Be careful not to choose B, since nothing in the passage suggests that Clay previously believed this option to be viable, and has now changed his mind. A (which mostly reflects negatively on Calhoun's character) and D (which overstates the extent of Clay's optimism about a solution) can also be eliminated, since they are both unsubstantiated by the passages.

40. C is the correct answer.

See the previous answer explanation for analysis of the correct line reference. A describes the decision-making stage at which the proposed Compromise has arrived, while B describes the gravity and scope of the decision to be made about the Compromise. D focuses on the attitudes and feelings that Clay hopes his audience will be able to set aside. None of the other answers illustrate why Clay sees Calhoun's proposal as unrealistic, and all should be rejected.

41. A is the correct answer.

In Passage 1, Clay urges an audience of people who may possess diverse opinions about slavery to put aside differing interests in order to act for mutual benefit by adopting the Compromise. In Passage 2, Calhoun urges those who do not support slavery to openly admit to their perspective so that there can be transparency and fair dealings. Given the authors' differing aims of fostering collaboration and responding to an unsympathetic group, choose A. B can be dismissed since Clay does NOT provide evidence of relevant expertise, while C can be rejected because Calhoun does not carefully engage with counter-arguments. D can also be eliminated since Calhoun never signals that he means to offer deliberately provocative ideas, even though his stance may strike some readers as divisive.

Passage 5, Pages 20-23

42. D is the correct answer.

The passage begins by defining red nuggets and describing their main qualities. The focus then shifts to discussing black holes as one element of a situation involving red nuggets. Choose D to support this content. B can be eliminated since it describes a progression that reverses the actual structure of the passage, while A is incorrect because the focus of the passage is description, NOT the resolution of a previously uncertain question. C is illogical because the passage does NOT focus on methods for detecting black holes, even though black holes are of high interest.

43. C is the correct answer.

In line 5, "formation" refers to the activity of stars that have the potential to appear in a physical form that can be "squelched" and thus means emergence or "generation" (as in creation or growth). Choose C to support this content. A (inappropriately implying balance or agreement), B (inappropriately referring to a system or structure being put in place), and D (implying design or decoration) all introduce improper contexts and should thus be eliminated.

44. <u>B</u> is the correct answer.

In line 23, "unscathed" refers to "untouched" red nuggets and thus means unchanged or undamaged. Choose B to reflect this meaning. A (inappropriately implying a moral situation), C (inappropriately referring to an idea or philosophy going unchallenged), and D (implying security and protection) all introduce improper contexts and should thus be eliminated.

45. <u>B</u> is the correct answer.

Lines 32-35 describe how hot gas provides an indication of black hole activity, implying that this relationship reveals one reason that hot gas is of interest to researchers. Choose B to support this content. Be careful not to choose C, since hot gas is linked to activity within one aspect of red nuggets but NOT necessarily to red nugget formation. A and D can both be dismissed as illogical, since hot gas is neither described as something escaping a black hole nor discussed in relation to the Eddington limit.

46. <u>B</u> is the correct answer.

See the previous answer explanation for analysis of the correct line reference. A focuses on how new technology has allowed for hot gas to be studied, while C summarizes the findings of a particular study. D describes the measurements of some specific black holes. None of these other answers explain why hot gas is important to researchers, and therefore all should be dismissed.

47. <u>D</u> is the correct answer.

In lines 44-47, the author notes that astronomers have been aware of the effect of magnetic fields on matter interacting with black holes for a long time. This information indicates that this knowledge was NOT discovered in Werner's research. Choose D to support this content. A, B, and C all involve content which reflects new conclusions emerging from Werner's studies, and thus CONTRADICT the question requirement.

48. <u>B</u> is the correct answer.

See the previous answer explanation for analysis of the correct line reference. A describes the long period in which red nugget galaxies have existed without interacting with each other, while C focuses on a characteristic that appears to signal the presence of a black hole at a particular location within the galaxy. D describes the mass of these galaxies by comparing such mass to that of the Sun. None of these other answers describe findings that preceded Werner's research, and therefore all should be eliminated.

49. <u>A</u> is the correct answer.

The information described in the final paragraph of the passage is best characterized as a plausible hypothesis that has not yet been fully confirmed, since the author calls attention to situations that "may" (lines 70 and 72) be valid on the basis of research findings. Choose A to support this content. Be careful not to choose C or

Answer Explanations, Diagnostic Test

D, since the information is NOT discussed in terms of whether it is accepted, problematic, or disputed within the scientific community, but simply as well-supported by a particular study. B can also be eliminated since the information reflects a description of scientific phenomena which is not intended to be either imaginative or practical.

50. <u>D</u> is the correct answer.

The graph shows the difference between the minimum and maximum estimate of the number of black holes in the Milky Way (indicated by two dotted lines) steadily increasing over the past 3 billion years and reaching its peak difference in the present day. Choose D to support this content. A and B can be rejected since at 9 billion and 6 billion years ago the difference between minimum and maximum was relatively small, with little change occurring between these two time points. C can be rejected since 3 billion years ago the difference was larger but still not as large as it is shown to be for the present day.

51. <u>C</u> is the correct answer.

Lines 20-21 describe how "most red nuggets merged with other galaxies over billions of years." This theory is reflected in the graph, which shows the total number of red nuggets declining over time. Choose C to support this content. A and B can be rejected, since nothing in the passage indicates that red nuggets tend to transform into individual black holes or disintegrate into hot gas. D can be dismissed as illogical since it describes content that does not align with the relationship between black holes and red nuggets described in the passage, since the passage indicates that black holes impede star formation in red nugget galaxies, NOT that black holes cause red nuggets themselves to explode or detonate..

52. <u>C</u> is the correct answer.

The "new study" described at the start of the passage hypothesizes that the presence of black holes within red nugget galaxies has limited star formation and led to the growth of the black holes themselves. The chart only documents trends in the number of red nuggets and black holes, not information about the sizes of either or about the number of stars, and therefore does not support the findings of the new study. Choose C to reflect this content. A and B can both be eliminated since they suggest that the chart DOES support the findings of the study, while D can be eliminated because the chart only shows fluctuations in the number of black holes and does NOT provide any information about their masses.

NOTES

- Passage 2 on Pages 11-12, "Country Food Sharing in the Canadian Arctic: Does It Feed the Neediest?" is adapted from the article of the same name published by the PLOS Blogs network. 10 May 2018, Worth a Thousand Words. https://blogs.plos.org/everyone/2018/05/10/country-food-sharing-canada/. Accessed 3 November 2018.

- Passage 3 on Page 14, "Bigger human brain prioritizes thinking hub—at a cost.," is adapted from the article of the same name published by the National Institutes of Health. 31 May 2018, NIH. https://www.nih.gov/news-events/news-releases/bigger-human-brain-prioritizes-thinking-hub-cost. 3 November 2018.

- Passage 5 on Page 20, "Red Nuggets Are Galactic Gold for Astronomers," is adapted from the article of the same name that appeared on nasa.gov. 21 June 2018, NASA. https://www.nasa.gov/mission_pages/chandra/news/red-nuggets-are-galactic-gold-for-astronomers.html. 3 November 2018.

Part 1

Main Issue
Strategy and Practice

Strategy 1
Main Issues in the Passage

Passage Types

As explained in the introductory portions of this book (pages 3-7), the SAT Reading section will ALWAYS feature five passages that break down into fairly predictable passage types. This chapter is designed to show you the fundamentals of how to read the passages, understand their content, and answer the various "big picture" questions that accompany the readings.

For now, the emphasis will be single passages, since paired passages follow a format that requires its own set of specialized strategies. The first passage on every SAT Reading test, however, will normally be a single passage. This passage will also normally be a work of narrative fiction.

Fiction: Classic and Contemporary

In order to master the Fiction element of the SAT Reading section, you must be prepared to read, comprehend, and analyze classic fiction from the early 19th to the early 20th century. However, more recent works will also appear. In fact, literature readings from later in history have become increasingly common. Both the tests in the Official SAT Study Guide and the most recent College Board tests are, arguably, dominated by relatively recent fiction.

All of these readings do have a few traits in common, despite in some cases being initially published several decades apart. Each one can be roughly described as a sample of "realism"—a piece of literature that attempts to portray human society and psychology as they really are. Each one also has well-defined characters. Some official SAT readings do mention various side characters in quick succession, yet close reading of even these passages will reveal clear specifics—family status, age, occupation, personality traits, or some combination—for each individual designated.

You can safely assume that many of the Fiction passages that you will see on the SAT will have the following characteristics.

1. An emphasis on realistic or at least plausible social structures, ways of thinking, and everyday events

2. Characters whose roles and identities are clearly explained, often with a focus on one or two main perspectives

3. Little or no content (controversies in politics or religion, or depictions of violence, drug use, or sexuality) that would be considered controversial

4. Little or no experimentation with prose form (fragments, bizarre time jumps, unexplained fantastical or surreal elements) that might disorient a reader

For the most part, the Fiction passages that you will read have a high probability of being selected from the works of various social, psychological, and occasionally satirical writers. There is some chance that you may read a portion of a work that has adventure or science fiction elements—for instance, part of a work by H.G. Wells, Robert Louis Stevenson, or Kurt Vonnegut—so long as these elements do not make the passage unduly difficult to comprehend. After all, authors from the 19th century to the present often combined outlandish motifs with realistic character portraits that would be, on the basis of past tests, appropriate to the SAT.

But there is almost NO chance that you will read a passage heavy on content that a reader—any reader at all—would find deeply offensive or upsetting. Even death scenes are mostly off-limits in SAT readings, to say nothing of the potentially controversial content noted above. A passage may of course be taken from a larger work with politically-charged, even disturbing themes; among the authors who have appeared on administered SATs, both Nikolai Gogol and Philip Roth are in fact *famous* for addressing such content. However, it is highly unlikely that a literature reading will address dark, disturbing content head-on. There are few test prep precedents for doing so, and with good reason. The risk of distracting from the test, and of alienating a large group of test-takers, is simply too great.

For a different reason, you can also safely assume that the SAT will present nothing truly bizarre in terms of perspective, structure, or vocabulary. The 20th century was a time of outlandish experimentation with prose form, and the 21st century continues to be an era of structural and stylistic innovation in fiction of all genres. Still, you will probably not need to deal with anything comparable to the dreamlike monologues of Virginia Woolf's *The Waves*, the fusion of scriptwriting and prose of F. Scott Fitzgerald's *The Beautiful and the Damned*, or the PowerPoint-inspired vignettes of Jennifer Egan's *A Visit from the Goon Squad*. You MAY, of course, need to deal with more approachable passages of first-person or third-person realism from these authors.

Part 1: Main Issues in the Passage

As you read through SAT Fiction selections, try to clarify any given passage by determining the following elements with as much clarity as possible.

1. Major characters and how they relate to one another

2. Conflicts, motives, or goals apparent in the text

3. Passage structure, including any important changes or shifts (tone, action, revelations)

While you work through the passages, you must also keep in mind the following guidelines.

1. DO NOT evaluate or interpret what you are reading

2. DO NOT bring in any outside knowledge

Remember, each Reading question that you will confront is PURELY evidence-based. You should be finding important ELEMENTS of the passage as you read—elements that will give you strong comprehension for these questions—not creating independent ideas or value judgments of your own.

If you feel that you can work with the Fiction passages without ANY risk of distracting yourself from the fundamentals of evidence, details, and comprehension, you might also look for some of the following elements as you read.

1. Themes and Messages (built into or clearly articulated in the passage)

2. Significant or Recurring Phrases, Details, or Images

The danger with these issues is that, in your present English courses, you may be used to analyzing themes, phrases, or images in a manner that involves interpretation. You CANNOT do this, under any circumstances, on the SAT. Any themes or significant details will be themselves extremely clear from a literal comprehension of the passage's evidence. No interpretive flights are necessary: just go with what the narrator directly states about WHY the passage's significant portions are significant.

To perform the task of breaking down each SAT Fiction passage with the highest possible precision and efficiency, confront important reading comprehension issues one by one. The following checklist addresses important matters that can appear in virtually ANY passage.

Fiction Checklist
Main Issue Strategy

Can you identify the following elements as they appear in the passage?

Important Characters

Character 1: _____ ; Role/Traits: _____
_____

Character 2: _____ ; Role/Traits: _____
_____

Character 3: _____ ; Role/Traits: _____
_____

Character 4: _____ ; Role/Traits: _____
_____

Overall Issues

Setting: _____

Shifts in Tone or Topic: 1: _____ ➡ _____

2: _____ ➡ _____

Structure: _____

Themes: 1. _____   2. _____

3. _____   4. _____

Part 1: Main Issues in the Passage

How to Use the Checklists

Each SAT Reading passage has its own UNIQUE checklist, which is designed to reflect the type of content that naturally occurs in the specific passage type.

1. As you begin your practice, NOTE the passage features that each checklist gives you. These features will help you to answer the Main Issue questions that occur, most often, as the first few questions after the passage.

2. As much as possible, UNDERLINE content that is related directly to checklist items, especially important individuals and important shifts.

3. As your practice progresses, READ for the checklist features and note them independently. Of course, you will not have the checklists to help you on the actual SAT, but you will have the METHODS that the checklists have helped you to absorb.

The Fiction checklist will help you to achieve clarity and to locate useful information REGARDLESS of whether you are reading an excerpt from a relatively old (late 1700s to early 1900s) or a relatively new (early 1900s to present) work of fiction. Each type, however, has its own challenges.

Classic Fiction (late 1700s to early 1900s)

1. Stylistic Challenges (tendency towards long, intricate sentences; some especially tough vocabulary)

2. Tonal Challenges (emotions, attitudes, and ironies that are difficult to see at a glance)

3. Information-Based Challenges (shifts to new characters and shifts in emphasis)

Newer Fiction (early 1900s to present)

1. Perspective-Based Challenges (roughly even split between first-person and third-person readings)

2. Coherence-Based Challenges (absence of one main perspective; absence of an extremely clear theme)

The purpose of your read-through of the passages is to glean as much important information as you POSSIBLY can. Indeed, the checklists will help you to clarify some issues (tone, theme). Still, you must make sure NOT to over-think an issue if it is not clearly evident in the passage, especially for those issues (again, tone and theme) that present special risks of over-interpretation. In addition, if you cannot find information for one of the checklist categories, do NOT fill the category in. (The passage may not have the relevant information in the first place.) The trick is to run every Fiction passage, regardless of historical era or authorial style, through the same predictable and precise method, without distorting the passage itself.

To see how this process works, read through the passage on the next page, and complete its checklist.

Questions 1-4 are based on the following Fiction passage.

This passage is adapted from Saachika Reddy, "Winter Orchids" (2017).

Another Wednesday arrived, and with it another not-quite-self-consciously resplendent message from Monsieur Tremblay. Avni followed
Line along as his prose, after alighting on the briefest
5 yet warmest of greetings, swept off over the autumny tundras of Saskatchewan and Manitoba, tentatively returned back to inspect the contents of a few curiously dog-eared volumes in Monsieur Tremblay's book collection, and finally settled
10 down in the grotto-like eateries and slow-falling dusks of Old Montreal. As always, it was hard to say where distant recollection ended and the more recent past began. Monsieur Tremblay's narrations, in sweeping over so much space,
15 seemed to find it necessary to suspend time; the acrobatics of moving so deftly from sight to sight allowed no time to pause for the necessary *when* and *how* of a more mundane account. His words suspended both the dull mechanics of travel—the
20 waits, the rides, the rain, the headaches—and the threatening absurdity of trying to commit any rich thought to e-mail. Somehow, thought Avni, Monsieur Tremblay restored dignity to a medium that had none of the inherent dignity of pen and
25 ink.
    Then, as an anticlimax, there would be a perfectly unimportant and perfectly edited business letter attached. "For your review, please find . . ." the message would conclude, and Avni
30 would—as a matter of habit—ask herself yet again why Monsieur Tremblay and his Henry James*-ian command of English required a proofreading service.
    Whether writing provided Monsieur Tremblay
35 a refuge or whether he poured out his experiences in mulled bronze prose out of a sort of compulsion was impossible, even now, for Avni to determine.

---

*Henry James (1843-1916): American novelist and critic famous for the complex imagery and syntax of his writing

From the headshot, resume, and questionnaire answers in his client profile she had deduced
40 everything she could; she had constructed an image of this diminutive 50-year-old wandering around Prince Edward Island and twining together the serpentine sentences of his next letter. Yet she knew nothing of *why* he wrote like this, why he
45 wrote *at all*. Wouldn't it be enough to have these transcendent thoughts all to oneself?
    Avni thought it would be. To have a world such as Monsieur Tremblay's all to oneself would be enough. In such a place, needling messages from
50 one's brother and mother would have no way to pierce through. Her mother was the more direct of the two, and should have been the more irksome: Avni had received dozens of e-mails with links to marketing jobs and research fellowships. "Perhaps
55 you should look at this" and "This one looks interesting" had become interchangeable with her mother's presence. Avni's response was always indifference. Her brother didn't send "helpful" e-mails, for his part. Instead he called at strange
60 hours and asked Avni a series of harmless day-to-day questions, though the worry and annoyance in his voice were both unmistakable to her. Beneath an inquiry about an unimportant movie would be the thought, "Are you still just patching together
65 part-time work, really, seriously?" Beneath a remark about an election that neither of them cared about would be the sentiment, "Please, find something to do, a real job. I'm not saying this to insult you. I'm saying this because I have an
70 MBA and you have a PhD, and only one of us is making good on these facts." Avni would want to sigh the loudest possible sigh of relief at the end of each of these conversations. She was not trying to convince him of anything at this point, and she
75 had won enough arguments with herself to feel convinced that she was in the right, that the $18 per hour she made as a proofreader was a measure of so few of the things that made life worthwhile.

CONTINUE

Fiction Checklist
Practice Exercise 1.1

Can you identify the following elements as they appear in the passage?

Important Characters

Character 1: _____ ; Role/Traits: _____
_____

Character 2: _____ ; Role/Traits: _____
_____

Character 3: _____ ; Role/Traits: _____
_____

Character 4: _____ ; Role/Traits: _____
_____

Overall Issues

Setting: _____

Shifts in Tone or Topic: 1: _____ ➡ _____

2: _____ ➡ _____

Structure: _____

Themes: 1. _____ 2. _____

3. _____ 4. _____

CONTINUE TO ANSWER PASSAGE QUESTIONS 1-4

1

The passage primarily depicts

A) a central character who finds unexpected parallels in her memories of antagonistic characters.

B) a central character who has decisive emotional responses to various other characters.

C) a group of characters who offer guidance and compassion to a conflicted central character.

D) two characters who have formed an emotional bond despite mutual misunderstandings.

2

In relation to Avni, Monsieur Tremblay can best be described as

A) a confidante who reaches out to Avni in the expectation that her responses will intensify their friendship.

B) an acquaintance who has disregarded professional formalities order to better cultivate Avni's sense of imagination.

C) a colleague who tactfully urges Avni to take a proactive and individualistic approach to life.

D) a contact whose detailed communication with Avni does not fulfill a pressing practical purpose.

3

Which of the following statements summarizes a theme present in the passage?

A) Education frequently leads to self-doubt.

B) Inspiring narratives are most often written in obscurity.

C) Professional recognition and material wealth do not correlate with satisfaction.

D) Family members will embrace conflict if they feel that doing so will strengthen their bonds.

4

Over the course of the passage, the narration as a whole shifts from

A) recording a typically pleasing experience to explaining interactions that are informed by tension.

B) pointing out the fundamental similarities between two characters to explaining why these characters are seen as outsiders.

C) surveying a set of unlikely ambitions to analyzing why those same goals are regarded as disreputable.

D) conveying the impact of a single transformative moment to showing how the same moment later resulted in disillusionment.

STOP
**After you have finished the questions, consult the relevant answers on Page 72.
Do not turn to any other section.**

Social Studies

In terms of time period, the Social Studies passages that appear on the SAT represent a departure from the Fiction selections: so far, most of the Social Studies content has been taken from the relatively recent past. You can expect to see articles that deal with contemporary urban life, public health, popular communications platforms, and present-day trends in journalism. While consistently designed to address 21st-century problems in a rigorously evidence-based manner, Social Studies passages regularly return to a few core topics: the psychology of decision-making, population and cultural studies, economics, marketing, ethics, and the media.

What you will NEVER see in the Social Studies passages are topics that are blatantly or divisively political. As with all sections of the SAT Reading, discussions of material—religious debates, partisan arguments, sexuality, substance abuse—that could offend a large group of test-takers are strictly off-limits. Keep in mind, though, that issues such as impassioned political agendas and stances may be addressed in passing.

In general, Social Studies passages will call upon your ability to sort through different perspectives and evidence-based studies—some of which may build upon one another, some of which may be in complete disagreement. There are a few natural starting points for your analysis. Keep these in mind, but keep in mind as well that the questions may depend on fine points of passage details and passage transitions.

Topic, Sources, and Positions

There is one feature of Social Studies passages that, in the right circumstances, can make the entire reading experience move along in a wonderfully predictable manner. For Fiction passages, reading the blurb that introduces a given reading can be helpful (since the Fiction blurbs can clarify character and plot points), but is not always essential (since the titles, for this passage type, can be puzzling and may not be accompanied by further information). However, for Social Studies AND for Science passages, try to make a habit of reading the short introductory content. The reason will soon become obvious.

> ## ALWAYS read Social Studies and Science blurbs
> ## since passage titles often indicate TOPIC and MAIN IDEA

This approach is helpful, but is not a complete giveaway—since you will STILL need to read the passage thoroughly in order to understand how the topic, dilemma, or debate at hand is being investigated. What you should do is keep the title in mind and use it to orient your reading.

Consider the titles that appeared in the Diagnostic test, for both Social Studies and Science.

- "Country Food Sharing in the Canadian Arctic: Does It Feed the Neediest?"

- "Bigger human brain prioritizes thinking hub—at a cost"

- "Red Nuggets Are Galactic Gold for Astronomers"

On their own, these titles are most helpful for helping you to understand what kinds of topics (local economics, neuroscience, astronomy) are being addressed. To make the best possible sense of such topics, you will need to ask the right questions as your reading moves along: how a process referenced in the title works, why a specific idea indicated in the title is important, whether a theory contained in the title is valid. The food-sharing article gives an obvious instance. Quite simply, does food sharing feed the neediest? Your reading of the article should return an answer of some sort to this question.

Of course, passage titles do not have a perfect track record of pointing readers towards key passage information, and some of them may be too short or too cryptic to be particularly useful. You may need to work through a Social Studies passage entirely on its own terms. Knowing what to look for, in this case, is key—and, often enough, you will need to work through a few different types of information related to a key topic area.

As you read, stay alert for the following types of information.

1. Key Sources (named experts, institutions, or the author himself or herself)

2. Key Pieces of Evidence (statistics, quotations, studies, experimental outcomes)

3. Key Perspectives (common beliefs, new explanations, proposals, criticisms)

Some of these pieces of information may be quite closely related; in fact, the Social Studies checklist integrates a few of them, since you should work as much as possible to trace evidence and perspectives BACK to key sources. You should also keep in mind that how these elements are combined can vary considerably from passage to passage. Some Social Studies readings will present you with several viewpoints or studies that conflict with one another, while other readings in this category will focus on meticulously-described individual experiments—sometimes devoting almost all of the discussion to a single research project.

Notice, though, that so far you have not been called upon to weigh in on a potentially important element for any SAT Social Studies reading: the passage's thesis. The reason, here, is that the thesis will NOT occur in a single predictable place. Drawing hasty conclusions about a passage's viewpoint—even when the title seems like a giveaway—can do more harm than good. However, once you have worked through a passage's key pieces of information, you will be ready to discern what kind of a thesis the passage possesses.

Working with the Thesis

The central question with the thesis of any Social Studies passage is how strong, exactly, the author's position is. Some authors will be highly opinionated; others may simply be recording results or viewpoints. Think in terms of the following questions.

• Does the author present a single side of an issue or multiple sides?

• Does the author take a strong tone towards any side, or instead avoid bias?

• Does the author endorse or set forward a theory, or instead remain ambivalent or uncertain?

Note that an author may shift topic, tone, or degree of certainty considerably. These are the issues that you should use the Social Studies checklist, and the sample activity that follows, to clarify as you move forward.

Social Studies Checklist
Main Issue Strategy

Can you identify the following elements as they appear in the passage?

Overall Content

Core Topic or Question: _____

Source/Study 1: _____; Position: _____
Evidence/Support: _____

Source/Study 2: _____; Position: _____
Evidence/Support: _____

Source/Study 3: _____; Position: _____
Evidence/Support: _____

Author: _____; Position: _____
Evidence/Support: _____

Overall Issues

Thesis: _____

Conclusive: __ or Inconclusive: __ and WHY: _____

Shifts in Tone or Topic: 1: _____ ➡

2: _____ ➡

Structure: _____

Visuals Summary: _____

Visuals Related to Passage: _____

Questions 5-8 are based on the following Social Studies passage.

This passage is adapted from "Game Corrects Children's Misreading of Emotional Faces to Tame Irritability," a 2016 Science Update article posted* by the National Institute of Mental Health.

A computer game that changes a tendency to misread ambiguous faces as angry is showing promise as a potential treatment for irritability in
Line children. The game shifts a child's judgment for
5 perceiving ambiguous faces from angry to happy. In a small pilot study, irritable children who played it experienced less irritability, accompanied by changes in activation of mood-related brain circuitry. Researchers are now following up with a
10 larger study to confirm its effectiveness.

Melissa Brotman, Ph.D., Ellen Leibenluft, M.D., Joel Stoddard, M.D., of the NIMH Emotion and Development Branch, and colleagues, reported on findings of their pilot study of
15 "interpretation bias training" for child irritability online on January 8, 2016 in the *Journal of Child and Adolescent Psychopharmacology.*

About 3 percent of youth experience chronic severe irritability. They are prone to temper
20 outbursts and are often in a grumpy mood. Parents complain of having to "walk on eggshells" to avoid unleashing verbal—and sometimes physical—outbursts. These behaviors can lead to problems with friends, with family, and at school.
25 While irritability is common in disorders such as attention deficit hyperactivity disorder (ADHD) and oppositional defiant disorder, it is a core feature of disruptive mood dysregulation disorder (DMDD), which is associated with risk
30 for developing mood and anxiety disorders—and socioeconomic underachievement later in life.

While research suggests that parent training, psychotherapy, and some medications may be helpful for severe irritability, there are no
35 established treatments for DMDD. Evidence suggests that irritable youth with DMDD tend to misperceive emotional expressions. Compared

to healthy controls, children with DMDD were more prone to rate ambiguous faces as angry. So
40 Leibenluft's team set out to test interpretation bias training (IBT), a computer game designed to diminish irritable children's tendency to view ambiguous faces as angry.

Participants rated a continuum of 15
45 ambiguous faces appearing on a computer monitor as either happy or angry. After computer training, the children shifted their ratings toward seeing some of these ambiguous faces as "happy." This effect was maintained for at least 2 weeks and was
50 associated with decreased irritability, as rated by parents and by clinicians who interviewed both parents and children.

Some of these DMDD participants also performed a face-viewing task while their brain
55 activity was being measured by functional magnetic resonance imaging (fMRI). They showed activity changes in emotional learning areas suggesting that the computer-based training may alter neural responses to emotional faces.
60 Encouraged by these findings, the researchers have launched a larger, more controlled study to learn whether IBT might be effective as a treatment. They are also testing cognitive behavioral therapy (CBT), a talk therapy that aims
65 to change behaviors in response to frustrating events. These are among the first non-drug interventions that seek to help those with DMDD.

Families with affected children can choose to receive CBT alone, IBT alone, or IBT followed
70 by CBT. Those who elect IBT will perform most computer training sessions at home, over the course of a training program which can last from 3 to 13 weeks. Participants who are interested in brain scanning will also undergo before-and-
75 after fMRI scans while they are looking at the same ambiguous faces presented in the training sessions. The researchers hope these scans will show changes in brain activity that relate to symptom improvement following treatment.
80 "The training may be calming irritability by altering circuit activity underlying interpretive biases and—hopefully—reducing anger-based reactions like outbursts," said Leibenluft.

*See Page 262 for the citation for this text.

CONTINUE →

Social Studies Checklist
Practice Exercise 1.2

Can you identify the following elements as they appear in the passage?

Overall Content

Core Topic or Question: _____

Source/Study 1: _____; Position: _____
Evidence/Support: _____

Source/Study 2: _____; Position: _____
Evidence/Support: _____

Source/Study 3: _____; Position: _____
Evidence/Support: _____

Author: _____; Position: _____
Evidence/Support: _____

. . . .

Overall Issues

Thesis: _____

Conclusive: ___ or Inconclusive: ___ and WHY: _____

Shifts in Tone or Topic: 1: _____ ➡ _____

2: _____ ➡ _____

Structure: _____

Visuals Summary: _____

Visuals Related to Passage: _____

CONTINUE TO ANSWER PASSAGE QUESTIONS 5-8 ➡

5

The main purpose of the passage is to

A) present experimental findings that could prove useful in addressing irritability disorders.

B) describe how the scientific community as a whole responded to single study of adolescent irritability.

C) explain the origins and expected effects of chronic severe irritability in adolescents.

D) demonstrate that unusual patterns of brain activity can be linked to aggressive tendencies.

6

Which choice best describes the developmental pattern of the passage?

A) A few different terms are explained and an experiment that suggests new definitions is documented.

B) An approach to a psychological problem is outlined and possible shortcomings are briefly discussed.

C) An unconventional method is endorsed and diverging perspectives on its future uses are presented.

D) A specific technology is introduced and its applicability to psychological problem is examined.

7

On the basis of the passage, it can be reasonably inferred that irritability in children

A) may be treatable without the use of medications.

B) is not comparable to any condition observed among adults.

C) can become more severe as a result of exposure to technology.

D) is a direct outcome of specific parenting styles.

8

The passage is written from the point of view of

A) a concerned citizen whose response to irritability in children is based on personal experience.

B) a researcher who wishes to promote constructive changes to current pediatric practices.

C) an observer who possesses precise information about therapeutic methods for children.

D) a specialist in irritability disorders who aims to institute a new system of classification.

STOP
**After you have finished the questions, consult the relevant answers on Page 72.
Do not turn to any other section.**

Natural Science

The two Science passages that appear on each SAT Reading section can be drawn from a variety of topics: biology, chemistry, physics, ecology, earth science, and astronomy among them. In fact, passages that address issues in psychology and technology—fields that may seem oriented towards Social Studies—are eligible to appear under Natural Science. Keep in mind, also, that one graph WILL always appear and that one paired passage MAY appear in this passage category.

Fortunately, the designated Science passages can be quite approachable at times. Although you may be challenged to adapt to a new scientific concept, you will ALWAYS be given enough background information to approach such content; as ever, outside knowledge may help but is not in any way a necessity. Moreover, there will be relatively few stylistic difficulties. Because Science passages (unlike Fiction passages) are almost always taken from the past 75 years—and often from the extremely recent past—the possibility of encountering older-fashioned expressions and syntax decreases considerably.

Perhaps the most fortunate feature of Science passages, though, is their relative predictability in structure and intent. Though there are certainly some exceptions, a typical Science passage will be devoted to a single well-defined area of inquiry that is addressed in the following format.

1. Inquiry or Issue Established

2. Experiment or Research Explained

3. Broader Outcomes Addressed (Applications, Problems, Debates, Future Inquiries)

In some cases, Science passages will break down into EXACTLY these stages, with one following the next in an orderly fashion. In other cases, the different stages may be harder to discern—that is, until you learn to identify and comprehend each stage with speed and efficiency.

Inquiry or Issue

Your first priority should be to determine what theory, fact, or problem in scientific inquiry the author has chosen to address. This is in some ways a fairly straightforward task since 1) the TITLE can be extremely informative in some cases and 2) the FIRST FEW PARAGRAPHS can lay out a considerable amount of information. Of course, there may be SAT passages that deal with main issues that are extremely complex, that are elaborated over the course of rather long paragraphs, or that are accompanied by several counter-examples and counter-arguments. If you find yourself faced with such a passage, maintain high precision with the following questions—which are relevant to ANY Science passage.

• What information does the title provide? What ADDITIONAL questions does it raise?

• What is the theory, idea, or assumed fact that is being evaluated in the passage? Is there an EXPLICIT statement that defines the topic under investigation?

• What factors COMPLICATE the main inquiry or issue? Are competing theories, explanations, or examples mentioned anywhere?

Once you have clarified these issues—whether by finding information provided by the author or by researchers quoted in the article—you can easily move on to consider how, exactly, the investigations described in the passage proceeded.

Experiment or Research

In some passages, "experiments" and "research" may seem loosely defined at best. Official SAT passages have included informative and theoretical discussions of topics such as DNA and the Higgs boson particle; in these cases, the authors provided overviews of major scientific issues. Still, passages that are walk-throughs of specific experiments and research projects continue to dominate the test, and passages that deviate from this classic format can still be approached using a similar method.

As you read any given Science passage, divide up information in terms of methods of inquiry. These are often experiments, but can also be ideas or proposals (such as the nature of a molecule or a particle) that are given some logical explanation. Be aware, also, that experiment-oriented passages may proceed in stages, with two or even three related inquiries outlined one after another. Overall, try to think in terms of the following questions for every method or mode of investigation present.

• What idea or premise is this experiment, project, or line of reasoning meant to evaluate?

• What are the fine points of design and execution for the research? Did the researchers meet any obstacles?

• What are the immediate outcomes? Do they confirm or contradict any ideas—or lead to a new inquiry?

If you can think about immediate outcomes, you will also have a firm basis for considering the broad research outcomes that, frequently, are addressed in the final stages of Science passages.

Broader Outcomes

The last few paragraphs of a Science passage will, with some regularity, broaden the topic outward. A variety of new issues raised by the topic or research at hand may be considered, and some of the most common are listed below.

• Validation of an earlier theory

• Contradiction of an assumed explanation

• Formulation of a new or improved theory

• Sources of continuing uncertainty

• Proposal for a new or modified experiment

• Intensification of a debate or dispute

• Approval or agreement from the scientific community

• Dissent from a specific expert or a group of specialists

These issues may be raised by the author, by researchers quoted or described throughout the passage, or by researchers who are quoted for the first time near the passage's closing. Note also that some passages may terminate WITHOUT raising broad issues such as these, or may raise them towards a midpoint. Your task is to use your comprehension skills—and the checklist on the next page—to approach each passage on its unique terms, as helpful as knowing the standard Inquiry/Research/Outcome format can be.

Science Checklist
Main Issue Strategy

Can you identify the following elements as they appear in the passage?

Inquiry or Issue

Core Topic: _____ Core Question: _____

Source 1: _____; Hypothesis: _____

Source 2: _____; Hypothesis: _____

Other Hypotheses: _____

Research and Experiments

Method 1: _____

Outcome 1: _____ Conclusion 1: _____

Method 2: _____

Outcome 2: _____ Conclusion 2: _____

Broad Outcomes: _____

Overall Issues

Shifts in Tone or Topic: 1: _____ ➡ _____

2: _____ ➡ _____

Structure: _____

Visuals Summary: _____

Visuals Related to Passage: _____

Questions 9-12 are based on the following Science passage.

This passage is adapted from Charlotte Bhaskar, "A New Fossil Lace Bug with Unusual Antennae Joins the 'Big' Club." Originally published* in 2015 in *Worth a Thousand Words.*

Have you ever seen a lace bug? Don't let their pretty name fool you—even though they're dainty as a doily, they're tough little bugs. You may have encountered lace bugs in your garden or on houseplants, since they're herbivorous sap-drinkers. Though they only feed on plants, their bite can sting!

Named for their translucent delicate wings, little lace bugs make up the big family Tingidae within the order Hemiptera. Currently, there are over 2100 species of lace bugs living all over Earth. This globetrotting goes way back: Places as diverse as the Dominican Republic, Paris, and Myanmar all have amber deposits containing lace bug fossils from millions of years ago.

Most recently, as described in a study in PLOS ONE, scientists found four male lace bugs in the Eocene Green River Formation, a group of basins with exceptional fossil deposits in Colorado, Utah, and Wyoming.

These fossilized lace bugs are unusual for their remarkable preservation and flashy golf club-shaped antennae.

Their unusual antennae led the authors to suspect that they had a totally new species of lace bug on their hands. It can be difficult to categorize a new species, though—especially when looking at fossils. Time renders DNA, proteins, and other biological material low quality, making it often impossible to use common genetic or molecular tools.

Using phylogenetic analysis, which enables researchers to look at evolutionary links between organisms to determine relationships between ancestors and descendants, the authors were still able to assess the relationship of these fossils with other living and fossilized Tingidae species. In this case, instead of using genetic material, the authors compared physical characteristics of these fossils with other known Tingidae specimens.

The results of this detective work? The authors classified these fossils as a new species, Gyaclavator kohlsi. Since it's hard to miss the antennae on these guys, the authors constructed their genus name from a combination of the terms Gyas, who was a mythical giant from the *Aeneid*, and clavator, Latin for "club."

The authors of this study suspect Gyaclavator's showy antenna may be a rare fossil example of a visual display structure that could have played a role in mate attraction. In other words, Gyaclavator might have used its antennae like a male peacock uses its striking tail feathers: to advertise its appeal as a capable, healthy mate.

The authors also speculate that Glaclavator may have used its antennae as part of male-male competition, in the same way that male deer fight over resources using their antlers. Scientists have not found any other examples of lace bugs from the present or past that have features like these spectacular antennae.

However, other Hemiptera members do show similar enlarged physical structures akin to Gyaclavator's fancy antennae. Some species of leaf-footed bugs from the Coreidae family, for example, have large, petal-shaped antennae segments. They wave their conspicuous antennae through the air as part of a display that seems to function both in courtship as well as male-male competition.

It seems possible that Gyaclavator may have used its specialized antennae in a similar fashion, though it's hard to say for certain. Whatever function Gyaclavator's club-shaped antennae performed, it's clear this little lace bug marched to the beat of its own drum.

*See Page 262 for the citation for this text.

CONTINUE →

Science Checklist
Practice Exercise 1.3

Can you identify the following elements as they appear in the passage?

Inquiry or Issue

Core Topic: _____ Core Question: _____

Source 1: _____; Hypothesis: _____

Source 2: _____; Hypothesis: _____

Other Hypotheses: _____

Research and Experiments

Method 1: _____

Outcome 1: _____ Conclusion 1: _____

Method 2: _____

Outcome 2: _____ Conclusion 2: _____

Broad Outcomes: _____

Overall Issues

Shifts in Tone or Topic: 1: _____ ➡ _____

2: _____ ➡ _____

Structure: _____

Visuals Summary: _____

Visuals Related to Passage: _____

CONTINUE TO ANSWER PASSAGE QUESTIONS 9-12

9

The main purpose of the passage is to

A) challenge a series of common assumptions.

B) recommend modifications to a method.

C) examine the implications of a discovery.

D) spur discussion of an unsettling finding.

10

Which choice best describes the structure of the passage?

A) The common beliefs surrounding a group of insects are outlined, and a theory that challenges these beliefs is then assessed.

B) The genetic profile of a group of insects is presented, and this information is then used to explain a few different behaviors.

C) The traits of a group of insects are described, and an investigation that revolves around a single feature of these insects is then documented.

D) The best-known experiments involving a group of insects are assessed, and a new experiment that builds on various earlier results is then profiled.

11

As described in the passage, the researchers involved in the Eocene Green River Formation study relied on

A) DNA modeling that considered lace bugs alongside invertebrates that are not insects.

B) fieldwork that called attention to how lace bugs fight and communicate.

C) computer modeling that helped to compare lace bug species.

D) logical conclusions drawn from available lace bug specimens.

12

It can be reasonably inferred from the passage as a whole that lace bugs

A) are typically of more interest to casual observers than to biologists.

B) have inhabited a large geographic range both at present and in earlier times.

C) exhibit defensive and mating strategies seen in other insect groupings.

D) have gradually become more diverse in terms of size and anatomy.

STOP
After you have finished the questions, consult the relevant answers on Page 72.
Do not turn to any other section.

Historical Documents

The Historical Documents readings that appear on the SAT are taken from a range of different eras. Selections from the 18th century to the near-present have been featured both in the College Board's practice materials and on the administered tests, though readings from the 19th century have been somewhat predominant recently. In a sense, these passages resemble the Fiction passages, which exhibit a similar range in time period. The signature difference, though, is that Fiction passages will never occur in a paired format; History passages will (as explained in Chapter 5), and these pairings are among the elements of the SAT that pose the greatest challenges to some test-takers.

Technically, all history documents readings are classified under the title "Founding Documents and Great Global Conversation." You don't need to know this wording; in fact, the College Board's own title is rather awkward. Just keep in mind that topics such as the origins of political democracy in the United States and the clash between different ideologies guide these readings as a group.

Although an area of study as vast as "historical documents" can be potentially difficult to navigate, there are a few issues, topics, and ideological debates that appear with some regularity on the SAT. Here are a few that, on the basis of past College Board tests, you might want to be prepared to address.

1. The structure of government (often democratic or representative government versus older forms) and the obligations that exist between citizens and their government

2. Various forms of injustice (slavery, racial discrimination, gender discrimination, economic suffering) and the question of the proper response to injustice (new legislation, civil disobedience)

3. Questions of historical progress and reform, including the possible connection between different aspects of reform or activism (such as the struggle for women's rights and the abolition of slavery)

4. The political, cultural, economic, and moral attributes of the United States, as analyzed both by leaders from within the country itself and by observers from other nations (particularly countries in Europe)

5. The motivating principles of the founding documents of the United States, and the ways in which later policies and ideologies have responded to the country's founding documents

In general, and in a measure that recalls the intent behind the Social Studies passages, the SAT avoids historical topics that could be seen as partisan or controversial. It is supremely unlikely that the test would feature a passage intended mainly to sway its audience to support a current political party, such as Democrats or Republicans. It is ALSO supremely unlikely that the test would feature a passage on gun rights, abortion, evolution, or prayer in schools. Official test-makers tend to edit out even passing references to Christianity, and material related to a religious or ideological dispute that would sharply divide current American voters would not fit the current emphasis of the material.

Approaching the Passages

The historical passages that appear on the SAT require attentive reading. Move at a reasonable pace and understand the wording, but do NOT allow yourself to get bogged down by the frequent stylistic complexity of these passages. You should be prepared to deal with the following difficulties, at least at first, for the history document readings that are taken from the 18th century and the 19th century.

1. Stylistic Challenges (tendency towards long, intricate sentences; some especially tough vocabulary)

2. Tonal Challenges (ironies and shifts in attitude that are difficult to see at a glance)

However, some of the other challenges in these passages are matters of core content—and are linked to the nature of each reading as an excerpt from a document that takes a momentous historical position.

3. Concept- and Definition-Based Challenges (historical terms and ideas such as "suffrage," "abolition," and "capitalism" that may be unfamiliar, and may require attentive reading for context and comprehension)

4. Position-Based Challenges (intricacies of or qualifications to an author's argument that, though important, will NOT be easy to detect without practice or attention to detail)

There are, fortunately, a few main questions that should be useful on ANY History passage that you are given. Keep these in mind in order to read actively and to maintain focus.

• What is the author's main point or position? Why has the author written this piece (to connect issues, to correct a misconception, to promote a policy . . .) and what are the main justifications for the author's stance?

• What stylistic techniques (quotations, collective voice, direct address, metaphors, analogies, rhetorical questions . . .) dominate the author's discussion? What points in particular do these techniques help to convey?

• What kind of evidence (historical precedents, statistics, etc.) does the author employ? Or does the author rely mostly on tactics (hypothetical examples, broad claims about human nature, speculations, theories) that are not necessarily evidence based?

• What opponents does the author have? What points are these opponents making, and how does the author address these other sides of the argument?

• What shifts in topic, tone, stance, or strategy (if any) are present in the passage?

For a systematic presentation of these issues, consult the History checklist. You will notice that the categories that are given are EXTREMELY perspective-based. This emphasis is perfectly intentional: while some history authors may not use especially much empirical evidence or may stay very thesis-bound, these authors do with some regularity consider differing and disagreeing positions. In most cases, the point is to explain and refute flawed lines of reasoning—NOT to weaken an author's own approach.

History Checklist
Main Issue Strategy

Can you identify the following elements as they appear in the passage?

Main Idea

Core Topic: _____

Author's Position: _____

Author's Purpose: _____

Author's Argument

Reason 1: _____ Tone: _____

Reason 2: _____ Tone: _____

Reason 3: _____ Tone: _____

Opponent 1: _____ Idea: _____ Flaw: _____

Opponent 2: _____ Idea: _____ Flaw: _____

Passage Organization

Shifts in Tone or Topic: 1: _____ ➡ _____

2: _____ ➡ _____

3: _____ ➡ _____

Structure: _____

Main Writing Techniques: _____

Exercise 1.4

Questions 13-16 are based on the following History passage.

The following passage is adapted from Helen Hamilton Gardener, "Woman as an Annex." This essay appeared in Gardener's book *Facts and Fictions of Life* (1893).

It is the fashion in this country now-a-days to say that women are treated as equals. Some of the most progressive and best of men truly
Line believe what they say in this regard. One of
5 our leading daily papers, which insists that this is true, and even goes so far as to say that American gentlemen believe in and act upon the theory that their mothers and daughters are of a superior quality—and are always of the very
10 first consideration to and by men—recently had an editorial headlined "Universal Suffrage the Birthright of the Free Born." I read it through, and if you will believe me, the writer had so large a bump of sex arrogance that he never once thought
15 of one-half of humanity in the entire course of an elaborate and eloquent two-column article! "Universal" suffrage did not touch but one sex. There was but one sex "free born." There was but one which was born with "rights." The words
20 "persons," "citizens," "residents of the state," and all similar terms were used quite freely, but not once did it dawn upon the mind of the writer that every one of those words, every argument for freedom, every plea for liberty and justice,
25 equality and right, applied to the human race and not merely to one-half of that race.

Sex bias, sex arrogance, sex pride, sex assumption is so ingrained that it simply does not occur to the male logicians, scientists,
30 philosophers and politicians that there is a humanity. They see, think of and argue for and about only a sex of man—with an annex to him—woman. They call this the race; but they do not mean the race—they mean men. They write
35 and talk of "human beings;" of their needs, their education, their capacity and development; but they are not thinking of humanity at all. They are thinking of, planning for, and executing plans

which subordinate the race—the human entity—
40 to a subdivision, the mark and sign of which is the lowest and most universal possession of male nature—the mere procreative instinct and possibility. And this has grown to be the habit of thought until in science, in philosophy, in religion,
45 in law, in politics—one and all—we must translate all language into other terms than those used. For the word "universal" we must read "male;" for the "people," the "nation," we must read "men." The "will of the majority—majority rule"—
50 really means the larger number of masculine citizens. And so with all our common language, it is in a false tense. It is mere democratic verbal gymnastics, clothing the same old monarchial, aristocratic mental beliefs, with man now the
55 "divine right" ruler and with woman his subject and perquisite. Its gender is misstated and its import multiplied by two. It does not mean what it says, and it does not say what it means.

Our thoughts are adjusted to false verbal forms,
60 and so the thoughts do not ring true. They are merely hereditary forms of speech. All masculine thought and expression up to the present time has been in the language of sex, and not in the language of race; and so it has come about that
65 the music of humanity has been set in one key and played on one chord.

It has been well said that an Englishman cannot speak French correctly until he has learned to think in French. It is far more true that no one
70 can speak or write the language of human liberty and equality until he has learned to think in that language, and to feel without stopping to argue with himself, that right is not masculine only and that justice knows no sex.

CONTINUE

History Checklist
Practice Exercise 1.4

Can you identify the following elements as they appear in the passage?

Main Idea

Core Topic: _____

Author's Position: _____

Author's Purpose: _____

Author's Argument

Reason 1: _____ Tone: _____

Reason 2: _____ Tone: _____

Reason 3: _____ Tone: _____

Opponent 1: _____ Idea: _____ Flaw: _____

Opponent 2: _____ Idea: _____ Flaw: _____

Passage Organization

Shifts in Tone or Topic: 1: _____ ➡ _____

2: _____ ➡ _____

3: _____ ➡ _____

Structure: _____

Main Writing Techniques: _____

CONTINUE TO ANSWER PASSAGE QUESTIONS 13-16 ➡

13

Gardener's main purpose in the passage is to

A) demonstrate that men have intentionally damaged women's social status.

B) advocate a policy that would help to re-structure current reform movements.

C) prompt her audience to reject a limited understanding of democracy and injustice.

D) justify recent calls for a change in the leadership of the suffrage reform movement.

14

Over the course of the passage, Gardener transitions from

A) analyzing popular perceptions of women to relating women's rights to her own experience.

B) citing the opinions of a divisive figure to noting the possible merits of those opinions.

C) offering a critical assessment of a source to urging a broader perspective.

D) expressing disagreement with a figure of authority to endorsing a spirit of cooperation.

15

One of the central ideas present in the passage is that

A) those who think and write about politics instinctively consider only a single gender.

B) new political institutions should be created to address the historical disadvantages of women.

C) traditional definitions of political concepts have been altered by the emergence of democracy.

D) women's own unwillingness to assert themselves has been a key flaw of the women's suffrage movement.

16

Which of the following is a technique that Gardener uses to advance her argument throughout the passage?

A) Comparing the types of voting rights present in different nations

B) Acknowledging and dismissing the presumed weaknesses of her own argument

C) Quoting political activists whom she regards as sources of wisdom

D) Pinpointing terms and phrases that are deemed fundamentally inaccurate

STOP
**After you have finished the questions, consult the relevant answers on Page 72.
Then turn the page for additional exercises.**

Questions 17-20 are based on the following Fiction passage.

This passage is adapted from *Vandover and the Brute* (1914) by Frank Norris.

As he looked back over his life, Vandover could recall nothing after this, his mother's death, for nearly five years. Even after that lapse of time
Line the only scene he could picture with any degree
5 of clearness was one of the greatest triviality in which he saw himself, a rank thirteen-year-old boy, sitting on a bit of carpet in the back yard of the San Francisco house playing with his guinea-pigs.
10 In order to get at his life during his teens, Vandover would have been obliged to collect these scattered memory pictures as best he could, rearrange them in some more orderly sequence, piece out what he could imperfectly recall and
15 fill in the many gaps by mere guesswork and conjecture.

It was the summer of 1880 that they had come to San Francisco. Once settled there, Vandover's father began to build small residence houses and
20 cheap flats which he rented at various prices, the cheapest at ten dollars, the more expensive at thirty-five and forty. He had closed out his business in the East, coming out to California on account of his wife's ill health. He had made his
25 money in Boston and had intended to retire.

But he soon found that he could not do this. At this time he was an old man, nearly sixty. He had given his entire life to his business to the exclusion of everything else, and now when his
30 fortune had been made and when he could afford to enjoy it, discovered that he had lost the capacity for enjoying anything but the business itself. Nothing else could interest him. He was not what would be called in America a rich man, but he had
35 made money enough to travel, to allow himself any reasonable relaxation, to cultivate a taste for art, music, literature, or the drama, to indulge in any harmless fad, such as collecting etchings, china, or bric-à-brac, or even to permit himself
40 the luxury of horses. In the place of all these he

found himself, at nearly sixty years of age, forced again into the sordid round of business as the only escape from the mortal ennui and weariness of the spirit that preyed upon him during every leisure
45 hour of the day.

Early and late he went about the city, personally superintending the building of his little houses and cheap flats, sitting on saw-horses and piles of lumber, watching the carpenters at work.
50 In the evening he came home to a late supper, completely fagged, bringing with him the smell of mortar and of pine shavings.

On the first of each month when his agents turned over the rents to him he was in great spirits.
55 He would bring home the little canvas sack of coin with him before banking it, and call his son's attention to the amount, never failing to stick a twenty-dollar gold-piece in each eye, monocle fashion, exclaiming, "Good for the masses," a
60 meaningless jest that had been one of the family's household words for years.

His plan of building was peculiar. His credit was good, and having chosen his lot he would find out from the banks how much they would
65 loan him upon it in case he should become the owner. If this amount suited him, he would buy the lot, making one large payment outright and giving his note for the balance. The lot once his, the banks loaned him the desired amount. With
70 this money and with money of his own he would make the final payment on the lot and would begin the building itself, paying his labour on the nail, but getting his material, lumber, brick, and fittings on time. . . . Real estate was flourishing
75 in the rapidly growing city, and the new houses, although built so cheaply that they were mere shells of lath and plaster, were nevertheless made gay and brave with varnish and cheap mill-work. They rented well at first; scarcely a one was ever
80 vacant. People spoke of the Old Gentleman as one of the most successful realty owners in the city. So pleased did he become with the success of his new venture that in course of time all his money was reinvested after this fashion.

CONTINUE

17

The passage as a whole primarily describes

A) the impact of an unlikely death within a prosperous family.

B) the differing goals of an otherwise compatible father and son.

C) the pleasing routines agreed upon by members of a household.

D) the pursuits of a man who is regarded as a local success.

18

In the passage, one significant shift in focus is from

A) Vandover's attempts to remember his childhood to conflicting perspectives on Vandover's father.

B) Vandover's recollections to the projects and personality of Vandover's father.

C) Vandover's sense of isolation to the deep-seated pride of Vandover's father.

D) Vandover's creativity in childhood to the troubled old age of Vandover's father.

19

As described in the passage, Vandover's father is notable for his

A) vocal contempt for seemingly impractical pursuits.

B) immersion in the details of business operations.

C) unwillingness to show mercy to his competitors.

D) skill in quickly winning new friends and confidantes.

20

One way that the narrator of the passage provides insight into the character of Vandover's father is by

A) paraphrasing Vandover's own statements about his father.

B) recording the changing ways in which Vandover's mother saw her husband.

C) noting a few fairly reliable habits and tendencies.

D) presenting a single counterintuitive analogy.

CONTINUE

Part 1

This passage is adapted from "The Dreams Ideas Are Made Of" (2014) by Alex Camarota. Originally published* in InventorsEye, a newsletter of the United States Patent and Trademark Office.

The Internet is brimming with stories about inventions and discoveries that appeared in dreams. Einstein is said to have begun
Line contemplating the theory of relativity after
5   dreaming about cows when he was a teenager. There's also the story of Elias Howe, inventor of the sewing machine, who got the idea for a needle with the eye at its tip after dreaming about an incident involving spear-wielding cannibals.
10 The list of dream-born creations goes on and on, from the lyrics of famous songs to the molecular structures for common chemicals. . .

Inventors Eye's most recent spark of genius, Kim Meckwood, also got the idea for her Click &
15 Carry in a dream. She needed to solve the problem of carrying multiple bags of groceries up long flights of stairs to her apartment, and that's exactly what she did. But for Meckwood, getting ideas while asleep is nothing new. She said dreaming
20 is a way for her to process her thoughts and allow ideas to percolate and rise to the surface. As it turns out, this is also what some experts say dreaming is all about.

Most dreaming occurs during rapid eye
25 movement (REM), the period of sleep when the eyes erratically dart to and fro beneath the eyelids. REM sleep is also marked by increased brain activity. Various theories (none of which have a consensus in the scientific community) attempt
30 to explain the purpose of dreaming and REM. According to one, REM is the result of the brain processing and organizing the day's thoughts, sights, and sounds. In this way, dreams might be a way for us to contemplate things that we
35 are unable to or unwilling to contemplate during waking hours—or a way for us to finally grasp the solution to a problem that puzzled us.

Aside from the occasional dream, inventors get their ideas in many different ways. While
40 stories of invention often start with a common problem that needs fixing, the way inventors arrive at the solution can be varied. Most solutions are the result of trial and error, thinking and perseverance—like the Wright Brothers' flying
45 machine. Others still are the result of mere accident—Post-It Notes and vulcanized rubber were stumbled upon while their inventors were pursuing a different angle. And then there is the proverbial light bulb moment, when inspiration
50 feels so new and disruptive it seems almost miraculous. But there's a rub: it turns out a lot of good ideas are really just additions to, or new directions taken from, already existing ideas.

One thing is clear: innovation happens
55 in increments. Even during today's rapid technological expansion, most new mindboggling creations are the result of teams of researchers and engineers analyzing previous devices and processes, and figuring out how to make them
60 better. Even independent inventors solving everyday problems are adding their own ideas to ones that already exist. Invention does not occur in a vacuum.

This collaborative system of productivity
65 is common today, but that wasn't always the case. Ideas have not always had free reign to intermingle and bounce off each other. In fact, some experts, including notable science and technology writer Steven Johnson, credit the
70 arrival of a truly collaborative "marketplace of ideas" to something that many of us take a warming to: coffee.

First appearing on the European continent in the mid-1600s, coffee houses quickly took hold
75 as everyone from noblemen to street sweepers clamored in for a caffeine kick. The result, says Johnson, was that people from all walks of life began mingling and rubbing shoulders. Naturally, so did their ideas. Coffee houses were gathering
80 places to talk about every subject, from politics and philosophy to science and technology. The collaborative environment that sprung up in European coffee houses in the 17th century gave

---

*See Page 262 for the citation for this text.

CONTINUE

rise to what became known as the Enlightenment,
85 itself leading to scientific and technological
revolutions and even the modern patent system. . .

Every time an inventor receives a patent, he
or she adds to the archive of mankind's collective
good ideas. Patents force new ideas to enter the
90 marketplace and replace or improve the old. The
state of the art advances, and the process repeats
itself *ad infinitum*. You might even say that the
patent system is the coffee house of intellectual
property, where inventors and their inventions
95 come together to mingle and learn and take new
directions.

So go ahead: have another cup of Joe, but
always remember to dream.

21

The main purpose of the passage is to

A) present scientific research that lends credibility
to ideas about invention that would otherwise
appear outlandish.

B) show how a seemingly outdated set of beliefs has
led to revolutionary new inventions.

C) survey a range of factors in order to consider how
influential inventions and ideas were conceived.

D) emphasize the fact that inventors see isolation
from one another as essential to their work.

22

Overall, the passage is structured as

A) a synopsis of theoretical debates that do not fully
align with current practices.

B) a set of anecdotes that suggest conflicts involving
prominent figures.

C) a series of facts that are individually intriguing
but fundamentally dissimilar.

D) a group of examples that offer possibilities related
to a common theme.

23

One of the author's central ideas in the passage is that

A) dreams have inspired more potent inventions than
collaborative approaches have inspired.

B) inventors value extended REM sleep as a means
of cultivating new ideas.

C) some of the processes linked to invention have
not yet met with scientific consensus.

D) explanations of how inventions emerge have
changed little since the 1600s.

24

The passage as a whole indicates that inventions of
different kinds are inspired by

A) new ideas and a desire to make improvements.

B) community-driven endeavors to gain recognition.

C) personal expression as opposed to profitability.

D) everyday nuisances that require quick resolutions.

CONTINUE

Questions 25-28 are based on the following Science passage.

This passage is adapted from "NIH researchers discover highly infectious vehicle for transmission of viruses among humans," a 2018 news release* from the National Institutes of Health.

Researchers have found that a group of viruses that cause severe stomach illness—including the one famous for widespread outbreaks
Line on cruise ships—get transmitted to humans
5 through membrane-cloaked "virus clusters" that exacerbate the spread and severity of disease. Previously, it was believed that these viruses only spread through individual virus particles. The discovery of these clusters, the scientists
10 say, marks a turning point in the understanding of how these viruses spread and why they are so infectious. This preliminary work could lead to the development of more effective antiviral agents than existing treatments that mainly target
15 individual particles.

The researchers studied norovirus and rotavirus—hard-to-treat viruses that are the most common cause of stomach illness, or gastroenteritis, and that afflict millions of
20 people each year. The viruses cause symptoms ranging from diarrhea to abdominal pain and can sometimes result in death, particularly among young children and the elderly. Their highly contagious nature has led to serious outbreaks in
25 crowded spaces throughout many communities, most notably in cruise ships, daycare centers, classrooms, and nursing homes. Fortunately, vaccines against rotavirus are now available and are routinely given to babies in the United States.
30 "This is a really exciting finding in the field of virology because it reveals a mode of virus spread that has not been observed among humans and animals," said study leader Nihal Altan-Bonnet, Ph.D., senior investigator and head of
35 the Laboratory of Host-Pathogen Dynamics at the National Heart, Lung, and Blood Institute (NHLBI). "We hope that it will provide new clues

to fighting a wide range of diseases involving many types of viruses, including those that cause
40 gastrointestinal illnesses, heart inflammation, certain respiratory illnesses, and even the common cold."

The study was supported in part by the Intramural Research programs of the NHLBI and
45 the National Institute of Allergy and Infectious Diseases (NIAID), both part of the National Institutes of Health. It is featured as the cover story of *Cell Host & Microbe* and appears online on August 8.
50 Until a few years ago, most scientists believed that viruses, particularly those responsible for stomach illnesses, could only behave as independent infectious agents. However, in 2015 Altan-Bonnet and her colleagues showed that
55 polioviruses could transmit themselves in packets, or membrane-bound vesicles containing multiple virus particles. The scientists compared this new model of viral transmission to a Trojan horse: a group of membrane-bound viruses arrives at a
60 host cell and deposits viruses in the cell while dodging detection by the immune system. The scientists did not know whether this system applied to animals and humans, or how effective these packets were in infecting host cells.
65 To find out, they focused on rotaviruses and noroviruses, which mainly get spread through accidental ingestion of tiny particles of an infected person's stool—through, for example, contaminated food or liquids. The
70 researchers obtained fecal samples of humans and animals (pigs and mice) and found that the viruses are shed in the stool as virus clusters inside membrane-bound packets. In addition, they found that these virus-containing vesicles
75 were significantly more infectious than the free, unbound viruses within the samples.

The researchers determined that the high level of infectiousness was likely due to the vesicles delivering many viruses at once to the target
80 tissues; protecting their viral cargo from being destroyed by prolonged exposure to enzymes; and possibly by making their viral cargo invisible to the antibodies that are in the stool or gut of the

*See Page 262 for the citation for this text.

CONTINUE

host. More studies are needed, but the extreme
85 potency of the virus packets, they said, has a
clear consequence: it not only enhances the
virus' ability to spread more aggressively; it also
increases the severity of the disease it causes.
Handwashing with soap and water helps prevent
90 the spread of viruses.

"Our findings indicate that vesicle-cloaked
viruses are highly virulent units of fecal-oral
transmission, and highlight a need for antivirals
targeting vesicles and virus clustering," Altan-
95 Bonnet noted.

25

The passage as a whole primarily serves to

A) underscore a failure of earlier therapeutic methods, then celebrate a newly-developed technique.

B) assess a single scientific field, then promote an interdisciplinary approach.

C) describe a health liability, then record experimental findings.

D) explain a humanitarian crisis, then endorse one possible solution.

26

As described in the passage, Altan-Bonnet and the other researchers were mainly interested in viruses that

A) had adapted over time to resist a variety of treatment methods.

B) were known from their symptoms but had never been directly studied.

C) lead to infamous and occasionally fatal problems.

D) continue to be too diverse to classify formally.

27

Over the course of the passage, the main focus shifts from

A) statements that put a research endeavor in perspective to documentation of experimental procedures and results.

B) explanations of how an experiment was conducted to remarks that summarize public responses to that experiment.

C) assertions that celebrate the ingenuity of how an experiment was designed to statements that complicate such praise.

D) criticisms of proposed approaches to a dilemma to firsthand accounts from the researchers who addressed that dilemma.

28

It can be reasonably inferred that the study that is the focus of the passage was

A) disputed by experts who were receptive to Altan-Bonnet's earlier work.

B) not entirely conclusive but still suggestive of useful applications.

C) embraced by specialists in public health despite its apparent shortcomings.

D) eventually instrumental in preventing virus outbreaks on cruise ships.

Part 1

This passage is adapted from "The Theory of Social Revolutions" (1913) by Brooks Adams.

Questions 29-32 are based on the following History passage.

The same acceleration of the social movement which has caused this centralization of capital has caused the centralization of another form of
Line human energy, which is its negative: labor unions
5 organize labor as a monopoly. Labor protests against the irresponsible sovereignty of capital, as men have always protested against irresponsible sovereignty, declaring that the capitalistic social system, as it now exists, is a form of slavery. Very
10 logically, therefore, the abler and bolder labor agitators proclaim that labor levies actual war against society, and that in that war there can be no truce until irresponsible capital has capitulated. Also, in labor's methods of warfare the same
15 phenomena appear as in the autocracy of capital. Labor attacks capitalistic society by methods beyond the purview of the law, and may, at any moment, shatter the social system, while, under our laws and institutions, society is helpless.
20   Few persons, I should imagine, who reflect on these phenomena, fail to admit to themselves, whatever they may say publicly, that present social conditions are unsatisfactory, and I take the cause of the stress to be that which I have
25 stated. We have extended the range of applied science until we daily use infinite forces, and those forces must, apparently, disrupt our society, unless we can raise the laws and institutions which hold society together to an energy and
30 efficiency commensurate to them. How much vigor and ability would be required to accomplish such a work may be measured by the experience of Washington, who barely prevailed in his relatively simple task, surrounded by a generation
35 of extraordinary men, and with the capitalistic class of America behind him. Without the capitalistic class he must have failed. Therefore one most momentous problem of the future is the attitude which capital can or will assume in this
40 emergency.

That some of the more sagacious of the capitalistic class have preserved that instinct of self-preservation which was so conspicuous among men of the type of Washington is apparent
45 from the position taken by the management of the United States Steel Company, and by the Republican minority of the Congressional Committee which recently investigated the Steel Company; but whether such men very strongly
50 influence the genus to which they belong is not clear. If they do not, much improvement in existing conditions can hardly be anticipated.
     If capital insists upon continuing to exercise sovereign powers, without accepting
55 responsibility as for a trust, the revolt against the existing order must probably continue, and that revolt can only be dealt with, as all servile revolts must be dealt with, by physical force. I doubt, however, if even the most ardent and optimistic
60 of capitalists would care to speculate deeply upon the stability of any government capital might organize, which rested on the fundamental principle that the American people must be ruled by an army. On the other hand any government
65 to be effective must be strong. It is futile to talk of keeping peace in labor disputes by compulsory arbitration, if the government has not the power to command obedience to its arbitrators' decree; but a government able to constrain a couple
70 of hundred thousand discontented railway employees to work against their will, must differ considerably from the one we have. Nor is it possible to imagine that labor will ever yield peaceful obedience to such constraint, unless
75 capital makes equivalent concessions,—unless, perhaps, among other things, capital consents to erect tribunals which shall offer relief to any citizen who can show himself to be oppressed by the monopolistic price. In fine, a government, to
80 promise stability in the future, must apparently be so much more powerful than any private interest, that all men will stand equally before its tribunals; and these tribunals must be flexible enough to reach those categories of activity which now lie
85 beyond legal jurisdiction. If it be objected that the American people are incapable of an effort so

CONTINUE

prodigious, I readily admit that this may be true, but I also contend that the objection is beside the issue. What the American people can or cannot do
90 is a matter of opinion, but that social changes are imminent appears to be almost certain. Though these changes cannot be prevented, possibly they may, to a degree, be guided, as Washington guided the changes of 1789.

29

The main purpose of the passage is to

A) assert that democracy does not adequately represent those who most require aid.

B) explain that the labor movement in the United States should not be blamed for its recent excesses.

C) call into question the validity of a historical world view that omits economic considerations.

D) investigate the social and political circumstances that surround a troubling situation.

30

One central claim of the passage is that

A) conflict between social classes is impossible to avert.

B) compromise may be a way to address extremism and instability.

C) new laws inspire protest more often than they prompt compliance.

D) laborers will only embrace conformity if doing so will raise their social status.

31

As the author of the passage, Adams addresses his audience as

A) a concerned commentator who hopes to account for a few different perspectives.

B) an impartial historian who is skeptical of recent claims about scientific progress.

C) an advocate for workers who knowingly overstates the faults of the capitalistic class.

D) an engaged citizen who predicts the formation of an improved political system.

32

Throughout the passage, Adams develops his argument by

A) referring to a historical situation that may offer guidance.

B) citing common misinterpretations of the motives of antagonistic groups.

C) examining the origins of a few notable labor disputes.

D) directly addressing the American people to urge national harmony.

STOP
**After you have finished the questions, consult the relevant answers on Page 72.
Do not turn to any other section.**

Answer Key
Main Issue Questions

Passage 1	Passage 2	Passage 3	Passage 4
1. B	5. A	9. C	13. C
2. D	6. D	10. C	14. C
3. C	7. A	11. D	15. A
4. A	8. C	12. B	16. D

Passage 5	Passage 6	Passage 7	Passage 8
17. D	21. C	25. C	29. D
18. B	22. D	26. C	30. B
19. B	23. C	27. A	31. A
20. C	24. A	28. B	32. A

For detailed answer explanations for this practice section please visit **prepvantagetutoring.com/reading**.

Part 2

Passage Details
Strategy and Practice

Strategy 2
Passage Details

Question Fundamentals

While working through the Major Issue questions, you might have noticed that there were several false answers that could be readily eliminated. Some of these contained concepts that were present nowhere in the passage; others may have contained ideas that were in some ways present, but introduced subtle flaws in how ideas were connected or explained. Each passage checklist could direct you to the fundamental information that you would need to eliminate answers that deviated from the passage's content.

Working with Passage Details questions is in some ways a fundamentally similar task, since the SAT Reading section will continue to require attentive uses of evidence and conscientious elimination of problematic answer choices. However, the strategy here does NOT vary based on passage type. Instead, your challenge is to focus on specific line references, to read for context and comprehension, and to derive enough information to quickly cross off any false concepts, words, or tones that the answer choices offer.

Although this chapter does call attention to a few specialized question types—characterization, purpose, and logical inference among them—ALL Passage Details questions will follow roughly the same strategy. The only real difference, some times, is how much information you need to factor in to arrive at the correct answer.

The Core Strategy

Your first step, naturally, is to determine that you are in fact dealing with a Passage Detail question. This step itself relies on some process of elimination, since you must make sure that you are NOT dealing with a question that falls under Major Issue or Command of Evidence. Simply keep in mind the common formats.

- Major Issue: asks about OVERALL purpose, scenario, argument; may also ask about an issue (a major character or a broad writing technique) that CANNOT be localized to a few lines

- Command of Evidence: format includes four line references either as answer choices or as answer choices in the NEXT question

Here, instead, are the clues that you are dealing with a Passage Details question.

- Line References: "The first paragraph of the passage . . . " "In lines 27-34 . . . "

- Precise Detail: "As described early in the passage, Olga's friends . . . " "It can be inferred that high-salt diets can harm mice because . . . "

Once you have determined that you are in fact dealing with a set number of lines or a highly localized detail, perform the following steps REGARDLESS of the other details of the Passage Details question.

---

1. Determine the EXACT TOPIC that the question requires you to address and CIRCLE the key words or concepts in the question itself

2. Locate the LINE REFERENCE, then READ CLOSELY and READ AROUND for comprehension

3. Use the information from your reading to write a SHORT ANSWER and TONE (positive or negative) in response to the question

4. Perform a first round of PROCESS OF ELIMINATION using your predicted answer and (if appropriate) comprehension from your overall reading of the passage, so that all false words and false tones are crossed off

5. Revisit the lines to gather more information (if you have any REMAINING false answers) or to check your chosen answer against the text (if you have ELIMINATED ALL false answers)

Part 2: Passage Details

These steps will allow you to see the most valuable components of the information at hand—or at least ENOUGH components to reliably eliminate false answers. However, some differentiation may be necessary from here. Different Passage Details questions call upon you to focus on special features of a text, and perhaps—while still working with evidence—to place emphasis on different features of your predicted best answer.

Summary

The various Summary questions on the SAT Reading section call upon you to find precise information, often with the goal of offering a paraphrase or an accurate overall statement. You may be directed to a specific line or paragraph; in fact, the main variation in Summary questions involves HOW MUCH information you must factor in. A few of the Summary tasks that you may need to perform are as follow.

- Determining the traits, mood, or reactions of a fictional character or a real individual

- Explaining the important features of a process, situation, or setting

- Finding a specific detail or set of details that relates to a specific point or idea

- Explaining the content of a few key sentences or of a paragraph as a whole

To see how to work with the first—and somewhat more localized—of these possibilities, consider the following demonstration. The question below is new, but returns (as many of the questions in the next few chapters will) to content from the Diagnostic Test.

Olga Ivanovna was twenty-two, Dymov
was thirty-one. They got on splendidly together
when they were married. Olga Ivanovna hung
Line all her drawing-room walls with her own and
5 other people's sketches, in frames and without
frames, and near the piano and furniture arranged
picturesque corners with Japanese parasols, easels,
daggers, busts, photographs, and rags of many
colours . . . In the dining-room she papered the
10 walls with peasant woodcuts, hung up bark shoes
and sickles, stood in a corner a scythe and a rake,
and so achieved a dining-room in the Russian
style. In her bedroom she draped the ceiling and
the walls with dark cloths to make it like a cavern,
15 hung a Venetian lantern over the beds, and at
the door set a figure with a halberd. And every
one thought that the young people had a very
charming little home.

3

As described in the first paragraph of the passage, the relationship between Olga and Dymov is best understood as

A) harmonious.

B) uneasy.

C) distant.

D) celebrated.

This question gives you a specific location ("first paragraph") and a specific topic ("relationship between Olga and Dymov"). Any content OUTSIDE of these constraints will be problematic; as the steps that follow will demonstrate, the Passage Details method is designed to maintain a reasonable focus on key items.

Steps 1-3

3

As described in the first paragraph of the passage, ~~the relationship between Olga and Dymov is~~ best understood as . . .

Olga Ivanovna was twenty-two, Dymov was thirty-one. They **got on splendidly together** when they were married. ~~Olga Ivanovna hung~~
Line   ~~all her drawing-room walls with her own and~~
5   ~~other people's sketches, in frames and without~~

- Question requires attention to the "relationship between Olga and Dymov" (CIRCLE) as designated (step 1)

- Go to the first paragraph and find the relevant content, which should relate to the characters and their interactions (step 2)

- Formulate an answer based on the content, which describes how Olga and Dymov "got on" or got along in a positive manner (step 3)

To make a reasonable prediction, you could simply write "get along, +" next to the question. This sort of annotation takes VERY little time if done well, and allows you to undertake process of elimination with high efficiency.

Steps 4-5

3

As described in the first paragraph of the passage, the relationship between Olga and Dymov is best understood as

A) harmonious.

B) uneasy.

C) distant.

D) celebrated.

"got on splendidly together . . . " = "harmonious"

- Use the prediction "get along, +" to eliminate ALL false concepts and false tones (step 4)

close to "get along," positive (KEEP)

negative (eliminate)

negative (eliminate)

positive, but raises the concept of reputation or joy, NOT of people who "get along" (eliminate)

- Check the passage to confirm that your chosen answer, "harmonious," does fit the content (step 5)

While the steps for Summary questions that only call attention to a few line references can be quite straightforward, questions that require you to examine full paragraphs can be a challenge at first. Even here, the same methods will apply. The main difference is that your predicted answer is somewhat less likely to direct you ENTIRELY to the right answer on a first run; if you find yourself in such a case, strategic re-reading for additional content may be necessary, as the following example from the Diagnostic Test shows.

Part 2: Passage Details

Olga Ivanovna was twenty-two, Dymov
was thirty-one. They got on splendidly together
when they were married. Olga Ivanovna hung
Line all her drawing-room walls with her own and
5 other people's sketches, in frames and without
frames, and near the piano and furniture arranged
picturesque corners with Japanese parasols, easels,
daggers, busts, photographs, and rags of many
colours . . . In the dining-room she papered the
10 walls with peasant woodcuts, hung up bark shoes
and sickles, stood in a corner a scythe and a rake,
and so achieved a dining-room in the Russian
style. In her bedroom she draped the ceiling and
the walls with dark cloths to make it like a cavern,
15 hung a Venetian lantern over the beds, and at
the door set a figure with a halberd. And every
one thought that the young people had a very
charming little home.

3

The first paragraph serves mainly to describe how

A) one character altered her surroundings in a
manner that met with approval.

B) one character assigned a series of meaningful
decisions to a second character.

C) one character reinvented a setting as an
expression of her unique personality.

D) two characters developed a collaborative method
for making improvements to their household.

Steps 1-3

- Consider the ENTIRE first paragraph, and read
this content for close comprehension. The topic
is how Olga chose decorations herself, and her
home is regarded as "charming" (steps 1-2)

- Formulate and write an answer that quickly
presents key concepts, such as "marriage, Olga's
decorations, +" (step 3)

Now, consider the answers. You will notice that ALL of these seem to have positive elements, but only a few
of them relate to the predictions that have been noted above.

Step 4

3

The first paragraph serves mainly to describe how

- Use the prediction "marriage, Olga's decorations
+" to eliminate ALL false concepts and false
tones

A) one character altered her surroundings in a
manner that met with approval.

close to "Olga's decorations" (KEEP)

B) one character assigned a series of meaningful
decisions to a second character.

shifts focus away from Olga (eliminate)

C) one character reinvented a setting as an
expression of her unique personality.

seems close to "Olga's decorations" (POSSIBLE?)

D) two characters developed a collaborative method
for making improvements to their household.

shifts focus away from Olga, raises faulty theme of
"collaborative method" (eliminate)

You may recall from the Diagnostic Test that the answer is in fact A. Still, under the time constraints, C may appear to be an appealing choice since it DOES reference the core topic of the prediction. Answers of this sort will often feature incorrect LOGIC (when the key terms are present) or inaccurate SIDE TOPICS (when the main theme or topic is nonetheless addressed in some manner). In cases such as this one, return to the passage and re-read to account for ALL content.

Step 5

- A: Does the paragraph mention that Olga's alterations "met with approval"? YES (lines 16-18, "And every one thought that the young people had a very charming little home.")

- C: Does the paragraph connect the setting to Olga's "unique personality"? NO (objects are mentioned but are not EXPLICITLY connected to her specific character traits)

There are two important notes on this stage of the method.

1. Checking for more evidence is NOT the same as double-guessing. If you genuinely cannot decide between two choices such as A and C, your task is to factor in MORE content. If you used the method to successfully get A and detected a critical flaw in C using an early prediction, be cautious of ANY further analysis. As you complete more tests, you should start using the methods instinctively—and should never over-think your way out of correct answers.

2. Some answers, such as C, may rely on extrapolation, interpretation, or indeterminate content. For instance, it is possible that Olga's decorations do reflect her personality—but it also possible that they do not, since the passage does not EXPLICITLY raise this point. An answer that "seems logical" or "sounds good" but is not directly backed by content should be automatically eliminated.

Purpose

Despite their different designation, Purpose questions do not always differ from Summary questions in major ways. These two question types can share wording—for instance, "serves to," which is used both for entire paragraphs for Summary questions and for various Purpose questions—and for the sake of efficiency you should NOT spend much time thinking about fine distinctions here.

Overall, Purpose questions call attention to the following issues.

- The effects of specific word choices or turns of phrase within a passage

- The author's motive for including a specific image, phrase, or piece of information

- The ways in which different parts of a passage relate to one another (setting up examples, returning to key ideas, defining central terms, etc.)

Part 2: Passage Details

To work with these questions, you typically do NOT need any specialized training in rhetorical terminology (although some background in this area, as part of your vocabulary training, may increase your comfort with the test as a whole). What you MAY need is significantly more reading around or more consideration of a passage's main issues than Summary questions tend to require. Consider, here, the following example, which returns to the Diagnostic Test content.

must be of use. I don't understand them, but not understanding does not imply disbelieving in them."

80   "Let me shake your honest hand!"
After dinner Olga Ivanovna would drive off to see her friends, then to a theatre or to a concert, and she returned home after midnight. So it was every day.

10

The final sentence of the passage serves primarily to indicate that

A) Olga is eager to make changes in her way of living.

B) the reader is meant to see the passage's characters as unwilling to change.

C) Dymov and Olga are not fully aware of the psychological effects of their marriage.

D) the passage as a whole describes a predictable lifestyle.

Although a question that calls attention to a single sentence and what it "serves primarily to indicate" may seem to require clever analysis, the answer can be quite straightforward. Just work through the method as carefully as possible.

Steps 1-3

10

The final sentence of the passage serves primarily to indicate that . . .

After dinner Olga Ivanovna would drive off to see her friends, then to a theatre or to a concert, and she returned home after midnight. **So it was every day.**

- Question requires attention to the "final sentence" (CIRCLE) as designated (step 1)

- Go to the final paragraph and find the sentence, then read around to clarify that the words "So it was" refer to Olga's pleasant lifestyle (step 2)

- Formulate an answer based on the content, which describes a lifestyle that continues every day in a positive manner (step 3)

Now, use your predictions from the cited content and the required reading around to work through the answer choices.

Steps 4-5

10

The final sentence of the passage serves primarily to indicate that

A) Olga is eager to make changes in her way of living.

B) the reader is meant to see the passage's characters as unwilling to change.

C) Dymov and Olga are not fully aware of the psychological effects of their marriage.

D) the passage as a whole describes a predictable lifestyle.

- Use the prediction "lifestyle continues, +" to eliminate ALL false concepts and false tones (step 4)

directly contradicts the prediction (eliminate)

negative towards the characters (eliminate)

somewhat negative, false theme of limited awareness (eliminate)

theme or idea of predictability, avoids a tone but possible positive (CORRECT)

"every day . . . " = "predictable lifestyle"

- Check the passage to confirm that your chosen answer, "predictable lifestyle," does fit the content (step 5)

Inference

The Inference questions on the SAT Reading section require you to draw logical conclusions based on information available in the text. Verbs such as "suggest," "indicate," "support," and of course "infer" will signal this question type. Although each Inference question can be answered using the standard method, some of these questions may require you to consider new and direct consequences of the information present. Such consequences will ALWAYS be evidence-based. For instance, if the passage indicates that "a majority of students did not vote in the recent election," a reasonable inference—and one that COULD appear in the answer choices—would involve the other side of this situation, that "only a minority of students cast election ballots."

Here are a few of the topics or aptitudes that Inference questions have incorporated on recent SAT tests.

- Determining what conclusion is supported (or undermined) by information present in the passage

- Explaining the correct cause-and-effect relationship involving information from the passage

- Deciding which situation supports (or contradicts) an idea or finding present in the passage

- Selecting a situation or scenario that is similar to content from the passage

Part 2: Passage Details

Note that you will NEVER deviate from information that is given to you "in the passage." This fundamental is important to keep in mind even as you work with Inference questions that become complex and that might tempt you to try either a shortcut or a "creative" approach. Just stay with the Passage Details method, and even a complicated Inference question such as the one that follows will soon resolve itself.

65   Since people with certain mental disorders show alterations in brain size related to genetic influences, the new cortex maps may improve understanding of altered brain organization in disorders. The higher expanding regions are also
70   implicated across diverse neurodevelopmental disorders, so the new insights may hold clues to understanding how genetic and environmental changes can impact higher mental functions.
     "Our study shows there are consistent
75   organizational changes between large brains and small brains," said Raznahan. "Observing that the brain needs to consistently configure itself differently as a function of its size is important for understanding how the brain functions in health
80   and disease states."
     "Notably, we saw the same patterns for scaled-up brains across three large independent datasets," noted Seidlitz.

30

Which of the following findings would most clearly CONTRADICT the primary findings of the study described in the passage?

A) The quickest-growing areas of the brain can take over functions often assigned to slower-growing areas.

B) The typical neurodevelopmental disease renders the brain completely incapable of growing or changing.

C) The regions of the brain that govern higher-order thinking can experience unusually high growth rates in the brains of subjects who have psychological disorders.

D) The growth of brain regions related to analysis and problem solving can lead to impaired physical coordination.

Begin by reading the question carefully, and notice that you need to evaluate the "primary findings" of the passage. From your work with the Main Issues in the passage, you should know that—for this Diagnostic Test reading—the findings are provided in the final few paragraphs. Note also that you need an answer that contradicts one of these findings (NOT one that supports a finding) and keep this fact firmly in mind as you set the techniques to work.

Steps 1-3

30

Which of the following findings would most clearly CONTRADICT the primary findings of the study described in the passage?

⬇

Since people with certain mental disorders show alterations in brain size related to genetic influences . . . The higher expanding regions are also implicated across diverse neurodevelopmental disorders . . . "Our study shows there are consistent organizational changes between large brains and small brains" . . . "the brain needs to consistently configure itself differently as a function of its size" . . . "Notably, we saw the same patterns for scaled-up brains"

- Question requires attention to something that would "CONTRADICT" a finding (CIRCLE) as designated (step 1)

- Read through the findings and note main conclusions, such as "disorders and expansion" and "brains consistently changing" (step 2)

- Formulate an answer based on the content, which describes how brains at different levels of size and mental health can change (step 3)

Steps 4-5

30

Which of the following findings would most clearly CONTRADICT the primary findings of the study described in the passage?

- Use the prediction "brains changing" to determine the answer, which should CONTRADICT the idea that the brain changes (step 4)

A) The quickest-growing areas of the brain can take over functions often assigned to slower-growing areas.

indicates that brains DO grow (eliminate)

B) The typical neurodevelopmental disease renders the brain completely incapable of growing or changing.

indicates that some brains to NOT grow (KEEP)

C) The regions of the brain that govern higher-order thinking can experience unusually high growth rates in the brains of subjects who have psychological disorders.

indicates that brains DO grow (eliminate)

D) The growth of brain regions related to analysis and problem solving can lead to impaired physical coordination.

indicates that brains DO grow (eliminate)

"neurodevelopmental disorders . . . " in lines 70-71, "neurodevelopmental disease . . . " in the answer

- Check the passage to confirm that your chosen answer fits an appropriate concept from the relevant content (step 5)

Now that you are familiar with the fundamental strategy and the core classifications for Passage Details questions, put your skills to the test with the practice questions that follow. You may see some question formats and topics that are unfamiliar at first, but your approach should be consistent throughout.

Questions 1-6 are based on the following Fiction passage.

This passage is adapted from Saachika Reddy, "Winter Orchids" (2017).

Another Wednesday arrived, and with it another not-quite-self-consciously resplendent message from Monsieur Tremblay. Avni followed
Line along as his prose, after alighting on the briefest
5 yet warmest of greetings, swept off over the autumny tundras of Saskatchewan and Manitoba, tentatively returned back to inspect the contents of a few curiously dog-eared volumes in Monsieur Tremblay's book collection, and finally settled
10 down in the grotto-like eateries and slow-falling dusks of Old Montreal. As always, it was hard to say where distant recollection ended and the more recent past began. Monsieur Tremblay's narrations, in sweeping over so much space,
15 seemed to find it necessary to suspend time; the acrobatics of moving so deftly from sight to sight allowed no time to pause for the necessary *when* and *how* of a more mundane account. His words suspended both the dull mechanics of travel—the
20 waits, the rides, the rain, the headaches—and the threatening absurdity of trying to commit any rich thought to e-mail. Somehow, thought Avni, Monsieur Tremblay restored dignity to a medium that had none of the inherent dignity of pen and
25 ink.
    Then, as an anticlimax, there would be a perfectly unimportant and perfectly edited business letter attached. "For your review, please find . . . " the message would conclude, and Avni
30 would—as a matter of habit—ask herself yet again why Monsieur Tremblay and his Henry James*-ian command of English required a proofreading service.
    Whether writing provided Monsieur Tremblay
35 a refuge or whether he poured out his experiences in mulled bronze prose out of a sort of compulsion was impossible, even now, for Avni to determine.

From the headshot, resume, and questionnaire answers in his client profile she had deduced
40 everything she could; she had constructed an image of this diminutive 50-year-old wandering around Prince Edward Island and twining together the serpentine sentences of his next letter. Yet she knew nothing of *why* he wrote like this, why he
45 wrote *at all*. Wouldn't it be enough to have these transcendent thoughts all to oneself?
    Avni thought it would be. To have a world such as Monsieur Tremblay's all to oneself would be enough. In such a place, needling messages from
50 one's brother and mother would have no way to pierce through. Her mother was the more direct of the two, and should have been the more irksome: Avni had received dozens of e-mails with links to marketing jobs and research fellowships. "Perhaps
55 you should look at this" and "This one looks interesting" had become interchangeable with her mother's presence. Avni's response was always indifference. Her brother didn't send "helpful" e-mails, for his part. Instead he called at strange
60 hours and asked Avni a series of harmless day-to-day questions, though the worry and annoyance in his voice were both unmistakable to her. Beneath an inquiry about an unimportant movie would be the thought, "Are you still just patching together
65 part-time work, really, seriously?" Beneath a remark about an election that neither of them cared about would be the sentiment, "Please, find something to do, a real job. I'm not saying this to insult you. I'm saying this because I have an
70 MBA and you have a PhD, and only one of us is making good on these facts." Avni would want to sigh the loudest possible sigh of relief at the end of each of these conversations. She was not trying to convince him of anything at this point, and she
75 had won enough arguments with herself to feel convinced that she was in the right, that the $18 per hour she made as a proofreader was a measure of so few of the things that made life worthwhile.

---

*Henry James (1843-1916): American novelist and critic famous for the complex imagery and syntax of his writing

CONTINUE

1

The first paragraph of the passage serves to establish

A) one of Monsieur Tremblay's motives for confiding in Avni.

B) a few of the broad characteristics of Monsieur Tremblay's style of writing.

C) the role of a formative experience in altering Monsieur Tremblay's character.

D) a point of similarity between Avni and Monsieur Tremblay.

2

As mentioned in the passage, "Old Montreal" (line 11) is best understood as

A) an area that Monsieur Tremblay has only recently seen for the first time.

B) a site that Monsieur Tremblay has persuaded Avni to visit.

C) a destination that Avni finds more intriguing than Saskatchewan or Manitoba.

D) a location that Monsieur Tremblay knows well enough to describe in some detail.

3

Which choice best captures an important irony related to the business letters that Monsieur Tremblay sends Avni?

A) Monsieur Tremblay routinely asks Avni to edit work that is too well-written to require attention.

B) Monsieur Tremblay normally requests small edits to documents that are seldom read carefully.

C) Monsieur Tremblay is unaware that his business letters resemble his casual correspondence.

D) Monsieur Tremblay's talents as a writer in fact undermine a few of his business instincts.

4

The question in lines 45-46 mainly functions to

A) resolve a few of the questions surrounding Monsieur Tremblay's background.

B) address a few of the apprehensions raised by Avni's mother.

C) demonstrate Monsieur Tremblay's fundamental impracticality.

D) suggest an area of certainty in Avni's way of thinking.

5

It can be inferred that Avni's mother wants Avni to

A) take greater pride in material accomplishment.

B) keep in closer touch with the family as a whole.

C) pursue opportunities that are of little interest to Avni herself.

D) abandon a fear of personal and professional change.

6

As described in the passage, Avni's brother interacts with Avni in a manner notable for its

A) cleverness and contempt.

B) earnestness and incoherence.

C) indirection and vexation.

D) despair and unpredictability.

CONTINUE ➤

Part 2

This passage is adapted from "Game Corrects Children's Misreading of Emotional Faces to Tame Irritability," a 2016 Science Update article posted* by the National Institute of Mental Health.

A computer game that changes a tendency to misread ambiguous faces as angry is showing promise as a potential treatment for irritability in
Line children. The game shifts a child's judgment for
5 perceiving ambiguous faces from angry to happy. In a small pilot study, irritable children who played it experienced less irritability, accompanied by changes in activation of mood-related brain circuitry. Researchers are now following up with a
10 larger study to confirm its effectiveness.
   Melissa Brotman, Ph.D., Ellen Leibenluft, M.D., Joel Stoddard, M.D., of the NIMH Emotion and Development Branch, and colleagues, reported on findings of their pilot study of
15 "interpretation bias training" for child irritability online on January 8, 2016 in the *Journal of Child and Adolescent Psychopharmacology*.
   About 3 percent of youth experience chronic severe irritability. They are prone to temper
20 outbursts and are often in a grumpy mood. Parents complain of having to "walk on eggshells" to avoid unleashing verbal—and sometimes physical—outbursts. These behaviors can lead to problems with friends, with family, and at school.
25   While irritability is common in disorders such as attention deficit hyperactivity disorder (ADHD) and oppositional defiant disorder, it is a core feature of disruptive mood dysregulation disorder (DMDD), which is associated with risk
30 for developing mood and anxiety disorders—and socioeconomic underachievement later in life.
   While research suggests that parent training, psychotherapy, and some medications may be helpful for severe irritability, there are no
35 established treatments for DMDD. Evidence suggests that irritable youth with DMDD tend to misperceive emotional expressions. Compared

to healthy controls, children with DMDD were more prone to rate ambiguous faces as angry. So
40 Leibenluft's team set out to test interpretation bias training (IBT), a computer game designed to diminish irritable children's tendency to view ambiguous faces as angry.
   Participants rated a continuum of 15
45 ambiguous faces appearing on a computer monitor as either happy or angry. After computer training, the children shifted their ratings toward seeing some of these ambiguous faces as "happy." This effect was maintained for at least 2 weeks and was
50 associated with decreased irritability, as rated by parents and by clinicians who interviewed both parents and children.
   Some of these DMDD participants also performed a face-viewing task while their brain
55 activity was being measured by functional magnetic resonance imaging (fMRI). They showed activity changes in emotional learning areas suggesting that the computer-based training may alter neural responses to emotional faces.
60   Encouraged by these findings, the researchers have launched a larger, more controlled study to learn whether IBT might be effective as a treatment. They are also testing cognitive behavioral therapy (CBT), a talk therapy that aims
65 to change behaviors in response to frustrating events. These are among the first non-drug interventions that seek to help those with DMDD.
   Families with affected children can choose to receive CBT alone, IBT alone, or IBT followed
70 by CBT. Those who elect IBT will perform most computer training sessions at home, over the course of a training program which can last from 3 to 13 weeks. Participants who are interested in brain scanning will also undergo before-and-
75 after fMRI scans while they are looking at the same ambiguous faces presented in the training sessions. The researchers hope these scans will show changes in brain activity that relate to symptom improvement following treatment.
80   "The training may be calming irritability by altering circuit activity underlying interpretive biases and—hopefully—reducing anger-based reactions like outbursts," said Leibenluft.

---

*See Page 262 for the citation for this text.

7

The first paragraph primarily characterizes the "computer game" (line 1) as

A) significantly flawed but capable of being adjusted.

B) useful as a therapeutic tool but still difficult to explain in theoretical terms.

C) immensely entertaining but incapable of countering severe problems.

D) rich with potential but requiring additional investigation.

8

On the basis of the information present in the passage, which of the following children most clearly exhibits symptoms of chronic severe irritability?

A) A boy who refuses to talk to his parents any time that they reprimand him for misbehavior

B) A boy who vandalizes houses in his neighborhood with the assistance of his friends

C) A boy who screams at his parents when asked to perform his assigned chores

D) A boy who has difficulty making friends despite attending a small school

9

Leibenluft's initial experiment was structured with the goal of evaluating

A) how much two comparable disorders overlap.

B) whether a computer game can serve an educational purpose.

C) the role of parenting styles in cognitive behavioral therapy.

D) the effectiveness of interpretation bias training.

10

The primary effect of placing the word "happy" in quotation marks in line 48 is to

A) indicate the difficulty of defining a concept.

B) imply that expert testimony is being quoted.

C) signal that a designation is questionable.

D) allude to a consensus among parents.

11

Which of the following situations suggests that CBT could be an effective treatment for DMDD?

A) Children who discuss their problems with licensed specialists exhibit relatively low risk of developing mood disorders.

B) Children who exhibit DMDD run very little risk of also developing ADHD.

C) Children whose parents avoid medication-based therapy are likely to enroll in talk therapy programs.

D) Children whose parents took medication to treat DMDD run a relatively low risk of developing DMDD themselves.

12

According to the passage, fMRI scans may be useful as a means of

A) clarifying the dangers that can attend drug-based psychotherapy methods.

B) exploring how children with ADHD deal with stress as they mature.

C) determining whether therapy changes brain circuitry.

D) comparing the abilities of children who have overcome DMDD.

CONTINUE

Part 2

Questions 13-18 are based on the following Science passage.

This passage is adapted from Charlotte Bhaskar, "A New Fossil Lace Bug with Unusual Antennae Joins the 'Big' Club." Originally published* in 2015 in *Worth a Thousand Words*.

Have you ever seen a lace bug? Don't let their pretty name fool you—even though they're dainty as a doily, they're tough little bugs. You
Line may have encountered lace bugs in your garden or
5 on houseplants, since they're herbivorous sap-drinkers. Though they only feed on plants, their bite can sting!

Named for their translucent delicate wings, little lace bugs make up the big family Tingidae
10 within the order Hemiptera. Currently, there are over 2100 species of lace bugs living all over Earth. This globetrotting goes way back: Places as diverse as the Dominican Republic, Paris, and Myanmar all have amber deposits containing lace
15 bug fossils from millions of years ago.

Most recently, as described in a study in PLOS ONE, scientists found four male lace bugs in the Eocene Green River Formation, a group of basins with exceptional fossil deposits in Colorado, Utah,
20 and Wyoming.

These fossilized lace bugs are unusual for their remarkable preservation and flashy golf club-shaped antennae.

Their unusual antennae led the authors to
25 suspect that they had a totally new species of lace bug on their hands. It can be difficult to categorize a new species, though—especially when looking at fossils. Time renders DNA, proteins, and other biological material low quality, making it often
30 impossible to use common genetic or molecular tools.

Using phylogenetic analysis, which enables researchers to look at evolutionary links between organisms to determine relationships between
35 ancestors and descendants, the authors were still able to assess the relationship of these fossils with other living and fossilized Tingidae species. In

this case, instead of using genetic material, the authors compared physical characteristics of these
40 fossils with other known Tingidae specimens.

The results of this detective work? The authors classified these fossils as a new species, Gyaclavator kohlsi. Since it's hard to miss the antennae on these guys, the authors constructed
45 their genus name from a combination of the terms Gyas, who was a mythical giant from the *Aeneid*, and clavator, Latin for "club".

The authors of this study suspect Gyaclavator's showy antenna may have been a rare fossil example
50 of a visual display structure that could have played a role in mate attraction. In other words, Gyaclavator might have used its antennae like a male peacock uses its striking tail feathers: to advertise its appeal as a capable, healthy mate.

55 The authors also speculate that Gyaclavator may have used its antennae as part of male-male competition, in the same way that male deer fight over resources using their antlers. Scientists have not found any other examples of lace bugs from
60 the present or past that have features like these spectacular antennae.

However, other Hemiptera members do show similar enlarged physical structures akin to Gyaclavator's fancy antennae. Some species
65 of leaf-footed bugs from the Coreidae family, for example, have large, petal-shaped antennae segments. They wave their conspicuous antennae through the air as part of a display that seems to function both in courtship as well as male-male
70 competition.

It seems possible that Gyaclavator may have used its specialized antennae in a similar fashion, though it's hard to say for certain. Whatever function Gyaclavator's club-shaped antennae
75 performed, it's clear this little lace bug marched to the beat of its own drum.

---

*See Page 262 for the citation for this text.

CONTINUE

13

In the first paragraph, the words "pretty" and "dainty" primarily have the effect of

A) establishing contrasts involving characteristics of lace bugs.

B) construing the topic matter of the passage as ultimately trifling.

C) critiquing the reader's method of interpretation as irrational.

D) paraphrasing a pair of seemingly antagonistic opinions.

14

As characterized in the passage, the Eocene Green River Formation is

A) an important landmark in a lightly populated area.

B) a site that has yielded a surprisingly large number of lace bug specimens.

C) a promising place to search for the remains of ancient life.

D) a location that was of little scientific interest before it was discovered to contain insect remains.

15

It can be inferred from the passage that the newly-discovered lace bugs were difficult to classify as a new species because

A) the lace bugs did not resemble any living insects.

B) past attempts to categorize lace bugs have resulted in incompatible classification systems.

C) genetic methods of species identification are best adapted to living and recently-deceased animals.

D) amber fossilization warps the DNA signature of a fossilized organism.

16

The author presents the imagery of "a male peacock" (line 53) and "male deer" (line 57) in order to

A) challenge an earlier depiction of lace bugs as fragile.

B) clarify a few plausible Gyaclavator behaviors.

C) add humor to an unusually technical analysis.

D) draw analogies that reference various zoological experiments.

17

One possible similarity between Gyaclavator and "other Hemiptera members" (line 62) involves

A) the male-dominated nature of their typical interactions.

B) the use of antennae in mating and competition.

C) their ability to adjust to resource scarcity.

D) the prominence of massive and club-shaped antennae.

18

The main purpose of the final paragraph is to

A) depart from the informal tone present elsewhere in the passage.

B) reject a group of well-publicized explanations.

C) connect an important topic to a seemingly insignificant detail.

D) highlight a point that has not been fully resolved.

Part 2

Questions 19-24 are based on the following History passage.

The following passage is adapted from Helen Hamilton Gardener, "Woman as an Annex." This essay appeared in Gardener's book *Facts and Fictions of Life* (1893).

It is the fashion in this country now-a-days to say that women are treated as equals. Some of the most progressive and best of men truly

Line believe what they say in this regard. One of
5   our leading daily papers, which insists that
this is true, and even goes so far as to say that
American gentlemen believe in and act upon the
theory that their mothers and daughters are of
a superior quality—and are always of the very
10 first consideration to and by men—recently had
an editorial headlined "Universal Suffrage the
Birthright of the Free Born." I read it through, and
if you will believe me, the writer had so large a
bump of sex arrogance that he never once thought
15 of one-half of humanity in the entire course of
an elaborate and eloquent two-column article!
"Universal" suffrage did not touch but one sex.
There was but one sex "free born." There was
but one which was born with "rights." The words
20 "persons," "citizens," "residents of the state,"
and all similar terms were used quite freely, but
not once did it dawn upon the mind of the writer
that every one of those words, every argument
for freedom, every plea for liberty and justice,
25 equality and right, applied to the human race and
not merely to one-half of that race.

Sex bias, sex arrogance, sex pride, sex
assumption is so ingrained that it simply does
not occur to the male logicians, scientists,
30 philosophers and politicians that there is a
humanity. They see, think of and argue for and
about only a sex of man—with an annex to
him—woman. They call this the race; but they do
not mean the race—they mean men. They write
35 and talk of "human beings;" of their needs, their
education, their capacity and development; but
they are not thinking of humanity at all. They
are thinking of, planning for and executing plans

which subordinate the race—the human entity—
40 to a subdivision, the mark and sign of which
is the lowest and most universal possession of
male nature—the mere procreative instinct and
possibility. And this has grown to be the habit of
thought until in science, in philosophy, in religion,
45 in law, in politics—one and all—we must translate
all language into other terms than those used. For
the word "universal" we must read "male;" for
the "people," the "nation," we must read "men."
The "will of the majority—majority rule"—
50 really means the larger number of masculine
citizens. And so with all our common language,
it is in a false tense. It is mere democratic verbal
gymnastics, clothing the same old monarchial,
aristocratic mental beliefs, with man now the
55 "divine right" ruler and with woman his subject
and perquisite. Its gender is misstated and its
import multiplied by two. It does not mean what it
says, and it does not say what it means.

Our thoughts are adjusted to false verbal forms,
60 and so the thoughts do not ring true. They are
merely hereditary forms of speech. All masculine
thought and expression up to the present time
has been in the language of sex, and not in the
language of race; and so it has come about that
65 the music of humanity has been set in one key and
played on one chord.

It has been well said that an Englishman cannot
speak French correctly until he has learned to
think in French. It is far more true that no one
70 can speak or write the language of human liberty
and equality until he has learned to think in that
language, and to feel without stopping to argue
with himself, that right is not masculine only and
that justice knows no sex.

CONTINUE

19

Gardener primarily criticizes the writer of the "editorial" (line 11) for exhibiting

A) contempt for women who embrace household roles.

B) incomprehension of the history of women's suffrage.

C) an eagerness to harm the cause of women's rights.

D) a presumptuous and narrow perspective on politics.

20

On the basis of the passage, Gardener would regard the qualities mentioned in lines 24-25 ("freedom . . . right") as

A) signs of integrity that few men actually manifest.

B) meaningful goals that have been pursued mainly by remarkable women.

C) important concepts that most male writers avoid mentioning.

D) worthwhile principles that men understand in a flawed manner.

21

In lines 27-46 ("Sex bias . . . used"), Gardener argues that men's ideas about gender have become

A) irreversible.

B) automatic.

C) abstract.

D) incoherent.

22

Gardener explains that the rule of the majority is

A) infamous for gradually depriving women of their few existing rights.

B) influential under most forms of monarchical government.

C) often protested against as a force that oppresses both men and women.

D) not necessarily representative of the majority of women.

23

Which of the following terms best reflects the idea or concept indicated by the "key" (line 65) and "chord" (line 66)?

A) Fortitude

B) Limitation

C) Honesty

D) Rebellion

24

Which of the following examples would most clearly stand in opposition to Gardener's line of reasoning in the final paragraph?

A) Educated commentators who understand their own cultures often make poor assessments of foreign cultures.

B) People who come from different nations often develop similar ideas about democracy.

C) Representative governments can become provincial and oppressive over time.

D) Tyrannical leaders have written convincing defenses of democracy and personal liberty.

CONTINUE

Questions 25-30 are based on the following Fiction passage.

This passage is adapted from *Vandover and the Brute* (1914) by Frank Norris.

As he looked back over his life, Vandover could recall nothing after this, his mother's death, for nearly five years. Even after that lapse of time
Line the only scene he could picture with any degree
5 of clearness was one of the greatest triviality in which he saw himself, a rank thirteen-year-old boy, sitting on a bit of carpet in the back yard of the San Francisco house playing with his guinea-pigs.
10 In order to get at his life during his teens, Vandover would have been obliged to collect these scattered memory pictures as best he could, rearrange them in some more orderly sequence, piece out what he could imperfectly recall and
15 fill in the many gaps by mere guesswork and conjecture.

It was the summer of 1880 that they had come to San Francisco. Once settled there, Vandover's father began to build small residence houses and
20 cheap flats which he rented at various prices, the cheapest at ten dollars, the more expensive at thirty-five and forty. He had closed out his business in the East, coming out to California on account of his wife's ill health. He had made his
25 money in Boston and had intended to retire.

But he soon found that he could not do this. At this time he was an old man, nearly sixty. He had given his entire life to his business to the exclusion of everything else, and now when his
30 fortune had been made and when he could afford to enjoy it, discovered that he had lost the capacity for enjoying anything but the business itself. Nothing else could interest him. He was not what would be called in America a rich man, but he had
35 made money enough to travel, to allow himself any reasonable relaxation, to cultivate a taste for art, music, literature, or the drama, to indulge in any harmless fad, such as collecting etchings, china, or bric-à-brac, or even to permit himself
40 the luxury of horses. In the place of all these he

found himself, at nearly sixty years of age, forced again into the sordid round of business as the only escape from the mortal ennui and weariness of the spirit that preyed upon him during every leisure
45 hour of the day.

Early and late he went about the city, personally superintending the building of his little houses and cheap flats, sitting on saw-horses and piles of lumber, watching the carpenters at work.
50 In the evening he came home to a late supper, completely fagged, bringing with him the smell of mortar and of pine shavings.

On the first of each month when his agents turned over the rents to him he was in great spirits.
55 He would bring home the little canvas sack of coin with him before banking it, and call his son's attention to the amount, never failing to stick a twenty-dollar gold-piece in each eye, monocle fashion, exclaiming, "Good for the masses," a
60 meaningless jest that had been one of the family's household words for years.

His plan of building was peculiar. His credit was good, and having chosen his lot he would find out from the banks how much they would
65 loan him upon it in case he should become the owner. If this amount suited him, he would buy the lot, making one large payment outright and giving his note for the balance. The lot once his, the banks loaned him the desired amount. With
70 this money and with money of his own he would make the final payment on the lot and would begin the building itself, paying his labour on the nail, but getting his material, lumber, brick, and fittings on time. . . . Real estate was flourishing
75 in the rapidly growing city, and the new houses, although built so cheaply that they were mere shells of lath and plaster, were nevertheless made gay and brave with varnish and cheap mill-work. They rented well at first; scarcely a one was ever
80 vacant. People spoke of the Old Gentleman as one of the most successful realty owners in the city. So pleased did he become with the success of his new venture that in course of time all his money was reinvested after this fashion.

CONTINUE

25

The narrator presents the "scene" described in lines 3-9 as

A) uncharacteristically vivid compared to Vandover's other memories.

B) closely related to events surrounding the death of Vandover's mother.

C) indistinct compared to Vandover's recollections of his father's business enterprises.

D) influential in shaping Vandover's ideas about society and ambition generally.

26

The second and third paragraphs (lines 10-25) serve to transition from

A) criticisms of Vandover's father to a more affectionate tone towards this character.

B) Vandover's patchy ideas about Boston to his fascination with San Francisco.

C) reflections on Vandover's past to speculations about Vandover's future.

D) Vandover's perspective to the activities of Vandover's father.

27

It can be inferred from the passage that Vandover's father regards the possibility of retiring from the world of business as

A) subtly tantalizing.

B) profoundly undesirable.

C) dangerously energizing.

D) entertainingly laughable.

28

As described in lines 46-52, Vandover's father takes the position of

A) a discontented participant.

B) a conscientious spectator.

C) a relentless enforcer.

D) a gifted dabbler.

29

Which of the following situations most closely resembles the situation depicted in lines 53-61 ("On the . . . years")?

A) A lawyer good-naturedly pokes fun at the procedures followed by judges and juries during a family dinner.

B) A doctor gathers his children for an intensive discussion of the ethical flaws that he perceives in modern medicine.

C) An orator interrupts a serious analysis to impersonate his main opponents.

D) A celebrated biologist reaches a broad audience by producing accessible and humorous videos.

30

The final paragraph of the passage primarily serves to

A) foreshadow a few of the eventual problems with a method adopted by Vandover's father.

B) elaborate upon business practices that helped Vandover's father achieve respect.

C) paraphrase Vandover's own ideas about the value of his father's business methods.

D) prompt new questions about whether Vandover's father influenced the business community in a worthwhile manner.

CONTINUE

Part 2

This passage is adapted from "The Dreams Ideas Are Made Of" (2014) by Alex Camarota. Originally published* in InventorsEye, a newsletter of the United States Patent and Trademark Office.

The Internet is brimming with stories about inventions and discoveries that appeared in dreams. Einstein is said to have begun contemplating the theory of relativity after dreaming about cows when he was a teenager. There's also the story of Elias Howe, inventor of the sewing machine, who got the idea for a needle with the eye at its tip after dreaming about an incident involving spear-wielding cannibals. The list of dream-born creations goes on and on, from the lyrics of famous songs to the molecular structures for common chemicals. . .

Inventors Eye's most recent spark of genius, Kim Meckwood, also got the idea for her Click & Carry in a dream. She needed to solve the problem of carrying multiple bags of groceries up long flights of stairs to her apartment, and that's exactly what she did. But for Meckwood, getting ideas while asleep is nothing new. She said dreaming is a way for her to process her thoughts and allow ideas to percolate and rise to the surface. As it turns out, this is also what some experts say dreaming is all about.

Most dreaming occurs during rapid eye movement (REM), the period of sleep when the eyes erratically dart to and fro beneath the eyelids. REM sleep is also marked by increased brain activity. Various theories (none of which have a consensus in the scientific community) attempt to explain the purpose of dreaming and REM. According to one, REM is the result of the brain processing and organizing the day's thoughts, sights, and sounds. In this way, dreams might be a way for us to contemplate things that we are unable to or unwilling to contemplate during waking hours—or a way for us to finally grasp the solution to a problem that puzzled us.

Aside from the occasional dream, inventors get their ideas in many different ways. While stories of invention often start with a common problem that needs fixing, the way inventors arrive at the solution can be varied. Most solutions are the result of trial and error, thinking and perseverance—like the Wright Brothers' flying machine. Others still are the result of mere accident—Post-It Notes and vulcanized rubber were stumbled upon while their inventors were pursuing a different angle. And then there is the proverbial light bulb moment, when inspiration feels so new and disruptive it seems almost miraculous. But there's a rub: it turns out a lot of good ideas are really just additions to, or new directions taken from, already existing ideas.

One thing is clear: innovation happens in increments. Even during today's rapid technological expansion, most new mindboggling creations are the result of teams of researchers and engineers analyzing previous devices and processes, and figuring out how to make them better. Even independent inventors solving everyday problems are adding their own ideas to ones that already exist. Invention does not occur in a vacuum.

This collaborative system of productivity is common today, but that wasn't always the case. Ideas have not always had free reign to intermingle and bounce off each other. In fact, some experts, including notable science and technology writer Steven Johnson, credit the arrival of a truly collaborative "marketplace of ideas" to something that many of us take a warming to: coffee.

First appearing on the European continent in the mid-1600s, coffee houses quickly took hold as everyone from noblemen to street sweepers clamored in for a caffeine kick. The result, says Johnson, was that people from all walks of life began mingling and rubbing shoulders. Naturally, so did their ideas. Coffee houses were gathering places to talk about every subject, from politics and philosophy to science and technology. The collaborative environment that sprung up in European coffee houses in the 17th century gave

---

*See Page 262 for the citation for this text.

CONTINUE

rise to what became known as the Enlightenment,
85 itself leading to scientific and technological
revolutions and even the modern patent system. . .

Every time an inventor receives a patent, he
or she adds to the archive of mankind's collective
good ideas. Patents force new ideas to enter the
90 marketplace and replace or improve the old. The
state of the art advances, and the process repeats
itself *ad infinitum*. You might even say that the
patent system is the coffee house of intellectual
property, where inventors and their inventions
95 come together to mingle and learn and take new
directions.

So go ahead: have another cup of Joe, but
always remember to dream.

31

The author of the passage mentions Einstein and Elias
Howe as examples of innovators whose

A) idiosyncratic personalities were reflected both in
dreams and in inventions.

B) ideas were not entirely interchangeable with the
dreams that inspired them.

C) most important discoveries resulted from well-
coordinated sleep and relaxation regimens.

D) accomplishments may seem ridiculous in relation
to their dreams.

32

Which of the following findings would contradict
the ideas about REM and dreaming present in the
passage?

A) REM sleep has been definitively linked to the
objective of reducing stress.

B) Dreams that arise during REM sleep are harder to
remember than dreams from other sleep stages.

C) Humans developed REM sleep over time to serve
a practical function that remains mysterious.

D) A few brain areas exhibit only minor increases in
activity during REM sleep.

33

One example of an invention arrived at by "mere
accident" (lines 45-46) as understood by the author
would be

A) an synthetic fabric that originated from a
needlessly complex prototype.

B) a glue that was discovered while its inventor was
attempting to create a new rocket fuel.

C) a shower head that was adapted from a similar
device once used by soldiers in combat zones.

D) a chemical coating that protects car tires from
being punctured and is also found to prevent
rubber from cracking under low temperatures.

CONTINUE

Part 2

The author mentions "technological expansion" (line 56) and "independent inventors" (line 60) in order to

A) praise the pioneering spirit of figures mentioned earlier.

B) caution that current optimism about the pace of invention may not be justified.

C) outline an approach that is reliant on community and continuity.

D) assert that an individualistic perspective has often harmed inventors.

35

One repercussion of the popularization of coffee houses was

A) the creation of merchant fellowships that financially supported practical inventions.

B) the replacement of traditional ideas about the sources of genius.

C) closer contact of individuals from different social classes.

D) upheavals that re-structured vast political systems.

36

The author's attitude toward the "modern patent system" (line 86) is best described as

A) defensive.

B) disbelieving.

C) forgiving.

D) supportive.

Questions 37-42 are based on the following Science passage.

This passage is adapted from "NIH researchers discover highly infectious vehicle for transmission of viruses among humans," a 2018 news release* from the National Institutes of Health.

Researchers have found that a group of viruses that cause severe stomach illness—including the one famous for widespread outbreaks
Line on cruise ships—get transmitted to humans
5 through membrane-cloaked "virus clusters" that exacerbate the spread and severity of disease. Previously, it was believed that these viruses only spread through individual virus particles. The discovery of these clusters, the scientists
10 say, marks a turning point in the understanding of how these viruses spread and why they are so infectious. This preliminary work could lead to the development of more effective antiviral agents than existing treatments that mainly target
15 individual particles.

The researchers studied norovirus and rotavirus—hard-to-treat viruses that are the most common cause of stomach illness, or gastroenteritis, and that afflict millions of
20 people each year. The viruses cause symptoms ranging from diarrhea to abdominal pain and can sometimes result in death, particularly among young children and the elderly. Their highly contagious nature has led to serious outbreaks in
25 crowded spaces throughout many communities, most notably in cruise ships, daycare centers, classrooms, and nursing homes. Fortunately, vaccines against rotavirus are now available and are routinely given to babies in the United States.
30 "This is a really exciting finding in the field of virology because it reveals a mode of virus spread that has not been observed among humans and animals," said study leader Nihal Altan-Bonnet, Ph.D., senior investigator and head of
35 the Laboratory of Host-Pathogen Dynamics at

*See Page 262 for the citation for this text.

CONTINUE

the National Heart, Lung, and Blood Institute (NHLBI). "We hope that it will provide new clues to fighting a wide range of diseases involving many types of viruses, including those that cause
40 gastrointestinal illnesses, heart inflammation, certain respiratory illnesses, and even the common cold."

The study was supported in part by the Intramural Research programs of the NHLBI and
45 the National Institute of Allergy and Infectious Diseases (NIAID), both part of the National Institutes of Health. It is featured as the cover story of *Cell Host & Microbe* and appears online on August 8.

50 Until a few years ago, most scientists believed that viruses, particularly those responsible for stomach illnesses, could only behave as independent infectious agents. However, in 2015 Altan-Bonnet and her colleagues showed that
55 polioviruses could transmit themselves in packets, or membrane-bound vesicles containing multiple virus particles. The scientists compared this new model of viral transmission to a Trojan horse: a group of membrane-bound viruses arrives at a
60 host cell and deposits viruses in the cell while dodging detection by the immune system. The scientists did not know whether this system applied to animals and humans, or how effective these packets were in infecting host cells.

65 To find out, they focused on rotaviruses and noroviruses, which mainly get spread through accidental ingestion of tiny particles of an infected person's stool—through, for example, contaminated food or liquids. The
70 researchers obtained fecal samples of humans and animals (pigs and mice) and found that the viruses are shed in the stool as virus clusters inside membrane-bound packets. In addition, they found that these virus-containing vesicles
75 were significantly more infectious than the free, unbound viruses within the samples.

The researchers determined that the high level of infectiousness was likely due to the vesicles delivering many viruses at once to the target
80 tissues; protecting their viral cargo from being destroyed by prolonged exposure to enzymes; and

possibly by making their viral cargo invisible to the antibodies that are in the stool or gut of the host. More studies are needed, but the extreme
85 potency of the virus packets, they said, has a clear consequence: it not only enhances the virus' ability to spread more aggressively; it also increases the severity of the disease it causes. Handwashing with soap and water helps prevent
90 the spread of viruses.

"Our findings indicate that vesicle-cloaked viruses are highly virulent units of fecal-oral transmission, and highlight a need for antivirals targeting vesicles and virus clustering," Altan-
95 Bonnet noted.

37

The "discovery" (line 9) described in the first paragraph is notable for

A) rendering an approach useless.

B) popularizing a new discipline.

C) overturning an earlier belief.

D) spurring scholarly debate.

38

According to the passage, which of the following individuals is mostly likely to be suffering from "norovirus" (line 16) or "rotavirus" (line 17)?

A) A three year-old who has received regular anti-viral vaccinations since birth

B) A five year-old whose family has intentionally avoided any form of vaccination

C) A thirty year-old man who has recently missed a round of scheduled vaccinations

D) A sixty year-old woman who receives anti-viral vaccinations more often than is necessary

CONTINUE

Part 2

In the third paragraph (lines 30-42), Altan-Bonnet's comments primarily convey a tone of

A) tactful detachment.

B) abiding skepticism.

C) confrontational excitement.

D) enthusiastic optimism.

Which of the following is a relatively new discovery that the passage explicitly links to Altan-Bonnet's research?

A) Viruses that are linked to instances of polio can be transported in clusters.

B) Antibodies can easily mistake clustered viruses for healthy cells.

C) Noroviruses and rotaviruses require regular vaccination for successful treatment.

D) Humans are more vulnerable than other animals are to viruses that cause stomach ailments.

41

Which of the following is NOT, on the basis of the passage, a possible way in which virus packets are especially dangerous?

A) Antibody and enzyme resistance

B) Over-reaction by the immune system

C) Presence of multiple virus types

D) Fast-paced dispersion and infection

The author of the passage mentions "Handwashing" (line 89) as an example of

A) an underestimated piece of good advice.

B) an insufficiently rigorous practice.

C) a topic for future examination.

D) a recommended preventative measure.

CONTINUE

Questions 43-48 are based on the following History passage.

This passage is adapted from "The Theory of Social Revolutions" (1913) by Brooks Adams.

The same acceleration of the social movement which has caused this centralization of capital has caused the centralization of another form of
Line human energy, which is its negative: labor unions
5 organize labor as a monopoly. Labor protests against the irresponsible sovereignty of capital, as men have always protested against irresponsible sovereignty, declaring that the capitalistic social system, as it now exists, is a form of slavery. Very
10 logically, therefore, the abler and bolder labor agitators proclaim that labor levies actual war against society, and that in that war there can be no truce until irresponsible capital has capitulated. Also, in labor's methods of warfare the same
15 phenomena appear as in the autocracy of capital. Labor attacks capitalistic society by methods beyond the purview of the law, and may, at any moment, shatter the social system, while, under our laws and institutions, society is helpless.
20 Few persons, I should imagine, who reflect on these phenomena, fail to admit to themselves, whatever they may say publicly, that present social conditions are unsatisfactory, and I take the cause of the stress to be that which I have
25 stated. We have extended the range of applied science until we daily use infinite forces, and those forces must, apparently, disrupt our society, unless we can raise the laws and institutions which hold society together to an energy and
30 efficiency commensurate to them. How much vigor and ability would be required to accomplish such a work may be measured by the experience of Washington, who barely prevailed in his relatively simple task, surrounded by a generation
35 of extraordinary men, and with the capitalistic class of America behind him. Without the capitalistic class he must have failed. Therefore one most momentous problem of the future is the attitude which capital can or will assume in this
40 emergency.

That some of the more sagacious of the capitalistic class have preserved that instinct of self-preservation which was so conspicuous among men of the type of Washington is apparent
45 from the position taken by the management of the United States Steel Company, and by the Republican minority of the Congressional Committee which recently investigated the Steel Company; but whether such men very strongly
50 influence the genus to which they belong is not clear. If they do not, much improvement in existing conditions can hardly be anticipated.
If capital insists upon continuing to exercise sovereign powers, without accepting
55 responsibility as for a trust, the revolt against the existing order must probably continue, and that revolt can only be dealt with, as all servile revolts must be dealt with, by physical force. I doubt, however, if even the most ardent and optimistic
60 of capitalists would care to speculate deeply upon the stability of any government capital might organize, which rested on the fundamental principle that the American people must be ruled by an army. On the other hand any government
65 to be effective must be strong. It is futile to talk of keeping peace in labor disputes by compulsory arbitration, if the government has not the power to command obedience to its arbitrators' decree; but a government able to constrain a couple
70 of hundred thousand discontented railway employees to work against their will, must differ considerably from the one we have. Nor is it possible to imagine that labor will ever yield peaceful obedience to such constraint, unless
75 capital makes equivalent concessions,—unless, perhaps, among other things, capital consents to erect tribunals which shall offer relief to any citizen who can show himself to be oppressed by the monopolistic price. In fine, a government, to
80 promise stability in the future, must apparently be so much more powerful than any private interest, that all men will stand equally before its tribunals; and these tribunals must be flexible enough to reach those categories of activity which now lie
85 beyond legal jurisdiction. If it be objected that the American people are incapable of an effort so

CONTINUE

prodigious, I readily admit that this may be true, but I also contend that the objection is beside the issue. What the American people can or cannot do
90 is a matter of opinion, but that social changes are imminent appears to be almost certain. Though these changes cannot be prevented, possibly they may, to a degree, be guided, as Washington guided the changes of 1789.

43

In the first paragraph, Adams discusses the labor movement by

A) acknowledging both its practical motives and the threats that it poses.

B) mentioning the virtues of its leaders while dismissing their perceived failings.

C) implying that conflict between labor and capital is a greater threat to society than actual warfare is.

D) citing a policy that indicates the movement's unprecedented nature.

44

Adams's use of the word "we" in the second paragraph (lines 20-40) primarily serves to

A) counter the mis-perception that he is sympathetic to business interests.

B) call upon his audience to disregard regional and cultural differences.

C) define a group that should promote constructive social change.

D) inspire pride in and identification with a nation's political past.

45

Which piece of information would most effectively support Adams's statements about George Washington in lines 30-37 ("How . . . failed")?

A) Poorer Americans became enthusiastic supporters of Washington despite early opposition to his ideology.

B) Washington's initial approach to economic policy was abandoned early in his administration.

C) Aristocratic and merchant families in Europe were generally supportive of Washington's government.

D) Washington's most trusted advisors all possessed considerable amounts of land and family wealth.

46

Adams argues that "improvement in existing conditions" (lines 51-52) depends upon

A) the formation of new committees to regulate industrial activity.

B) the voluntary redistribution of wealth by influential households.

C) the ability of those with loyalties to business to set well-considered priorities.

D) the speed with which the largest businesses can re-organize their operations.

CONTINUE

47

On the basis of the final paragraph, which of the following would Adams view as an unstable government?

A) An oligarchy in which an unpopular group of aristocrats maintains its power by funding a private military.

B) A monarchy in which the ruling family is widely loved by the populace but despised by military leaders.

C) A republic in which voting rights are only granted to those citizens who hold a set amount of household wealth.

D) A democracy in which most citizens can vote but in which only the richest citizens exercise this right.

48

It can be inferred that Adams views the "American people" (lines 86 and 89) as

A) responsive to the use of coercion.

B) unaware of a pivotal social change.

C) faced with momentous consequences.

D) willing to be guided by history.

STOP

After you have finished the questions, consult the relevant answers on Page 102.
Do not turn to any other section.

Answer Key
Passage Details

Passage 1
1. B
2. D
3. A
4. D
5. C
6. C

Passage 2
7. D
8. C
9. D
10. C
11. A
12. C

Passage 3
13. A
14. C
15. C
16. B
17. B
18 D

Passage 4
19. D
20. D
21. B
22. D
23. B
24. D

Passage 5
25. A
26. D
27. B
28. B
29. A
30. B

Passage 6
31. B
32. A
33. B
34. C
35. C
36. D

Passage 7
37. C
38. B
39. D
40. A
41. B
42. D

Passage 8
43. A
44. C
45. D
46. C
47. A
48 C

For detailed answer explanations for this practice section please visit **prepvantagetutoring.com/reading**.

Part 3

Command of Evidence
Strategy and Practice

Strategy 3
Command of Evidence

Question Fundamentals

On each SAT Reading section, you will find roughly 10 questions with answer choices that are not statements or phrases; instead, the possible answers will be line references that fit an objective designated by the question prompt. These are your Command of Evidence questions, as defined by the College Board's test structure. Yet the official breakdown, here, is not especially helpful, since a large number of these 10 questions will be LINKED to other questions that must be solved in conjunction with them—questions that look like Passage Details questions but that can become unmanageable if solved in isolation.

Realistically, you can expect a maximum of 20 questions—some Single, some Paired—that require one of the Command of Evidence strategies outlined in this chapter. In some ways, the task is not too different from what you are accustomed to from working with Passage Details. You must still pay attention to key words, and must still rely on process of elimination. However, you should NOT spend time predicting answers when working with Command of Evidence. There is no need to, since—as the Single Command of Evidence questions reveal—all of the information that you need is contained in consolidated line references.

Single Command of Evidence

The questions classified under Single Command of Evidence consist of nothing more than a question prompt followed by four possible line references. Your task, with these, is simply to decide which of the given line references fits an objective or topic ("Which line reference indicates . . . "; "Which line reference provides the best evidence that . . . ") that is explicitly stated. In fact, you may remember questions of this sort from the Diagnostic Test.

9

Which choice best supports the idea that Dymov values pursuits that he does not fully comprehend?

A) Lines 66-68 ("I have . . . the arts")

B) Lines 70-72 ("Your . . . with it")

C) Lines 72-77 ("I don't . . . use")

D) Lines 77-79 ("I don't . . . them")

12

Which choice best indicates that Ready's work on food networks in Kangiqsujuaq had few effective or meaningful precedents?

A) Lines 16-19 ("However . . . studied")

B) Lines 23-26 ("Therefore . . . risk")

C) Lines 39-41 ("From . . . community")

D) Lines 71-73 ("Ready's . . . shocks")

Conscientious work with these questions can help you to build attention to small details and specific objectives. Still, there are a few realities of Single Command of Evidence questions that should be pointed out, in terms of prevalence and reception.

1. Some test takers find these considerably EASIER than Paired Command of Evidence questions

2. Some tests feature VERY FEW Single Command of Evidence questions

In some ways, indeed, Single Command of Evidence can appear to be relatively low-priority. These questions are nonetheless excellent training for the methods that you will need to approach the most difficult Paired Command of Evidence items.

Core Strategy: Single

1. Read the Prompt to determine ALL topics and ideas that the correct answer requires

2. Bracket the first line reference and read it carefully, checking again for all needed items

3. KEEP the reference if all items are present, or ELIMINATE if one or more are absent

4. Repeat for all line references until Process of Elimination yields the correct answer

The trick to working with Single Command of Evidence is to place an intense focus on EXACTLY what the prompt demands, content-wise. Often, trap answers will contain only one part of the required content, and some of the answers that can be eliminated most easily will refer to totally irrelevant parts of the passage. Do not over-think any of this: your entire task is to match item to item, perhaps with some paraphrasing and logical inference.

To see how the process works, consider the analysis of Question 9 that appears on the next page.

Part 3: Command of Evidence

9

Which choice best supports the idea that Dymov
values pursuits that he does not fully comprehend?

A) Lines 66-68 ("I have . . . the arts") . . . . About Dymov, but NOT about incomprehension X

B) Lines 70-72 ("Your . . . with it") . . . . About Dymov's lenience towards friends X

C) Lines 72-77 ("I don't . . . use") . . . . "I don't understand . . . sensible" CORRECT

D) Lines 77-79 ("I don't . . . them") . . . . About incomprehension but NOT about value X

In this question, each of the false answers refers to the appropriate character, Dymov, and references his opinions in some way. The real trick is that the false answers reference only a few of the needed items, while the correct answer will refer to both "pursuits" that Dymov values (positive) and a sense of incomprehension (negative). A does not capture the incomprehension theme, B refers primarily to a different quality (lenience), and D does not reflect the sense of "valuing" pursuits. C, however, properly indicates that Dymov values those who engage in pursuits that he does not "understand" as "sensible" and is thus a perfect fit.

This process is not especially difficult, but requires you to be extremely demanding when searching for evidence—and to avoid mis-readings and over-interpretations of the passage at all costs. Just remember that an answer that contains part of what you need, yet avoids a key piece of content, must be AUTOMATICALLY eliminated.

Important Tips

You MAY need to draw logical conclusions on the basis of passage information.

- References: On occasion, a line reference will refer to content from some other portion of the passage. Check for pronouns ("those," "it") and seemingly vague items ("this concept," "what was once believed to be true") and DEFINE THESE ITEMS by reading around. Even if a reference of this sort is oblique, it is STILL a part of the line reference that should be accounted for when you go to match your line reference to the topic in the prompt.

- Inferences: You may, when working with line references, find that the appropriate lines do not provide a direct paraphrase of topics from the question prompt. Instead, the correct lines may give a statement that logically yet somewhat indirectly supports the content that you need. For instance, a prompt may ask for "proof that honeybees do not favor purple flowers." The line reference may not mention "purple flowers" directly, but may indicate that "honeybees prefer yellow flowers over all other flower types." In this case and in others like it, a logical conclusion—here, that honeybees do not gravitate to "purple flowers" if they DO gravitate to "yellow flowers"—can be drawn with no dispute or uncertainty.

You should ALWAYS double-check to see if the question is Single or Double.

- A surprisingly large number of students solve Single Command of Evidence by wrongly creating pairings with previous questions—a tactic that leads to needless confusion and lost points. Simply read the questions carefully. Note also that some Single questions have prompts that are the same length (two lines) as the opening to the second component of a Paired question set. Do not breeze past these, and keep in mind that Single Command of Evidence, though still not as common as Paired Command of Evidence, IS becoming somewhat more popular on recent SAT tests.

You should NEVER rely completely on a nearby line reference to make your choice.

- Any line reference that you choose must, at the very least, contain an indirect and logical allusion to the topic that the prompt requires. If you find that some of the given line references are in the vicinity of the information that the question calls for—but do NOT fit this requirement—then these line references should be automatically eliminated. Proximity to a perfect fit line reference does not necessarily make a line reference correct. Topic, here, is the only standard.

Paired Command of Evidence

The skills that are honed through work with Single Command of Evidence—attention to detail, proficiency in matching concepts, and aptitude in topic-based process of elimination—all inform the strategies that you will need to approach the Double Command of Evidence questions. Look for these carefully: whenever you see the phrase "Which choice provides the best evidence for the answer to the previous question?" or something highly comparable in a question prompt, you are dealing with this question type, as shown below.

24

In describing his research, Raznahan makes use of

A) emphatic language that hints that earlier researchers were misguided.

B) anecdotes and recollections that make his ideas more accessible to a large audience.

C) an analogy that helps to explain a neurological process central to his inquiry.

D) general statements that are meant to spur meaningful debate.

25

Which choice provides the best evidence for the answer to the previous question?

A) Lines 23-25 ("An extra . . . brain")

B) Line 54 ("Not all . . . equal")

C) Lines 56-58 ("There's . . . tissue")

D) Lines 74-76 ("Our study . . . brains")

As in Single Command of Evidence, your first task is to identify exactly what information the question demands. From there, you should by NO MEANS treat the two questions in isolation. Instead, you will address them so that the topic for the initial question helps you locate the correct line reference—and so that the line references help you to address individual answers with high precision.

Part 3: Command of Evidence

Core Strategy: Paired

---

1. Read the Prompt to determine ALL topics and ideas that the correct answer requires (first question)

2. Bracket the first line reference and read it carefully, checking again for all needed items (second question)

3. KEEP the reference if all items are present, or ELIMINATE if one or more are absent (second question)

4. Repeat for all line references, and realize that you may need to keep MULTIPLE line references as appropriate to the prompt (second question)

5. Re-read first remaining line reference, then see if it MATCHES an answer to the previous question; if not, eliminate (second returning to first)

6. Repeat for all line references, performing process of elimination, until you have a perfect match between an answer and a line reference (second returning to first)

The successful use of this strategy is premised, naturally, on effective reading comprehension: you must be able to retain important details and see how the author is connecting ideas WITHOUT subjecting a line reference to your own interpretation. At first, the most challenging aspect may be the movement that occurs in steps 5-6. If you are not comfortable simply bracketing and analyzing the line references, try the following tactics.

1. Circle KEY WORDS in any one line reference to see if they effectively match answer phrases

2. Provide brief SUMMARIES of line references that stay close to the original wording

One danger of mis-reading a line reference is that your mis-reading may appear to justify an incorrect answer. In this case, you will cost yourself two points on a segment of the test that—with more practiced and effective reading comprehension—could have become quite simple.

To see how simple, consider how to work through the questions provided on the previous page.

24

In describing his research, Raznahan makes use of

A) emphatic language that hints that earlier researchers were misguided.

B) anecdotes and recollections that make his ideas more accessible to a large audience.

C) an analogy that helps to explain a neurological

Requires a **description by Raznahan** of his own research

Temporarily DISREGARD the answers and move to the line references

segmented, light-collecting mirror that will
85 ride on a shingle-like platform, is designed to
capture light directly from the planets themselves.
The light then can be split into a multi-colored
spectrum, a kind of bar code showing which gases
are present in the planet's atmosphere. Webb's
90 targets might include "super Earths," or planets
larger than Earth but smaller than Neptune—
some that could be rocky planets like super-sized
versions of our own.

Little is known about these big planets,
95 including whether some might be suitable for
life. If we're very lucky, perhaps one of them
will show signs of oxygen, carbon dioxide and
methane in its atmosphere. Such a mix of gases
would remind us strongly of our own atmosphere,
100 possibly indicating the presence of life.

But hunting for Earth-like atmospheres on
Earth-sized exoplanets will probably have to wait
for a future generation of even more powerful
space probes in the 2020s or 2030s.

16

The author of the passage indicates that indirect
methods for detecting exoplanets

A) are premised on random and unusual occurrences.

B) were generally efficient but made classification of
discovered exoplanets extremely difficult.

C) will slowly yet decisively be replaced by more
direct means of detecting exoplanets.

D) are no longer the only possibilities available to
astronomers who are searching for exoplanets.

17

Which choice provides the best evidence for the
answer to the previous question?

A) Lines 7-9 ("Some . . . types")

B) Lines 13-16 ("Direct . . . means")

C) Lines 18-20 ("The 'wobble' . . . planet")

D) Lines 23-26 ("This . . . Didier Queloz")

18

Which choice best supports the idea that the radial
velocity method has NOT offered researchers a
comprehensive approach for studying exoplanets?

A) Lines 26-28 ("Ground . . . so far")

B) Lines 34-35 ("The size . . . is")

C) Lines 44-46 ("Wobble . . . diameter")

D) Lines 56-59 ("The space-based . . . each other")

19

One of the assumptions present in the author's
discussion of Earth-like exoplanets is the idea that

A) an atmospheric composition that resembles
Earth's could indicate that a planet is inhabited by
organisms.

B) relatively large exoplanets are typically less dense
than Earth is.

C) a planet that exhibits varied climates and
geographical features is likely to foster life.

D) direct imaging of an Earth-like exoplanet is the
best way to confirm whether the planet has a
climate that could promote life.

20

Which choice provides the best evidence for the
answer to the previous question?

A) Lines 68-72 ("And while . . . own")

B) Lines 89-91 ("Webb's . . . Neptune")

C) Lines 94-96 ("Little . . . life")

D) Lines 98-100 ("Such a . . . life")

CONTINUE

Part 3

This passage is adapted from "The Ambiguities Abroad" by Nils Lundgarten (2016). Dominic, the main character of the short story from which this excerpt is taken, is a retired chemist who is on a sightseeing tour.

I doubt that many people would look out at a tan-and-black landscape under a gray sky and think, "I am free. I am free!" Had anyone other
Line than the vikings—had even they—ever landed
5 on Iceland on a rainy Thursday and found that "freedom! freedom!" was the first thing that came to mind?

As the bus bounded toward Reykjavik, I couldn't help thinking back to how all this would
10 have gone had I still been yoked to that tour group—how little freedom I would have enjoyed as I rode through that wind-whipped volcanic landscape. Again and again, I scanned the bus in satisfaction. Empty seats! A week ago, the entire
15 vehicle would have been populated by my "fellow travelers." I would have jealously guarded the seat next to me, my books and my hat situated on it in a manner designed to forbid companionship. Such attempts were never successful enough, but
20 now there were no companions. The interior of the bus was dark, the air that circulated through was crisp. I realized, now, how little I remembered of any one individual from the group tour, perhaps beyond our ever-voluble, ever-sunglassed guide
25 and the quiet, beleaguered fellow who actually drove the tour bus. I had remained aloof from them too, cautious of signaling to the younger and more raucous vacationers that I was ready to socialize at large. Of course, now, none of it
30 mattered. The only other people on the Reykjavik bus were a mother and her four children, all of them clustered towards the front seats and preoccupied with their iPads. For them, I had as little importance as my onetime fellow travelers
35 on the "Scandinavia Holiday Group Tour" now had for me.

The streets of Reykjavik itself were vacant; I kept on the lookout for another car, a woman with a baby carriage, a hardy soul on a bicycle,
40 and found myself disappointed at each new intersection. Finally, we reached the hotel. The family with the iPads disembarked promptly; I would never see them again. As for the hotel itself, it was not large or imposing by any means.
45 What it lacked in stature, though, it made up in its all-too-transparent positioning as an eminently modern establishment. The lobby was not so much a lobby as a machine made to deliver hospitality in the most efficient form possible—nothing but
50 navy blue furniture, pearl-white walls, fluorescent lighting. A bowl of flawlessly green apples and a large carafe of water—a pleasant change from the unruly collections of candies and pastries that every Russian hotel seemed to boast—were the
55 only attempts at refreshment.

When, in short order, I entered my room, I positively hurled my travel bags down in anticipation. The trip was not over, and this last stage would be mine to savor in the isolation
60 that I had craved for every preceding mile that I had traveled. Yet as those two bags hit the floor, something—not quite regret, but something comparable, something just as tangible—snuffed out my high spirits. The truth was that I had
65 waited so long for this moment that its arrival was quashingly underwhelming. There would no longer be a litany of complaints humming in the back of my mind; there would no longer be the tour guide's longwinded lectures, the pleasant
70 pointless chatter of my twenty-five "fellow travelers." I would miss them the way that one misses a tooth that had been aching consistently yet never too intensely before its extraction, and I would miss that quiet fellow who drove the bus—
75 and, having forgotten his name, I will always think of him as "that quiet fellow who drove the bus"—in a different way. I had felt that he and I were somehow united in this ordeal, trying to conduct our business while other people's
80 socialization clamored to get in the way, and I hadn't so much as offered him a perfunctory good-bye.

CONTINUE

21

Within the passage, the narrator characterizes Iceland's natural landscape as

A) remarkably unappealing to those who are most familiar with its features.

B) generally unlikely to inspire the positive sentiments that he experiences.

C) strangely uninteresting to those who would have the greatest motivation to examine it.

D) associated with a lingering sense of discomfort and alienation.

22

Which choice provides the best evidence for the answer to the previous question?

A) Lines 1-3 ("I doubt . . . free!")

B) Lines 13-14 ("Again . . . seats")

C) Lines 30-33 ("The only . . . iPads")

D) Lines 37-41 ("The streets . . . intersection")

23

The narrator would most likely characterize the bus driver from the "tour group" (lines 10-11) as

A) a peer who was capable of offering a new perspective.

B) an authority who disapproved of idle and irresponsible behavior.

C) an acquaintance who inspired a feeling of sympathy.

D) an ally who had difficulty expressing himself.

24

Which choice provides the best evidence for the answer to the previous question?

A) Lines 16-18 ("I would . . . companionship")

B) Lines 22-26 ("I realized . . . tour bus")

C) Lines 73-77 ("I would . . way")

D) Lines 77-80 ("I had felt . . . way")

25

Which choice best indicates that the narrator is not entirely pleased to be free of the tour group?

A) Lines 33-36 ("For them . . . for me")

B) Lines 56-58 ("When . . . anticipation")

C) Lines 64-66 ("The truth . . . underwhelming")

D) Lines 68-71 ("there would . . . fellow travelers")

CONTINUE

Part 3

This passage is adapted from Samantha Wallace, "Linking Isolated Languages: Linguistic Relationships of the Carabayo." Originally published* on EveryONE, the blog of the research site Plos One.

Line

5

10

15

20

25

30

35

In 2010, English clocked in at over 360 million native speakers, and it is the third-most-commonly used native language, right behind Mandarin Chinese and Spanish. While these languages spread, however, other indigenous languages decline at an accelerated pace. A fraction of these enigmatic languages belong to uncontacted indigenous groups of the Amazonian rainforest, groups of people in South America who have little to no interaction with societies beyond their own. Many of these groups choose to remain uncontacted by the rest of the world. Because of their isolation, not much is known about these languages beyond their existence.

The researchers of a recent PLOS ONE paper investigated one such language, that of the Carabayo people who live in the Colombian Amazon rainforest. Working with the relatively scarce historical data that exists for the Carabayo language—only 50 words have been recorded over time—the authors identified similarities between Carabayo and Yurí and Tikuna, two known languages of South America that constitute the current language family Ticuna-Yurí. Based on the correspondences, the authors posit a possible genealogical connection between these languages.

Few resources were available to the authors in this endeavor. They analyzed historical wordlists collected during the last encounter with the Carabayo people in 1969—the only linguistic data available from this group—against wordlists for the Yurí language. In addition, they sought the expertise of a native speaker of Tikuna, a linguist trained in Tikuna's many dialects. Using these resources, the authors broke down the Carabayo words into their foundational forms, starting with

40

45

50

55

60

65

70

75

80

consonants and vowels. They then compared them to similarly deconstructed words in Yurí and Tikuna.

The examination involved the evaluation of similarities in the basic building blocks of these words: the number of times a specific sound (or phoneme) appeared; the composition and patterns of the smallest grammatical units of a word (a morpheme); and the meanings attached to these words. When patterns appeared between Carabayo and either Yurí or Tikuna, the authors considered whether or not the languages' similarities constituted stronger correspondences. They also paid attention to the ways in which these words would have been used by the Carabayo when the lists were originally made many years ago.

The Yurí language was first recorded in the 19th century, but it is thought to have become extinct since then. From these lists, five words stood out: in Carabayo, ao 'father', hono 'boy', hako 'well!', and a complex form containing both the Yurí word from warm, noré, and the Yurí word, tʃau, which corresponds in English to 'I' or 'my'. Given the evidence, the authors contend that the strongest link between Carabayo and Yurí is found in the correspondence of tʃau. The study of other languages has indicated that first person pronouns are particularly resistant to "borrowing," or the absorption of one language's vocabulary into another. Therefore, the authors surmise it is unlikely in this instance that either of the languages absorbed tʃau from the other, but that they share a genealogical link.

Similarly, the comparison of Carabayo words to words of the living language of Tikuna provided a high number of matches, including in Carabayo gudda 'wait' and gu 'yes'. The matches especially exhibit sound correspondences of Carabayo g (or k) and the loss of the letter n in certain circumstances.

Although it is possible that the Carabayo language represents a language that had not yet been documented until the time of 1969, the results of the researchers' evaluation have led them to conclude that Carabayo more likely belongs to the language family of Ticuna-Yurí.

---

*See Page 262 for the citation for this text.

CONTINUE

The relationship of Carabayo to Yurí and
85 Tikuna changes the structure of the Ticuna-Yurí
family by placing Carabayo on the map as a
member of that family. The Tikuna language, once
considered to be the sole surviving member of
the Ticuna-Yurí family, might now have a sibling,
90 and the identity of a barely known language has
become that much more defined.

26

Another article on the Carabayo people claims that
indigenous people in the Amazon have changed their
languages and cultures in response to modernization.
Which piece of evidence from the passage above
most directly opposes this article's claim?

A) Lines 11-12 ("Many . . . world")

B) Lines 12-14 ("Because . . . existence")

C) Lines 18-24 ("Working . . . Ticuna-Yurí")

D) Lines 54-57 ("The Yurí . . . then")

27

The author indicates that one of the challenges faced
by the PLOS ONE researchers was

A) the difficulty of finding fluent speakers of
Carabayo.

B) the scarcity of useful information on the
Carabayo language.

C) the inaccuracy of previous research linking the
Carabayo and Tikuna languages.

D) the absence of parallels between Yuri and
Carabayo words.

28

Which choice provides the best evidence for the
answer to the previous question?

A) Lines 15-18 ("The researchers . . . rainforest")

B) Lines 29-33 ("They . . . language")

C) Lines 35-38 ("Using these . . . vowels")

D) Lines 47-50 ("When . . . correspondences")

29

According to the passage, the strongest evidence of a
connection between the Yurí and Carabayo languages
involves

A) the geographical proximity of speakers of
Carabayo, Yurí, and Tikuna.

B) the small number of changes in pronunciation
that the two languages have exhibited.

C) the presence of matching pronoun references in
the two languages.

D) the large number of everyday words shared by the
Carabayo and Tikuna languages.

30

Which choice provides the best evidence for the
answer to the previous question?

A) Lines 56-61 ("From these . . . my")

B) Lines 67-70 ("Therefore . . . link")

C) Lines 84-87 ("The relationship . . . family")

D) Lines 87-89 ("The Tikuna . . . sibling")

CONTINUE

Part 3

Questions 31-35 are based on the following Science passage.

This passage is adapted from "Fruit Fly Mating Driven by a Tweak in a Specific Brain Circuit" (July 2018). Originally published* by the National Institutes of Health.

According to a new National Institutes of Health-funded study, it is not destiny that brings two fruit flies together, but an evolutionary matchmaker of sorts that made tiny adjustments to their brains' mating circuits, so they would be attracted to one another while rejecting advances from other, even closely-related, species. The results, published in *Nature*, may help explain how a specific female scent triggers completely different responses in different male flies.

"This study reveals how a very small tweak in brain wiring can result in large changes in very complex social behaviors, which can ultimately determine the fate of a species," said Jim Gnadt, Ph.D., program director at the NIH's National Institute of Neurological Disorders and Stroke (NINDS), which supported the study. "Understanding how variation in brain circuits leads to changes in behavior is one of the primary goals of the NIH's BRAIN Initiative and this study provides a piece of the puzzle."

Vanessa Ruta, Ph.D., professor at Rockefeller University in New York City, and her colleagues used cutting-edge genetic tools to compare the brain circuits behind courtship behavior in two closely related species of fruit fly, D. melanogaster and D. simulans.

Previous studies showed that although males from both species could detect a specific pheromone, or scent, called 7,11-heptacosadiene (7,11-HD), their reactions to it were very different. Male D. melanogaster flies found it attractive while D. simulans males avoided females that carried it. In this study, Dr. Ruta and her team discovered that slight differences in the way the flies' brains are wired may control these opposite reactions.

"From a fly's perspective, courtship is the most important decision it will make, and so evolutionary processes have really fine-tuned flies' brains to ensure optimal behaviors, leading them to their ideal mates," said Dr. Ruta.

In fruit flies, pheromones are detected by sensory neurons on the legs, and that information travels to P1 neurons that sit in the lateral protocerebral complex (LPC) in the brain. In between the sensory and P1 neurons, the wiring splits so that the P1 cells can be either turned on or off.

P1 neurons trigger courtship activity in D. melanogaster males but have not been studied in other fly species. When the P1 neurons were turned on in D. simulans males, they tried mating with nearby objects including unsuitable targets such as females from different species as well as rotating magnets. This suggests that P1 neurons may be important for sparking courtship behaviors across species.

Dr. Ruta and her team used state-of-the-art technology to watch brain cells light up in real time as male flies were exposed to D. melanogaster and D. simulans females releasing 7,11-HD. When D. melanogaster males were exposed to females from their species, there was a lot of activity by the P1 neurons. Exposure to D. simulans females did not turn on those neurons. However, P1 neurons in the D. simulans males did not light up when they were exposed to females from their species, suggesting that differences in P1 neurons may underlie species-specific responses to 7,11-HD.

Additional experiments suggested that as pheromone signals traveled from the legs to P1 neurons, that information was conveyed differently in the two species of fruit fly by brain cells that communicate directly with P1 neurons. Specifically, P1 neurons appeared to receive lots of excitation in D. melanogaster flies but got more calming signals in D. simulans flies, which led to opposite responses when the animals were exposed to 7,11-HD. These findings also suggested that in some species of flies, absence of pheromone signaling may be more attractive than the presence of certain scents.

CONTINUE

85 Future experiments will look at similar behaviors in other species of fruit flies. More research is needed to learn the mechanisms that drive evolutionary changes in brain circuitry, which may have important consequences for
90 individual and social behavior.

31

As described in the passage, Dr. Ruta's study was notable for

A) proposing a new model for how a dominant species of fruit fly evolved.

B) building upon previous findings about fruit flies.

C) applying evolutionary models for other organisms to fruit flies.

D) replacing earlier ideas about fruit fly anatomy.

32

Which choice provides the best evidence for the answer to the previous question?

A) Lines 7-10 ("The results . . . flies")

B) Lines 34-37 ("In this . . . reactions")

C) Lines 43-46 ("In fruit flies . . . brain")

D) Lines 65-66 ("Exposure . . . neurons")

33

One of the important components in the design of Dr. Ruta's fruit fly experiment was

A) a process that could artificially intensify aggression responses.

B) technology that could directly monitor nervous system activity.

C) a new classification system that clarified the relationship between D. melanogaster and D. simulans.

D) a laboratory-produced pheromone that helped to reproduce a situation previously observable only in nature.

34

Which choice provides the best evidence for the answer to the previous question?

A) Lines 18-21 ("Understanding . . . puzzle")

B) Lines 22-27 ("Vanessa Ruta . . . D. simulans")

C) Lines 40-42 ("Evolutionary . . . Dr. Ruta")

D) Lines 59-63 ("Dr. Ruta . . . 7,11-HD")

35

Which choice most effectively indicates that D. melanogaster and D. simulans may respond to sensory information in ways that are not fully compatible?

A) Lines 11-15 ("This study . . . Jim Gnadt")

B) Lines 56-58 ("This . . . species")

C) Lines 72-76 ("Additional . . . P1 neurons")

D) Lines 85-86 ("Future . . . fruit flies")

CONTINUE

Questions 36-40 are based on the following History passage.

This passage is adapted from *The Impossibilities of Anarchism* (1895) by George Bernard Shaw. In its most extreme form, "anarchism" promotes the abolition of formal government; less extreme variants promote radical and expanded individual liberty.

If the individual chooses, as in most cases he will, to believe and worship as his fellows do, he finds temples built and services organized at a
Line cost to himself which he hardly feels. The clothes,
5 the food, the furniture which he is most likely to prefer are ready for him in the shops; the schools in which his children can be taught what their fellow citizens expect them to know are within fifteen minutes' walk of his door; and the red lamp
10 of the most approved pattern of doctor shines reassuringly at the corner of the street. He is free to live with the women of his family without suspicion or scandal; and if he is not free to marry them, what does that matter to him, since he does
15 not wish to marry them? And so happy may be his dole, in spite of his slavery.
   "Yes," cries some eccentric individual; "but all this is untrue of me. I want to marry my deceased wife's sister. I am prepared to prove that your
20 authorized system of medicine is nothing but a debased survival of witchcraft. Your schools are machines for forcing spurious learning on children in order that your universities may stamp them as educated men when they have finally lost all
25 power to think for themselves. The tall silk hats and starched linen shirts which you force me to wear, and without which I cannot successfully practice as a physician, clergyman, schoolmaster, lawyer, or merchant, are inconvenient, unsanitary,
30 ugly, pompous, and offensive. . . Under color of protecting my person and property you forcibly take my money to support an army of soldiers and policemen for the execution of barbarous and detestable laws; for the waging of wars which
35 I abhor; and for the subjection of my person to

those legal rights of property which compel me to sell myself for a wage to a class the maintenance of which I hold to be the greatest evil of our time. Your tyranny makes my very individuality a
40 hindrance to me: I am outdone and outbred by the mediocre, the docile, the time-serving. Evolution under such conditions means degeneracy: therefore I demand the abolition of all these officious compulsions, and proclaim myself an
45 Anarchist."
   The proclamation is not surprising under the circumstances; but it does not mend the matter in the least, nor would it if every person were to repeat it with enthusiasm, and the whole people
50 to fly to arms for Anarchism. The majority cannot help its tyranny even if it would. The giant Winkelmeier must have found our doorways inconvenient, just as men of five feet or less find the slope of the floor in a theatre not sufficiently
55 steep to enable them to see over the heads of those in front. But whilst the average height of a man is 5ft. 8in. there is no redress for such grievances. Builders will accommodate doors and floors to the majority, and not to the minority. For since either
60 the majority or the minority must be incommoded, evidently the more powerful must have its way. There may be no indisputable reason why it ought not; and any clever Tory can give excellent reasons why it ought not; but the fact remains that
65 it will, whether it ought or not. And this is what really settles the question as between democratic majorities and minorities. Where their interests conflict, the weaker side must go to the wall, because, as the evil involved is no greater than
70 that of the stronger going to the wall, the majority is not restrained by any scruple from compelling the weaker to give way.
   In practice, this does not involve either the absolute power of majorities, or "the infallibility
75 of the odd man." There are some matters in which the course preferred by the minority in no way obstructs that preferred by the majority. There are many more in which the obstruction is easier to bear than the cost of suppressing it. For it costs
80 something to suppress even a minority of one. The commonest example of that minority is the

CONTINUE

lunatic with a delusion; yet it is found quite safe
to entertain dozens of delusions, and be generally
an extremely selfish and troublesome idiot, in
85 spite of the power of majorities; for until you go
so far that it clearly costs less to lock you up than
to leave you at large, the majority will not take the
trouble to set itself in action against you. Thus a
minimum of individual liberty is secured, under
90 any system, to the smallest minority.

36

Shaw argues that the educational system of his era is

A) deeply unpopular among innovators and social reformers.

B) conveniently situated and effectively run for citizens who value conformity.

C) resistant to Anarchism despite a variety of institution-wide flaws.

D) hospitable to views that are bizarre and misguided.

37

Which choice provides the best evidence for the answer to the previous question?

A) Lines 6-9 ("The schools . . . door")

B) Lines 21-25 ("Your schools . . . themselves")

C) Lines 25-30 ("The tall . . . offensive")

D) Lines 82-85 ("yet it is . . . majorities")

38

Which choice most effectively indicates that the "eccentric individual" (line 17) believes that his worldview places him at a disadvantage?

A) Lines 19-20 ("I am . . . witchcraft")

B) Lines 30-34 ("Under . . . laws")

C) Lines 39-41 ("Your . . . time-serving")

D) Lines 43-45 ("therefore . . . Anarchist")

39

Shaw argues that the influence of the majority in political and civic life is

A) overwhelming, yet not fully justified on rational grounds.

B) widely admired, yet acknowledged by many as a source of injustice.

C) generally useful, yet of limited value in correcting dangerous or deranged behavior.

D) problematic, yet accepted since minorities tend to promote shortsighted policies.

40

Which choice provides the best evidence for the answer to the previous question?

A) Lines 47-50 ("but it . . . Anarchism")

B) Lines 62-65 ("There . . . not")

C) Lines 75-77 ("There . . . majority")

D) Lines 85-88 ("for until . . . you")

STOP

**After you have finished the questions, consult the relevant answers on Page 126.
Do not turn to any other section.**

Answer Key
Command of Evidence

Passage 1		Passage 2		Passage 3		Passage 4	
1.	C	6.	A	11.	B	16.	D
2.	C	7.	C	12.	D	17.	B
3.	B	8.	A	13.	B	18.	C
4.	D	9.	D	14.	C	19.	A
5.	B	10.	B	15.	D	20.	D

Passage 5		Passage 6		Passage 7		Passage 8	
21.	B	26.	A	31.	B	36.	B
22.	A	27.	B	32.	B	37.	A
23.	C	28.	B	33.	B	38.	C
24.	D	29.	C	34.	D	39.	A
25.	C	30.	B	35.	C	40.	B

For detailed answer explanations for this practice section please visit **prepvantagetutoring.com/reading**.

Part 4

Word in Context
Strategy and Practice

Strategy 4
Word in Context

Question Fundamentals

One of the major changes involved in the 2016 re-design of the SAT was the elimination of questions that tested relatively obscure vocabulary in isolation from complete passages. Now, almost all vocabulary that is tested directly on the SAT Reading section appears under a single question type: Word in Context. These questions, like some Command of Evidence questions, follow a fairly standard phrasing ("As used in line . . . most nearly means . . . ") that makes them readily identifiable. Yet the challenges of working with Word in Context content can be considerable—at least at first.

When approaching Word in Context items, you should NOT choose the "most obvious" or "dictionary" definition of the word that you must define. These questions typically feature words—"strength," "compromise," "range"—that can take on a variety of valid meanings, some of which may be relatively uncommon or may not initially come to mind. Your real task is to determine which of multiple plausible meanings fits the EXACT CONTEXT of the passage. Fortunately, there are a few different types of context clues that can be used in a highly systematic manner.

Working with Context Clues

In order to approach Word in Context questions effectively, you will need to locate or establish strong context clues for EVERY word that you are given (the one that appears in the question prompt, then the four answer choices). If you can do so, you will be able to perform process of elimination with high efficiency. You may not, of course, always use the same types of clues when working with the passage, though you will ALWAYS be able to make use of the same core method—one that is most open to modification in its early stages, when you are still mostly working with the word provided by the passage.

Core Strategy: Original Word

1. Locate the original word in the passage, but do NOT analyze its meaning

2. Determine whether there are any DIRECT clues for the original word

   • Synonyms that are the same part of speech

   • Antonyms that are the same part of speech

3. Determine whether there are any INDIRECT clues for the original word

   • What other word (especially for verbs, adjectives, or adverbs) the word describes or modifies

   • What general situation (context) and general tone (+/-) the word refers to

4. Using the clues, define the original word with a new word, context, or phrase that is AS CLOSE AS POSSIBLE to the content of the passage; note, if needed, TONE and CONTEXT

As you can see, the original word receives relatively little attention, and in some circumstances should be DIRECTLY REPLACED with a different word from the passage. For this reason, working with direct clues can yield easy answers if done properly. If you need to solve for the word "strong" and the passage gives you the phrase "her strong, unwavering stance," you should look for a direct synonym for "unwavering" in the answer choices. If you need to solve for the word "compromise" and the passage gives you the phrase "compromise rather than persevere," you should look for a word that means "NOT persevere."

Indirect clues can be more difficult to work with because they do not give word-to-word equivalences. Fortunately, they DO give plenty of context that can be analyzed in a straightforward manner. Consider how to work with a noun reference. If you need to solve for the word "range" and are given the phrase "the range of the experiment was considerable, drawing in well over 1000 volunteers," you should see that "range" refers to "experiment." Any words that raise other possible contexts for "range"—such as geographical location—will automatically be incorrect.

The same example also shows how well general context can help you to understand a given word in the absence of direct synonym or antonym. Here, "well over 1000 volunteers" is a clue that indicates the context of "size." You should thus, for your correct answers, predict a word that indicates "scope," "magnitude," or quite simply "size."

Part 4: Word in Context

Though vocabulary-oriented, the Word in Context strategy so far uses the same general principles of educated inference and prediction that appear in other SAT Reading question types. The answers still await, but you will need to perform one more round of analysis to deal with the individual choices appropriately.

Core Strategy: Answer Choices

5. Next to each answer choice, quickly define the context that is indicated; briefly note MULTIPLE contexts in special cases

6. Pair your predictions against the answer choices, and eliminate answer choices that do not fit ANY elements of your predictions

7. Check your final answer choice by plugging it into the passage in place of the original word

In essence, you must pair off the information that you have gathered from your comprehension of the reading to eliminate false choices that, WITHOUT this information, could be tempting. The point of the SAT is almost never what "sounds right" based on vague impressions. Like other question types, Word in Context calls upon your ability to adapt a predictable yet flexible method to the information given in a passage. Nonetheless, a few words of caution are necessary.

Important Tips

Do not rush to judgment on answer choices that themselves have MULTIPLE meanings.

- While several answer choices will in fact have obvious contexts, you may occasionally come across an answer choice that—like the word you are being asked to solve for—has important secondary or tertiary meanings. DO NOT disregard these. Note them instead, and realize that they might yield a correct answer.

Continue to build your vocabulary to ENHANCE your work, NOT to replace the strategy.

- Learning new and advanced words will help you to read through some passage types (particularly History) and can help you navigate Word in Context questions that feature tough vocabulary themselves. Still, stay method-bound. Words that are used every day, but with shades of meaning, still predominate.

Use a "plug-and-chug" method ONLY in crisis conditions, such as a time crunch or complete confusion.

- At first, test takers may get a fair number of right answers simply by "plugging in words and seeing what sounds best." This method is not absolutely terrible—and is, after all, incorporated into the final steps of the full method—but WILL NOT give you perfect accuracy. Instead, use plugging in as a way to check work that has already been approached methodically. The exception here is that simply plugging in may help you if you are completely confused or have two minutes left to finish five questions, though sufficient practice should remove BOTH of these problems.

of his college till time silvers his hairs; or he has
even been known to pass eighteen years among
his books, without once crossing the threshold
of his study. The young American, meanwhile,
90 satisfied at the end of three years that he knows
as much as his neighbours, settles in a home,
engages in farming or commerce, and plunges into
what alone he considers the business of life.

11

As used in line 17, "stronghold" most nearly means

A) boundary.

B) mainstay.

C) mansion.

D) buildup.

12

As used in line 29, "antique" most nearly means

A) picturesque.

B) elderly.

C) legendary.

D) outdated.

13

As used in line 43, "elastic" most nearly means

A) adaptive.

B) passive.

C) softening.

D) fanciful.

14

As used in line 58, "arise" most nearly means

A) escalate.

B) are created.

C) flare up.

D) spread forth.

15

As used in line 83, "pervading" most nearly means

A) universal and soulful.

B) dynamic and overbearing.

C) lingering and stubborn.

D) abiding and evident.

CONTINUE

Part 4

Questions 16-20 are based on the following Science passage.

This passage is adapted from "What in the World Is an Exoplanet?" by Pat Brennan (April 2018), originally published* on nasa. gov. The term "exoplanet" refers to any planet located outside our solar system.

We're standing on a precipice of scientific history. The era of early exploration, along with the first confirmed exoplanet detections,
Line is giving way to the next phase: sharper and
5 more sophisticated telescopes, in space and on the ground. They will go broad but also drill down. Some will be tasked with taking an ever more precise population census of these far-off worlds, nailing down their many sizes and types.
10 Others will make a closer inspection of individual planets, their atmospheres, and their potential to harbor some form of life.

Direct imaging of exoplanets—that is, actual pictures—will play an increasingly larger role,
15 though we've arrived at our present state of knowledge mostly through indirect means. The two main methods rely on wobbles and shadows. The "wobble" method, called radial velocity, watches for the telltale jitters of stars as they are
20 pulled back and forth by the gravitational tugs of an orbiting planet. The size of the wobble reveals the "weight," or mass, of the planet.

This method produced the very first confirmed exoplanet detections, including 51 Peg in 1995,
25 discovered by astronomers Michel Mayor and Didier Queloz. Ground telescopes using the radial velocity method have discovered nearly 700 planets so far.

But the vast majority of exoplanets have been
30 found by searching for shadows: the incredibly tiny dip in the light from a star when a planet crosses its face. Astronomers call this crossing a "transit."

The size of the dip in starlight reveals how big
35 around the transiting planet is. Unsurprisingly, this search for planetary shadows is known as the transit method.

NASA's Kepler space telescope, launched in 2009, has found nearly 2,700 confirmed
40 exoplanets this way. Now in its "K2" mission, Kepler is still discovering new planets, though its fuel is expected to run out soon.

Each method has its pluses and minuses. Wobble detections provide the mass of the planet,
45 but give no information about the planet's girth, or diameter. Transit detections reveal the diameter but not the mass.

But when multiple methods are used together, we can learn the vital statistics of whole planetary
50 systems—without ever directly imaging the planets themselves. The best example so far is the TRAPPIST-1 system about 40 light-years away, where seven roughly Earth-sized planets orbit a small, red star.
55 The TRAPPIST-1 planets have been examined with ground and space telescopes. The space-based studies revealed not only their diameters, but the subtle gravitational influence these seven closely packed planets have upon each other; from
60 this, scientists determined each planet's mass.

So now we know their masses and their diameters. We also know how much of the energy radiated by their star strikes these planets' surfaces, allowing scientists to estimate their
65 temperatures. We can even make reasonable estimates of the light level, and guess at the color of the sky, if you were standing on one of them. And while much remains unknown about these seven worlds, including whether they possess
70 atmospheres or oceans, ice sheets or glaciers, it's become the best-known solar system apart from our own.

The next generation of space telescopes is upon us. First up is the launch of TESS, the Transiting
75 Exoplanet Survey Satellite. This extraordinary instrument will take a nearly full-sky survey of the closer, brighter stars to look for transiting planets. Kepler, the past master of transits, will be passing the torch of discovery to TESS.
80 TESS, in turn, will reveal the best candidates for a closer look with the James Webb Space Telescope, currently scheduled to launch in 2020. The Webb telescope, deploying a giant,

*See Page 262 for the citation for this text.

CONTINUE →

segmented, light-collecting mirror that will
85 ride on a shingle-like platform, is designed to
capture light directly from the planets themselves.
The light then can be split into a multi-colored
spectrum, a kind of bar code showing which gases
are present in the planet's atmosphere. Webb's
90 targets might include "super Earths," or planets
larger than Earth but smaller than Neptune—
some that could be rocky planets like super-sized
versions of our own.

Little is known about these big planets,
95 including whether some might be suitable for
life. If we're very lucky, perhaps one of them
will show signs of oxygen, carbon dioxide and
methane in its atmosphere. Such a mix of gases
would remind us strongly of our own atmosphere,
100 possibly indicating the presence of life.

But hunting for Earth-like atmospheres on
Earth-sized exoplanets will probably have to wait
for a future generation of even more powerful
space probes in the 2020s or 2030s.

16

As used in line 2, "early" most nearly means

A) punctual.
B) primeval.
C) preliminary.
D) premature.

17

As used in line 31, "tiny" most nearly means

A) fragile.
B) meaningless.
C) subtle.
D) secondary.

18

As used in line 49, "vital" most nearly means

A) significant.
B) vibrant.
C) flourishing.
D) sustaining.

19

As used in line 69, "possess" most nearly means

A) are fixated on.
B) have taken.
C) are home to.
D) have occupied.

20

As used in line 98, "mix" most nearly means

A) sequence.
B) combination.
C) confusion.
D) assembly.

CONTINUE

Part 4

Questions 21-25 are based on the following Fiction passage.

This passage is adapted from "The Ambiguities Abroad" by Nils Lundgarten (2016). Dominic, the main character of the short story from which this excerpt is taken, is a retired chemist who is on a sightseeing tour.

I doubt that many people would look out at a tan-and-black landscape under a gray sky and think, "I am free. I am free!" Had anyone other
Line than the vikings—had even they—ever landed
5 on Iceland on a rainy Thursday and found that "freedom! freedom!" was the first thing that came to mind?

As the bus bounded toward Reykjavik, I couldn't help thinking back to how all this would
10 have gone had I still been yoked to that tour group—how little freedom I would have enjoyed as I rode through that wind-whipped volcanic landscape. Again and again, I scanned the bus in satisfaction. Empty seats! A week ago, the entire
15 vehicle would have been populated by my "fellow travelers." I would have jealously guarded the seat next to me, my books and my hat situated on it in a manner designed to forbid companionship. Such attempts were never successful enough, but
20 now there were no companions. The interior of the bus was dark, the air that circulated through was crisp. I realized, now, how little I remembered of any one individual from the group tour, perhaps beyond our ever-voluble, ever-sunglassed guide
25 and the quiet, beleaguered fellow who actually drove the tour bus. I had remained aloof from them too, cautious of signaling to the younger and more raucous vacationers that I was ready to socialize at large. Of course, now, none of it
30 mattered. The only other people on the Reykjavik bus were a mother and her four children, all of them clustered towards the front seats and preoccupied with their iPads. For them, I had as little importance as my onetime fellow travelers
35 on the "Scandinavia Holiday Group Tour" now had for me.

The streets of Reykjavik itself were vacant; I kept on the lookout for another car, a woman with a baby carriage, a hardy soul on a bicycle,
40 and found myself disappointed at each new intersection. Finally, we reached the hotel. The family with the iPads disembarked promptly; I would never see them again. As for the hotel itself, it was not large or imposing by any means.
45 What it lacked in stature, though, it made up in its all-too-transparent positioning as an eminently modern establishment. The lobby was not so much a lobby as a machine made to deliver hospitality in the most efficient form possible—nothing but
50 navy blue furniture, pearl-white walls, fluorescent lighting. A bowl of flawlessly green apples and a large carafe of water—a pleasant change from the unruly collections of candies and pastries that every Russian hotel seemed to boast—were the
55 only attempts at refreshment.

When, in short order, I entered my room, I positively hurled my travel bags down in anticipation. The trip was not over, and this last stage would be mine to savor in the isolation
60 that I had craved for every preceding mile that I had traveled. Yet as those two bags hit the floor, something—not quite regret, but something comparable, something just as tangible—snuffed out my high spirits. The truth was that I had
65 waited so long for this moment that its arrival was quashingly underwhelming. There would no longer be a litany of complaints humming in the back of my mind; there would no longer be the tour guide's longwinded lectures, the pleasant
70 pointless chatter of my twenty-five "fellow travelers." I would miss them the way that one misses a tooth that had been aching consistently yet never too intensely before its extraction, and I would miss that quiet fellow who drove the bus—
75 and, having forgotten his name, I will always think of him as "that quiet fellow who drove the bus"—in a different way. I had felt that he and I were somehow united in this ordeal, trying to conduct our business while other people's
80 socialization clamored to get in the way, and I hadn't so much as offered him a perfunctory good-bye.

CONTINUE

21

As used in line 10, "yoked to" most nearly means

A) lost to.

B) encumbered by.

C) interchangeable with.

D) dependent on.

22

As used in line 44, "imposing" most nearly means

A) virtuous.

B) sturdy.

C) sufficient.

D) impressive.

23

As used in line 53, "collections" most nearly means

A) assortments.

B) networks.

C) compositions.

D) stockpiles.

24

As used in line 60, "craved" most nearly means

A) felt helpless before.

B) worried about.

C) yearned to have.

D) been dependent on.

25

As used in line 76, "think of" most nearly means

A) show consideration for.

B) find ways to honor.

C) make reference to.

D) ask about.

CONTINUE

Part 4

This passage is adapted from Samantha Wallace, "Linking Isolated Languages: Linguistic Relationships of the Carabayo." Originally published* on EveryONE, the blog of the research site Plos One.

In 2010, English clocked in at over 360 million native speakers, and it is the third-most-commonly used native language, right behind Mandarin
Line Chinese and Spanish. While these languages
5 spread, however, other indigenous languages decline at an accelerated pace. A fraction of these enigmatic languages belong to uncontacted indigenous groups of the Amazonian rainforest, groups of people in South America who have
10 little to no interaction with societies beyond their own. Many of these groups choose to remain uncontacted by the rest of the world. Because of their isolation, not much is known about these languages beyond their existence.
15   The researchers of a recent PLOS ONE paper investigated one such language, that of the Carabayo people who live in the Colombian Amazon rainforest. Working with the relatively scarce historical data that exists for the Carabayo
20 language—only 50 words have been recorded over time—the authors identified similarities between Carabayo and Yurí and Tikuna, two known languages of South America that constitute the current language family Ticuna-Yurí. Based
25 on the correspondences, the authors posit a possible genealogical connection between these languages.
   Few resources were available to the authors in this endeavor. They analyzed historical wordlists
30 collected during the last encounter with the Carabayo people in 1969—the only linguistic data available from this group—against wordlists for the Yurí language. In addition, they sought the expertise of a native speaker of Tikuna, a linguist
35 trained in Tikuna's many dialects. Using these resources, the authors broke down the Carabayo words into their foundational forms, starting with

consonants and vowels. They then compared them to similarly deconstructed words in Yurí and
40 Tikuna.
   The examination involved the evaluation of similarities in the basic building blocks of these words: the number of times a specific sound (or phoneme) appeared; the composition and patterns
45 of the smallest grammatical units of a word (a morpheme); and the meanings attached to these words. When patterns appeared between Carabayo and either Yurí or Tikuna, the authors considered whether or not the languages' similarities
50 constituted stronger correspondences. They also paid attention to the ways in which these words would have been used by the Carabayo when the lists were originally made many years ago.
   The Yurí language was first recorded in the
55 19th century, but it is thought to have become extinct since then. From these lists, five words stood out: in Carabayo, ao 'father', hono 'boy', hako 'well!', and a complex form containing both the Yurí word from warm, noré, and the Yurí
60 word, tʃau, which corresponds in English to 'I' or 'my'. Given the evidence, the authors contend that the strongest link between Carabayo and Yurí is found in the correspondence of tʃau. The study of other languages has indicated that first person
65 pronouns are particularly resistant to "borrowing," or the absorption of one language's vocabulary into another. Therefore, the authors surmise it is unlikely in this instance that either of the languages absorbed tʃau from the other, but that
70 they share a genealogical link.
   Similarly, the comparison of Carabayo words to words of the living language of Tikuna provided a high number of matches, including in Carabayo gudda 'wait' and gu 'yes'. The matches
75 especially exhibit sound correspondences of Carabayo g (or k) and the loss of the letter n in certain circumstances.
   Although it is possible that the Carabayo language represents a language that had not yet
80 been documented until the time of 1969, the results of the researchers' evaluation have led them to conclude that Carabayo more likely belongs to the language family of Ticuna-Yurí.

---

*See Page 262 for the citation for this text.

CONTINUE ➡

The relationship of Carabayo to Yurí and
85 Tikuna changes the structure of the Ticuna-Yurí
family by placing Carabayo on the map as a
member of that family. The Tikuna language, once
considered to be the sole surviving member of
the Ticuna-Yurí family, might now have a sibling,
90 and the identity of a barely known language has
become that much more defined.

26

As used in line 7, "enigmatic" most nearly means

A) ultimately baffling.

B) purposefully bizarre.

C) completely hidden.

D) extremely localized.

27

As used in line 28, "available to" most nearly means

A) compliant with.

B) sympathetically inclined towards.

C) understandable to.

D) readily accessible to.

28

As used in line 46, "attached to" most nearly means

A) submissive to.

B) trailing from.

C) attributed to.

D) allied with.

29

As used in line 63, "study" most nearly means

A) experimentation.

B) examination.

C) estimation.

D) education.

30

As used in line 88, "considered" most nearly means

A) honored.

B) attempted.

C) solicited.

D) determined.

CONTINUE

Part 4

Questions 31-35 are based on the following Science passage.

This passage is adapted from "Fruit Fly Mating Driven by a Tweak in a Specific Brain Circuit" (July 2018). Originally published* by the National Institutes of Health.

According to a new National Institutes of Health-funded study, it is not destiny that brings two fruit flies together, but an evolutionary matchmaker of sorts that made tiny adjustments to their brains' mating circuits, so they would be attracted to one another while rejecting advances from other, even closely-related, species. The results, published in *Nature*, may help explain how a specific female scent triggers completely different responses in different male flies.

"This study reveals how a very small tweak in brain wiring can result in large changes in very complex social behaviors, which can ultimately determine the fate of a species," said Jim Gnadt, Ph.D., program director at the NIH's National Institute of Neurological Disorders and Stroke (NINDS), which supported the study. "Understanding how variation in brain circuits leads to changes in behavior is one of the primary goals of the NIH's BRAIN Initiative and this study provides a piece of the puzzle."

Vanessa Ruta, Ph.D., professor at Rockefeller University in New York City, and her colleagues used cutting-edge genetic tools to compare the brain circuits behind courtship behavior in two closely related species of fruit fly, D. melanogaster and D. simulans.

Previous studies showed that although males from both species could detect a specific pheromone, or scent, called 7,11-heptacosadiene (7,11-HD), their reactions to it were very different. Male D. melanogaster flies found it attractive while D. simulans males avoided females that carried it. In this study, Dr. Ruta and her team discovered that slight differences in the way the flies' brains are wired may control these opposite reactions.

"From a fly's perspective, courtship is the most important decision it will make, and so evolutionary processes have really fine-tuned flies' brains to ensure optimal behaviors, leading them to their ideal mates," said Dr. Ruta.

In fruit flies, pheromones are detected by sensory neurons on the legs, and that information travels to P1 neurons that sit in the lateral protocerebral complex (LPC) in the brain. In between the sensory and P1 neurons, the wiring splits so that the P1 cells can be either turned on or off.

P1 neurons trigger courtship activity in D. melanogaster males but have not been studied in other fly species. When the P1 neurons were turned on in D. simulans males, they tried mating with nearby objects including unsuitable targets such as females from different species as well as rotating magnets. This suggests that P1 neurons may be important for sparking courtship behaviors across species.

Dr. Ruta and her team used state-of-the-art technology to watch brain cells light up in real time as male flies were exposed to D. melanogaster and D. simulans females releasing 7,11-HD. When D. melanogaster males were exposed to females from their species, there was a lot of activity by the P1 neurons. Exposure to D. simulans females did not turn on those neurons. However, P1 neurons in the D. simulans males did not light up when they were exposed to females from their species, suggesting that differences in P1 neurons may underlie species-specific responses to 7,11-HD.

Additional experiments suggested that as pheromone signals traveled from the legs to P1 neurons, that information was conveyed differently in the two species of fruit fly by brain cells that communicate directly with P1 neurons. Specifically, P1 neurons appeared to receive lots of excitation in D. melanogaster flies but got more calming signals in D. simulans flies, which led to opposite responses when the animals were exposed to 7,11-HD. These findings also suggested that in some species of flies, absence of pheromone signaling may be more attractive than the presence of certain scents.

CONTINUE

85 Future experiments will look at similar behaviors in other species of fruit flies. More research is needed to learn the mechanisms that drive evolutionary changes in brain circuitry, which may have important consequences for
90 individual and social behavior.

31

As used in line 9, "triggers" most nearly means

A) inflames.

B) produces.

C) releases.

D) undertakes.

32

As used in line 36, "wired" most nearly means

A) transmitted.

B) suspended.

C) structured.

D) aggravated.

33

As used in line 45, "sit in" most nearly means

A) watch over.

B) linger near.

C) are located at.

D) assert themselves for.

34

As used in line 68, "exposed to" most nearly means

A) defined for.

B) vulnerable to.

C) pinpointed by.

D) presented with.

35

As used in line 79, "more calming" most nearly means

A) less agitating.

B) less ambivalent.

C) less inspiring.

D) less timid.

CONTINUE

Part 4

This passage is adapted from *The Impossibilities of Anarchism* (1895) by George Bernard Shaw. In its most extreme form, "anarchism" promotes the abolition of formal government; less extreme variants promote radical and expanded individual liberty.

If the individual chooses, as in most cases he will, to believe and worship as his fellows do, he finds temples built and services organized at a
Line cost to himself which he hardly feels. The clothes,
5   the food, the furniture which he is most likely to prefer are ready for him in the shops; the schools in which his children can be taught what their fellow citizens expect them to know are within fifteen minutes' walk of his door; and the red lamp
10 of the most approved pattern of doctor shines reassuringly at the corner of the street. He is free to live with the women of his family without suspicion or scandal; and if he is not free to marry them, what does that matter to him, since he does
15 not wish to marry them? And so happy may be his dole, in spite of his slavery.
      "Yes," cries some eccentric individual; "but all this is untrue of me. I want to marry my deceased wife's sister. I am prepared to prove that your
20 authorized system of medicine is nothing but a debased survival of witchcraft. Your schools are machines for forcing spurious learning on children in order that your universities may stamp them as educated men when they have finally lost all
25 power to think for themselves. The tall silk hats and starched linen shirts which you force me to wear, and without which I cannot successfully practice as a physician, clergyman, schoolmaster, lawyer, or merchant, are inconvenient, unsanitary,
30 ugly, pompous, and offensive. . . Under color of protecting my person and property you forcibly take my money to support an army of soldiers and policemen for the execution of barbarous and detestable laws; for the waging of wars which
35 I abhor; and for the subjection of my person to

those legal rights of property which compel me to sell myself for a wage to a class the maintenance of which I hold to be the greatest evil of our time. Your tyranny makes my very individuality a
40 hindrance to me: I am outdone and outbred by the mediocre, the docile, the time-serving. Evolution under such conditions means degeneracy: therefore I demand the abolition of all these officious compulsions, and proclaim myself an
45 Anarchist."
      The proclamation is not surprising under the circumstances; but it does not mend the matter in the least, nor would it if every person were to repeat it with enthusiasm, and the whole people
50 to fly to arms for Anarchism. The majority cannot help its tyranny even if it would. The giant Winkelmeier must have found our doorways inconvenient, just as men of five feet or less find the slope of the floor in a theatre not sufficiently
55 steep to enable them to see over the heads of those in front. But whilst the average height of a man is 5ft. 8in. there is no redress for such grievances. Builders will accommodate doors and floors to the majority, and not to the minority. For since either
60 the majority or the minority must be incommoded, evidently the more powerful must have its way. There may be no indisputable reason why it ought not; and any clever Tory can give excellent reasons why it ought not; but the fact remains that
65 it will, whether it ought or not. And this is what really settles the question as between democratic majorities and minorities. Where their interests conflict, the weaker side must go to the wall, because, as the evil involved is no greater than
70 that of the stronger going to the wall, the majority is not restrained by any scruple from compelling the weaker to give way.
      In practice, this does not involve either the absolute power of majorities, or "the infallibility
75 of the odd man." There are some matters in which the course preferred by the minority in no way obstructs that preferred by the majority. There are many more in which the obstruction is easier to bear than the cost of suppressing it. For it costs
80 something to suppress even a minority of one. The commonest example of that minority is the

CONTINUE

lunatic with a delusion; yet it is found quite safe
to entertain dozens of delusions, and be generally
an extremely selfish and troublesome idiot, in
85 spite of the power of majorities; for until you go
so far that it clearly costs less to lock you up than
to leave you at large, the majority will not take the
trouble to set itself in action against you. Thus a
minimum of individual liberty is secured, under
90 any system, to the smallest minority.

36

As used in line 25, "power" most nearly means

A) property.

B) fame.

C) ability.

D) motion.

37

As used in line 30, "color" most nearly means

A) the variation.

B) the drama.

C) the quality.

D) the premise.

38

As used in line 57, "grievances" most nearly means

A) injuries.

B) tragedies.

C) negligences.

D) inconveniences.

39

As used in line 67, "interests" most nearly means

A) fascinations.

B) specialties.

C) inclinations.

D) benefits.

40

As used in line 72, "give way" most nearly means

A) become forgiving.

B) ensure equality.

C) abandon individuality.

D) submit to authority.

STOP
**After you have finished the questions, consult the relevant answers on Page 148.
Do not turn to any other section.**

Answer Key
Word in Context

Passage 1

1. A
2. A
3. D
4. C
5. C

Passage 2

6. C
7. D
8. D
9. B
10. A

Passage 3

11. B
12. D
13. A
14. B
15. D

Passage 4

16. C
17. C
18. A
19. C
20. B

Passage 5

21. B
22. D
23. A
24. C
25. C

Passage 6

26. D
27. D
28. C
29. B
30. D

Passage 7

31. B
32. C
33. C
34. D
35. A

Passage 8

36. C
37. D
38. D
39. C
40. D

For detailed answer explanations for this practice section please visit **prepvantagetutoring.com/reading**.

Part 5

Paired Passages
Strategy and Practice

Strategy 5
Paired Passages

Passage Types

On each SAT Reading section, you will need to deal with EXACTLY one pairing: a selection in either Science or History that features two relatively short passages that address the same topic, and that are meant to be read and analyzed together. These paired passages can be difficult for readers who have trouble coordinating information and perspectives—but can be relatively easy for test-takers who comprehend topics more effectively by factoring in multiple sources. Regardless of your current aptitudes, each paired passage can be run through the same strategy, with careful modifications depending on passage type.

Science Pairings

The paired Science passages cover the same range of topics as the single Science passages, as described on Page 52. Stylistically, these readings can also be much more accessible than paired History passages. Still, paired Science can be more difficult for readers who are accustomed to a straightforward pro-con structure, which appears with great regularity in paired History but NOT in paired Science. These readings, instead, can give you a sound early sense of the many different ways in which two SAT passages can play off one another.

Possible combinations include

*   Sharp disagreement (two contradictory theories or experiments)

*   Moderate disagreement (two passages that point out exceptions or convey skepticism)

- One neutral or balanced author, one extremely biased author

- One passage providing essential background, one pointing out a new approach or a new aspect of the topic

- One passage explaining a finding, one analyzing a specific point or repercussion of that finding

As this list of statements indicates, there will ALMOST ALWAYS be a core relationship between the two passages that can be summed up in a fairly concise statement. Your task is to determine what this relationship is—since the SAT features questions on exactly this topic—and then to determine a few of the smaller similarities and differences that the passages involve.

For ALL paired passages, ask yourself the following core questions.

1. What is the main idea and main tone (positive or negative, if relevant) of each passage?

2. How can the relationship between the passages be summed up in a single phrase or sentence?

3. In what smaller ways are the passages the same or different?

You will find that thinking analytically about this information will prepare you for the standard passage questions, for BOTH Science and History. Here is a list of the Paired Passage questions that have appeared prominently on the SAT.

- Relationship between the passages (opposition, agreement, one expanding upon the other, etc.)

- Purposes of the passages (sometimes BOTH passages serving the same purpose, despite other differences)

- Point of similarity (even if the passages are in overall disagreement) or point of difference (even if the passages are in overall agreement)

- Techniques used by the authors (often similarity, though noting differences may be required)

- How the author of one passage would respond to an element of the other passage (possibly a main idea or a main point, possibly a detail)

These questions will always be COMPLETELY evidence-based; in fact, the three or four questions that focus on passage comparison may include a Command of Evidence item. You must keep this rule firmly in mind even when dealing with question types that seem to require imagination or interpretation, as the final question type ("How would the author . . . ") appears to at first glance. In reality, this question type does NOT require any sort of cleverness. Simply determine one author's position, using either an effective overall read or a relevant set of lines, and use THAT information to determine a hypothetical response.

Working with paired Science passages is also made easier by similarities between these readings and the single Science entries. You will find that paired Science has its own checklist. On the whole, it adapts the standard "inquiry, experiment, outcomes" structure to account for the new, comparison-based analysis that you will need to perform.

Science Pairing
Passage Strategy

Can you identify and compare the main elements of the two passages?

Passage 1

Inquiry/Issue: _____

_____

Hypothesis 1: _____

_____

Hypothesis 2: _____

_____

Method 1: _____
Outcome 1: _____

Method 2: _____
Outcome 2: _____

Shifts: _____ ➡ _____

Final Outcomes: _____

_____

Passage 2

Inquiry/Issue: _____

_____

Hypothesis 1: _____

_____

Hypothesis 2: _____

_____

Method 1: _____
Outcome 1: _____

Method 2: _____
Outcome 2: _____

Shifts: _____ ➡ _____

Final Outcomes: _____

_____

Passage Comparison

Core Relationship: _____

Points of Similarity: _____

Present ONLY in Passage 1: _____

Present ONLY in Passage 2: _____

History Pairings

Like the single History passages, paired History passages have a track record of prioritizing readings from the late 18th to the early 20th century. All of the standard difficulties of the single History passages—vocabulary, sentence structure, challenging imagery, challenging lines of reasoning—can re-appear here. There is also the added difficulty of dealing with questions that require you to compare the authors' viewpoints, arguments, and rhetorical devices.

Though these passages are widely regarded as representing one of the test's supreme points of difficulty, here is some good news: these passages CAN be rather predictable. The College Board itself has repeatedly returned to the topics of women's rights and women's status in its paired History passages—though there are other forms that the predictability of this section can take. Perhaps the most important is the fact that, quite often, the paired authors are in DIRECT OPPOSITION to each other.

Consider the typical Official SAT passage devoted to the topic of women's rights. One author (often the first in the pair) typically argues in favor of measures that restrict women's opportunities and that would be considered sexist or chauvinistic by an enlightened reader today; another author (often the second in the pair) argues that women should be granted new rights, responsibilities, or respect. The passages will not always follow this opposition structure, but they do so often enough that you can expect author-against-author opposition with some regularity.

While the core strategy for Science and History passages will always remain consistent, History passages do call for some shifts in emphasis as you search for key elements. Remember, some History passages may be extremely light on empirical facts and examples. Look instead for the following features, which are central to working with this passage type in both single and paired form.

- Opponents and counter-arguments cited by each author (INCLUDING the author of the other passage and his or her points)

- Tones, attitudes, and emotions (INCLUDING possible shifts or modifications as each passage moves along

- Stylistic techniques and rhetorical strategies (including imagery, questions, hypothetical scenarios, addresses to an audience, direct uses of the author's own experience)

To approach these issues with clarity, use the checklist for paired History passages which is provided on the next page. You will find that this checklist mostly modifies the single History checklist to streamline your ideas about the most challenging features of this passage type and to account for the compare-and-contrast items that conclude each question set.

History Pairing
Passage Strategy

Can you identify and compare the main elements of the two passages?

Passage 1

Core Topic: _____
_____

Author's Position: _____
_____

Reason 1: _____
_____

Reason 2: _____
_____

Opponents: _____
_____

Shifts: _____ ➡ _____

Techniques: _____

Passage 2

Core Topic: _____
_____

Author's Position: _____
_____

Reason 1: _____
_____

Reason 2: _____
_____

Opponents: _____
_____

Shifts: _____ ➡ _____

Techniques: _____

Passage Comparison

Core Relationship: _____

Points of Similarity: _____

Present ONLY in Passage 1: _____

Present ONLY in Passage 2: _____

Practice Exercises Begin on the Next Page

Part 5

Questions 1-10 are based on the following passages.

Passage 1 is adapted from "New 3D Measurements Improve Understanding of Geomagnetic Storm Hazards," while Passage 2 is adapted from "Preparing the Nation for Intense Space Weather." Both passages are news releases* from the U.S. Geological Survey.

Passage 1

Space weather events such as geomagnetic storms can disturb the earth's magnetic field, interfering with electric power grids,
Line radio communication, GPS systems, satellite
5 operations, oil and gas drilling, and air travel. Scientists use models of the earth's structure and measurements of Earth's magnetic field taken at USGS observatories to determine which sections of the electrical grid might lose power during a
10 geomagnetic storm.

In a new U.S. Geological Survey study, scientists calculated voltages along power lines in the mid-Atlantic region of the U.S. using 3D data of the earth. These data, taken at Earth's surface,
15 reflect the complex structure of the earth below the measurement sites and were collected during the National Science Foundation EarthScope USArray project. The scientists found that for many locations, the voltages they calculated
20 were significantly different from those based on previous 1D calculations, with the 3D data producing the most precise results.

"Using the most accurate data available to determine vulnerable areas of the power grid
25 can help maintain life-saving communications and protect national security during severe geomagnetic storms," said Greg Lucas, a USGS scientist and the lead author of the study. "Our study suggests that 3D data of the earth should be
30 used whenever they are available."

Electric currents from a March 1989 geomagnetic storm caused a blackout in Québec and numerous glitches in the U.S. power grid. In past studies, scientists using simple 1D models of
35 the earth would have found that 16 high-voltage electrical transmission lines were disturbed in the mid-Atlantic region during the storm, resulting in the blackout. However, by using realistic 3D data to calculate the 1989 scenario, the new study
40 found that there might have actually been 62 vulnerable lines.

"This discrepancy between 1D- and 3D-based calculations of the 1989 storm demonstrates the importance of realistic data, rather than relying on
45 previous 1D models, to determine the impact that a geomagnetic storm has on power grids," Lucas said.

Passage 2

The entire Canadian province of Québec, which covers twice as much area as the State of
50 Texas, was plunged into darkness on the morning of March 13, 1989. An intense geomagnetic storm seized Québec's power-grid system, tripping relays, damaging high-voltage transformers, and causing a blackout.

55 This geomagnetic storm's impact on Québec pales in comparison to what could happen in the future. A report by the National Academy of Sciences suggests that a rare but powerful magnetic superstorm could cause continent-
60 wide loss of electricity and substantial damage to power-grid infrastructure that could persist for months and cost the Nation in excess of $1 trillion.

"Utility groups rely on historical data collected
65 by long-running USGS (U.S. Geological Survey) magnetic observatories to see what a worst-case scenario could look like," said Mark Olson, a standards developer with the North American Electric Reliability Corporation (NERC).
70 "These data help NERC draft standards aimed at maintaining reliable operations of the North American power grid."

When a large sunspot emerges, the likelihood of an abrupt emission of radiation and an intense
75 solar wind becomes greater. When these winds reach the Earth, electrically charged particles enter the Earth's magnetosphere, ionosphere, and interior, inducing a geomagnetic storm.

---

*See Page 263 for the citations for these texts.

CONTINUE

1

In Passage 1, Greg Lucas argues that 1D voltage calculation models should be

A) prioritized since they have proven useful in the past.

B) adjusted to more closely resemble 3D models.

C) investigated in light of data on recent crises.

D) abandoned in favor of a more accurate method.

2

Which choice provides the best evidence for the answer to the previous question?

A) Lines 14-18 ("These . . . project")

B) Lines 23-27 ("Using . . . Lucas")

C) Lines 33-38 ("In past . . . blackout")

D) Lines 42-47 ("This . . . said")

3

As used in line 36, "disturbed" most nearly means

A) vexed.

B) aggravated.

C) impaired.

D) removed.

4

As used in line 50, "plunged into" most nearly means

A) immersed in.

B) assailed by.

C) dependent on.

D) preoccupied with.

5

The author of Passage 2 mentions the report by the National Academy of Sciences in order to call attention to

A) the steep financial costs of studying environmental disasters.

B) the threats posed by magnetic superstorms.

C) the increasing frequency of superstorms.

D) gradual improvements in the technology used to study magnetic superstorms.

6

The final paragraph of Passage 2 mainly serves to

A) outline a process central to the author's analysis.

B) justify a standard method of classification.

C) summarize the most famous facts about a disaster.

D) support the thesis argued by a single researcher.

7

Which choice best describes the relationship between the two passages?

A) Passage 1 shows how a new consensus regarding a disaster described in Passage 2 has emerged over time.

B) Passage 1 describes a project that retrospectively analyzes an event explained in Passage 2.

C) Passage 1 presents an unexpected viewpoint that is given statistical support in Passage 2.

D) Passage 1 locates various objections to the research described in Passage 2.

CONTINUE ➤

8

One central tension between the passages is that

A) only Passage 1 points out the inconveniences that geomagnetic storms can cause for communities.

B) only Passage 1 presents a contrast that favors one procedure over another.

C) only Passage 2 describes how the 1989 geomagnetic storm influenced a national power grid.

D) only Passage 2 cites the widely-accepted definition of a geomagnetic storm.

9

On the basis of Passage 2, Marc Olson would respond to the information in Passage 1 by pointing out that

A) the passage rightly indicates the problems with 1D storm modeling, but neglects recent modifications to this modeling technique.

B) the passage may be too negative in its assessment, since past data collection has been important to maintaining infrastructure.

C) the passage presents useful data and suggests new possibilities for weather-related research.

D) the passage's valid arguments about the nature of geomagnetic storms are complicated by its unrealistic estimate of the extent of the 1989 storm.

10

Which choice provides the best evidence for the answer to the previous question?

A) Lines 51-54 ("An intense . . . blackout")

B) Lines 57-63 ("A report . . . $1 trillion")

C) Lines 64-67 ("Utility . . . Olson")

D) Lines 70-72 ("These . . . grid")

Questions 11-20 are based on the following passages.

Passage 1 is adapted from the article "Reconstruction" (1866) by Frederick Douglass. Passage 2 is adapted from *Up from Slavery: An Autobiography* (1901) by Booker T. Washington. Both men were African-American authors and activists.

Passage 1

The people . . . want a reconstruction such
as will protect loyal men, black and white, in
their persons and property; such a one as will
Line cause Northern industry, Northern capital, and
5 Northern civilization to flow into the South, and
make a man from New England as much at home
in Carolina as elsewhere in the Republic. No
Chinese wall can now be tolerated. The South
must be opened to the light of law and liberty,
10 and this session of Congress is relied upon to
accomplish this important work.
    The plain, common-sense way of doing this
work, as intimated at the beginning, is simply to
establish in the South one law, one government,
15 one administration of justice, one condition to
the exercise of the elective franchise, for men
of all races and colors alike. This great measure
is sought as earnestly by loyal white men as by
loyal blacks, and is needed alike by both. Let
20 sound political prescience but take the place of an
unreasoning prejudice, and this will be done.
    Men denounce the negro for his prominence
in this discussion, but it is no fault of his that in
peace as in war, that in conquering Rebel armies
25 as in reconstructing the rebellious States, the right
of the negro is the true solution of our national
troubles. The stern logic of events, which goes
directly to the point, disdaining all concern for
the color or features of men, has determined the
30 interests of the country as identical with and
inseparable from those of the negro.
    The policy that emancipated and armed
the negro—now seen to have been wise and
proper by the dullest—was not certainly more
35 sternly demanded than is now the policy of

CONTINUE

enfranchisement. If with the negro was success in war, and without him failure, so in peace it will be found that the nation must fall or flourish with the negro.

Passage 2

40   In every part of the South, during the Reconstruction period, schools, both day and night, were filled to overflowing with people of all ages and conditions, some being as far along in age as sixty and seventy years. The ambition

45   to secure an education was most praiseworthy and encouraging. The idea, however, was too prevalent that, as soon as one secured a little education, in some unexplainable way he would be free from most of the hardships of the world,

50   and, at any rate, could live without manual labour. There was a further feeling that a knowledge, however little, of the Greek and Latin languages would make one a very superior human being, something bordering almost on the supernatural.

55   I remember that the first coloured man whom I saw who knew something about foreign languages impressed me at the time as being a man of all others to be envied. . . .
     It is easy to find fault, to remark what might

60   have been done, and perhaps, after all, and under all the circumstances, those in charge of the conduct of affairs did the only thing that could be done at the time. Still, as I look back now over the entire period of our freedom, I cannot help

65   feeling that it would have been wiser if some plan could have been put in operation which would have made the possession of a certain amount of education or property, or both, a test for the exercise of the franchise, and a way provided by

70   which this test should be made to apply honestly and squarely to both the white and black races.
     Though I was but little more than a youth during the period of Reconstruction, I had the feeling that mistakes were being made, and

75   that things could not remain in the condition that they were in then very long. I felt that the Reconstruction policy, so far as it related to my race, was in a large measure on a false foundation, was artificial and forced.

11

The first paragraph of Passage 1 serves to

A) depict Douglass himself as moderate and open to compromise.

B) explain the difficulties inherent in a new attempt to promote civic freedom.

C) define the responsibilities that face both Congress and the nation as a whole.

D) urge cooperation between two vast regions that remain antagonistic.

12

In Passage 1, Douglass depicts white Americans as

A) cautious that the South will experience a new era of discord.

B) similar to black Americans in their desires for the future of the South.

C) confident that traditional prejudices can be eliminated by new laws.

D) uncomfortable with political measures that would involve new sacrifices.

13

Which choice provides the best evidence for the answer to the previous question?

A) Lines 17-19 ("This . . . both")

B) Lines 19-21 ("Let . . . done")

C) Lines 22-27 ("Men . . . troubles")

D) Lines 36-39 ("If with . . . negro")

CONTINUE

Part 5

14

The main purpose of Passage 2 is to

A) note the deficiencies of a broad endeavor.

B) justify the premises of an unpopular position.

C) question the virtues of a group of leaders.

D) propose a series of practical improvements.

15

As used in line 58, "envied" most nearly means

A) undermined.

B) exceeded.

C) admired.

D) disdained.

16

As used in line 79, "artificial" most nearly means

A) maliciously imitated.

B) outlandishly expressive.

C) unnaturally imposed.

D) carefully fabricated.

17

Which statement best describes the relationship between the two passages?

A) Passage 1 casts doubt on the wisdom of authority figures; Passage 2 praises those same figures.

B) Passage 1 lists a variety of objectives; Passage 2 establishes a more narrow focus on education.

C) Passage 1 states that reform is urgently needed; Passage 2 argues that reform should be avoided.

D) Passage 1 urges a spirit of harmony; Passage 2 suggests that such cooperation is impossible.

18

One central difference between how Douglass (Passage 1) and Washington (Passage 2) present their ideas is that

A) Douglass outlines the origins of slavery in the South while Washington emphasizes the need to move past historical barriers.

B) Douglass speaks on behalf of large groups while Washington draws on personal experience.

C) Douglass cites specific opponents while Washington seeks to foster a spirit of unity.

D) Douglass welcomes the possibility of further upheaval while Washington endorses moderation.

19

Washington would respond to Douglass's ideas about the "plain, common-sense way" (line 12) by

A) expressing the sentiment that racial prejudice rendered Douglass's plan impossible.

B) warning that Douglass's vision of political progress would find few supporters in the South.

C) sympathizing with Douglass's apparent belief that promoting political participation would naturally create an educated populace.

D) agreeing that regulating elective franchise in a way that did not put either black or white citizens at a disadvantage was a worthy goal.

20

Which choice provides the best evidence for the answer to the previous question?

A) Lines 44-46 ("The ambition . . . encouraging")

B) Lines 51-54 ("There . . . supernatural")

C) Lines 64-71 ("I cannot . . . races")

D) Lines 72-76 ("Though . . . long")

CONTINUE

Questions 21-30 are based on the following passages.

Passage 1 is adapted from Jyoti Madhusoodanan, "Could sleepless nights of terror be good for you?" (2012), published* on the PLOS One community blog EveryOne. Passage 2 is adapted from a news release* from the National Institute on Aging, "Does poor sleep raise risk for Alzheimer's disease?" (2016).

Passage 1

Lying awake and listening for demonic footsteps after *Paranormal Activity 4* may turn out to be more helpful to your mental health than
Line trying to fall asleep. A study published earlier this
5 month in PLOS ONE shows that losing sleep can prevent frightening memories from taking hold in the brain, at least in rats.

A good night's sleep has many advantages, including improving our ability to recollect facts
10 or learned motor skills. Losing sleep impairs these kinds of memory, but the impact of sleep deprivation on other kinds of memory, such as that of traumatic events, is still poorly understood.

In this study, the authors Tankesh Kumar and
15 Sushil Jha found that when rats were trained to develop a conditioned fear response to a sound they heard, this response was twice as strong in rats that slept for six hours after the training than in those that stayed awake for this period of time.
20 According to the authors, this result suggests that the rats that stayed awake hadn't learned to be afraid of the sound as well as the better-rested animals had.

Despite the ill effects of sleep deprivation
25 and associated poor memory under other circumstances, the authors suggest that losing sleep after a traumatic event can actually help prevent fearful memories from taking hold in the brain, potentially providing long-term benefits like
30 reducing the risk of post-traumatic stress disorder (PTSD) or anxiety disorders.

Related PLOS ONE research published last year studied the effects of a similar, odor-induced fear conditioning exercise in rats, and observed
35 changes in brain activity during sleep following the exercise. The researchers also found that these changes correlated with the strength of the fear response observed in rats the next day.

Passage 2

Disturbed sleep—whether due to illness, pain,
40 anxiety, depression, or a sleep disorder—can lead to trouble concentrating, remembering, and learning. A return to normal sleep patterns usually eases these problems. But in older people, disturbed sleep may have more dire and long-
45 lasting consequences.

Scientists long believed that the initial buildup of the beta-amyloid protein in the brain, an early biological sign of Alzheimer's, causes disturbed sleep, Dr. Mackiewicz said. Recently, though,
50 evidence suggests the opposite may also occur— disturbed sleep in cognitively normal older adults contributes to the risk of cognitive decline and Alzheimer's disease.

For example, in a study of older men free of
55 dementia, poor sleep, including greater nighttime wakefulness, was associated with cognitive decline over a period of more than 3 years (Blackwell et al., 2014). Sleep was assessed through participants' reports and a device worn on
60 the wrist that tracks movements during sleep.

Sleep disorders such as sleep apnea may pose an even greater risk of cognitive impairment. In a 5-year study of older women, those with sleep-disordered breathing (SDB)—repeated
65 arousals from sleep due to breathing disruptions, as happens in sleep apnea—had a nearly twofold increase in risk for mild cognitive impairment (a precursor to Alzheimer's in some people) or dementia (Yaffe et al., 2011).
70 In addition, certain types of poor sleep seem to be associated with risk of cognitive impairment, according to Kristine Yaffe, M.D., of the University of California, San Francisco. These include hypoxia (low oxygen levels that can be
75 caused by sleep disorders) and difficulty in falling or staying asleep.

Evidence of a link between sleep and risk of

---

*See Page 263 for the citations for these texts.

CONTINUE →

Alzheimer's has led to investigations to explain the brain activity that underlies this connection
80 in humans. Some recent studies suggest that poor sleep contributes to abnormal levels of beta-amyloid protein in the brain, which in turn leads to the amyloid plaques found in the Alzheimer's brain. These plaques might then affect sleep-
85 related brain regions, further disrupting sleep.

Studies in laboratory animals show a direct link between sleep and Alzheimer's disease. One study of mice, led by researchers at Washington University, St. Louis, showed that beta-amyloid
90 levels naturally rose during wakefulness and fell during sleep (Kang et al., 2009). Mice deprived of sleep for 21 days showed significantly greater beta-amyloid plaques than those that slept normally. Increasing sleep had the opposite
95 effect—it reduced the amyloid load.

21

Which piece of information would add certitude to the possibility raised by the author in lines 1-4 ("Lying awake . . . asleep")?

A) The effects of sleeplessness have often been depicted inaccurately in popular culture.

B) Kumar and Jha considered multiple age groups for the rats in their study.

C) Sleeplessness is now being promoted in the media as a factor that improves critical thinking.

D) The results of the study by Kumar and Jha are applicable to both rats and humans.

22

As used in line 24, "ill" most nearly means

A) weak.

B) harmful.

C) deadly.

D) repulsive.

23

Which piece of information, if true, would make the findings in the final two paragraphs (lines 24-38) of Passage 1 problematic?

A) Rats rely more on sound and and sight to navigate their surroundings than they do on smell.

B) Responses that indicate excitement among rats are indistinguishable from responses that indicate fear.

C) Rats have relatively weak long-term memory capacity under normal circumstances.

D) Odors that stimulate fear in rats are typically linked to substances that rats do not encounter in nature.

24

Which choice best indicates that the authors of Passage 2 see dementia as only one form of cognitive decline?

A) Lines 46-49 ("Scientists . . . said")

B) Lines 54-58 ("For example . . . 2014")

C) Lines 70-73 ("In addition . . . San Francisco")

D) Lines 87-91 ("One study . . . 2009")

25

As used in line 61, "pose" most nearly means

A) present.

B) simulate.

C) express.

D) position.

162

CONTINUE

26

The authors of Passage 2 characterize the "studies" mentioned in line 80 as

A) applicable to both humans and small animals.

B) authoritative yet currently under-appreciated.

C) contradicted by other experiments that focus on beta-amyloid proteins.

D) consequential but not completely verified.

27

On the basis of the information present in the passages, the author of Passage 1 would react to the first paragraph of Passage 2 with

A) profound surprise, since the assumed connection between sleeplessness in humans and memory loss had apparently been disproven.

B) open objection, since sleeplessness is in rare cases instrumental in preserving memories.

C) thorough skepticism, since there is not a useful consensus definition of a normal sleep pattern.

D) general concurrence, since a positive correlation between sound sleep and memory has been demonstrated.

28

Which choice provides the best evidence for the answer to the previous question?

A) Lines 1-4 ("Lying . . . asleep")

B) Lines 4-7 ("A study . . . rats")

C) Lines 8-10 ("A good . . . skills")

D) Lines 11-13 ("but the . . . understood")

29

Which choice best describes the relationship between the two passages?

A) Passage 1 traces a desirable connection between sleep deprivation and memory loss, while Passage 2 links sleep loss and impaired cognition.

B) Passage 1 indicates that sleep deprivation can increase the intensity of certain memories, while Passage 2 contradicts this same idea.

C) Passage 1 considers how studies of humans and animals relate to one another, while Passage 2 questions whether such studies are interchangeable.

D) Passage 1 outlines a scientific solution to a common problem, while Passage 2 debunks the idea that sleep research has such immediate practical applications.

30

One key similarity between how the two passages present recent research is that

A) both passages define technical terms that have become central to the study of neuroscience for animals and humans alike.

B) both passages consider multiple avenues of research that imply the virtues of an interdisciplinary approach.

C) both passages credit the work of specific scientists but do not offer exact quotes from research reports.

D) both passages suggest connections between the presence of particular stimuli and fundamental changes in brain structure.

CONTINUE

Part 5

Questions 31-40 are based on the following passages.

Passage 1 is adapted from *"The Girl of the Period" and Other Social Essays* (1883) by E. Lynn Linton. Passage 2 is adapted from *A Domestic Problem: Work and Culture in the Household* (1895) by A.M. Diaz.

Passage 1

To most men, indeed, the feminine strong-mindedness that can discuss immoral problems without blushing is a quality as unwomanly
Line as a well-developed biceps or a "shoulder-of-
5 mutton" fist. It is sympathy, not antagonism—it is companionship, not rivalry, still less supremacy, that they like in women; and some women with brains as well as learning—for the two are not the same thing—understand this, and keep their blue
10 stockings well covered by their petticoats. Others, enthusiasts for freedom of thought and intellectual rights, show theirs defiantly; and meet with their reward. Men shrink from them. Even clever men, able to meet them on their own ground, do not
15 feel drawn to them; while all but high-class minds are humiliated by their learning and dwarfed by their moral courage. And no man likes to feel humiliated or dwarfed in the presence of a woman, and because of her superiority.

20 But the brains most useful to women, and most befitting their work in life, are those which show themselves in common-sense, in good judgment, and that kind of patient courage which enables them to bear small crosses and great trials alike
25 with dignity and good temper. Mere intellectual culture, however valuable it may be in itself, does not equal the worth of this kind of moral power; for as the true domain of woman is the home, and her way of ordering her domestic life the best test
30 of her faculties, mere intellectual culture does not help in this; and, in fact, is often a hindrance rather than a help. What good is there in one's wife being an accomplished mathematician, a sound scholar, a first-rate musician, a deeply-read
35 theologian, if she cannot keep the accounts square, knows nothing of the management of children, lets herself be cheated by the servants and the tradespeople, has not her eyes opened to dirt and disorder, and gives way to a fretful temper on the
40 smallest provocation?

Passage 2

When a loving couple marry, they unite their interests, and it is in this union of interests that they find happiness. We often hear from a wife or a husband remarks like these: "I only half enjoyed
45 it, because he (or she) wasn't there;" "It will be no pleasure to me unless he (or she) is there too;" "The company was charming, but still I felt lonesome there without him (or her)." The phrase "half enjoy" gives the idea; for a sympathetic
50 couple are to such a degree one that a pleasure which comes to either singly can only be half enjoyed, and even this half-joy is lessened by the consciousness of what the other is losing.

If it be said that learned women are prone to
55 think lightly of home comforts and home duties, to despise physical labor, to look down on the ignorant, let us hasten to reply that learning is not culture, and that we want not learned mothers, but enlightened mothers, wisely educated mothers.
60 And let us steadfastly and perseveringly assert that enlightenment and a wise education are essential to the accomplishment of the mother's mission. When the housefather feels the truth of this, then shall we see him bringing home every publication
65 he can lay his hands on which treats intelligently of mental, moral, or physical training. Then shall we hear him saying to the house-mother, "Cease, I pray you, this ever-lasting toil. Read, study, rest. With your solemn responsibilities, it is madness
70 thus to spend yourself, thus to waste yourself." In his home shall the true essentials assume that position which is theirs by right, and certain occupations connected with that clamorous square inch of surface in the upper part of the mouth shall
75 receive only their due share of attention. For in one way or another, either by lessening the work or by hiring workers, the mother shall have her leisure.

CONTINUE

31

In Passage 1, Linton recommends which of the following as a suitable lifestyle for women?

A) Pursuit of skills and attainments that promote a spirit of practicality

B) Participation in political institutions in a thoughtful and unobtrusive manner

C) Abandonment of any education that does not relate to household duties

D) Cultivation of virtues that are completely different from those valued by men

32

Which choice provides the best evidence for the answer to the previous question?

A) Lines 10-13 ("Others . . . reward")

B) Lines 13-15 ("Even . . . them")

C) Lines 20-22 ("But . . . common-sense")

D) Line 28 ("the true . . . home")

33

As used in lines 16 and 18, "humiliated" most nearly means

A) rejected.

B) criticized.

C) demoted.

D) overshadowed.

34

Diaz in Passage 2 presents various quotations in lines 44-48 for the purpose of

A) signaling that a seemingly exaggerated situation is in fact realistic.

B) recounting scenes that occurred in the author's own household.

C) explaining a deficiency that men must address independently.

D) illustrating situations that are assumed to be familiar to the passage's readers.

35

Which choice most clearly indicates that Diaz in Passage 2 sees physical labor as unimportant relative to women's intellectual duties?

A) Lines 54-58 ("If . . . culture")

B) Lines 60-62 ("And . . . mission")

C) Lines 63-66 ("When . . . training")

D) Lines 71-75 ("In his . . . attention")

36

As used in line 63, "feels" most nearly means

A) is overwhelmed by.

B) learns to enjoy.

C) becomes aware of.

D) casually absorbs.

Part 5

37

One central point of disagreement between the two passages involves the issue of whether

A) women should pursue new legal rights and new forms of political leadership.

B) intellectual attainments that rival those of men can assist women in maintaining harmonious households.

C) traditional marriage arrangements make women financially and emotionally dependent on their husbands.

D) popular forms of culture and self-expression are sufficiently respected by educated men.

38

Each passage serves the purpose of

A) insisting that the struggle for gender equality has been accompanied by new challenges.

B) demonstrating that women have learned how to apply abstract ideas to everyday duties.

C) recommending activities and ways of thinking that the author considers appropriate for women.

D) convincing men that adhering to outdated ideas about women is detrimental to both genders.

39

Diaz in Passage 2 would respond to the ideas about "Men" (line 13) present in Passage 1 by arguing that

A) men have come to judge women based on personal merit rather than on appearance.

B) men can be pleased and invigorated by the company of properly educated women.

C) men who underestimate women's intellectual gifts still hold women's moral virtues in high regard.

D) men feel more threatened by intelligent members of their own gender than by intelligent women.

40

The two passages are similar in that both authors

A) fault men for limiting the educational opportunities available to women.

B) investigate how intelligent men normally react to strong-minded women.

C) encourage women to seek compromises that will ultimately promote better education.

D) imply that educated women have a tendency to avoid confrontation.

STOP
After you have finished the questions, consult the relevant answers on Page 168.
Do not turn to any other section.

Answer Key on the Next Page

Answer Key
Paired Passages

Reading 1		Reading 2		Reading 3		Reading 4	
1.	D	11.	C	21.	D	31.	A
2.	D	12.	B	22.	B	32.	C
3.	C	13.	A	23.	B	33.	D
4.	A	14.	A	24.	B	34.	D
5.	B	15.	C	25.	A	35.	D
6.	A	16.	C	26.	D	36.	C
7.	B	17.	B	27.	D	37.	B
8.	B	18.	B	28.	C	38.	C
9.	B	19.	D	29.	A	39.	B
10.	D	20.	C	30.	C	40.	B

For detailed answer explanations for this practice section please visit **prepvantagetutoring.com/reading**.

Part 6

Visual Evidence
Strategy and Practice

Strategy 6
Working with Visuals

Question Fundamentals

On each SAT Reading section, you will need to address TWO passages—the Social Studies reading and one of the Science readings—that are accompanied by visual evidence. The relevant questions will typically be the last few in a given passage's question set. For this reason, you will normally not need to work with the visuals until you have addressed all of the other question types.

Visuals can take a variety of forms: pie charts, bar charts, line graphs, maps, and tables among them. Regardless of form, each visual should be addressed using the same tactics, since SAT Reading visuals are surprisingly easy to misread. Fortunately, there is an efficient two-step process for comprehending the visuals—a process, moreover, that will often give you the information that you need to address standard question types.

Comprehending the Visuals

Step 1: Determine the Units

Effective work with the visuals requires a strong sense of WHAT quantities are being measured and of HOW exactly they are being measured. You need to make sure that you can evaluate these issues precisely; even though such work may seem basic, it is necessary. After all, SAT questions will often contain false answers that exploit elementary misreadings or faulty assumptions about what exactly a visual is measuring. Some of the traps to watch for are the following.

- Mistaking a raw number for a percentage, OR a percentage for a raw number

- Confusing two shaded regions in a graph   - Misreading a key that defines a numerical scale

Rather than constantly wondering if you are falling into one of these traps, prevent these problems in advance by simply defining the key properties of any visual that you are given. Here are a few to look for.

- Units measured on the x-axis
- Units measured on the y-axis

- What different shaded regions represent
- What boundary lines within a graph represent

- Whether any notes or keys determine how the graph should be read

Now, with these items in mind, consider how to analyze the main components of a graph that is already familiar from the Social Studies passage in the Diagnostic Test.

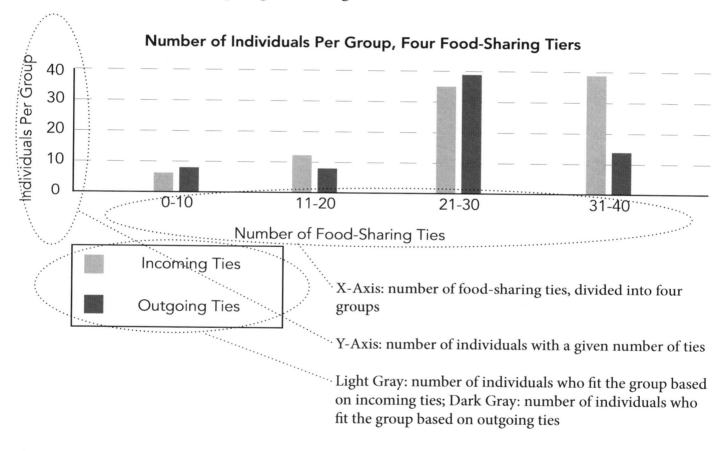

X-Axis: number of food-sharing ties, divided into four groups

Y-Axis: number of individuals with a given number of ties

Light Gray: number of individuals who fit the group based on incoming ties; Dark Gray: number of individuals who fit the group based on outgoing ties

The chart, as this analysis shows, measures how many individuals fit into any one of four different categories. It does NOT, to raise one possible trap, measure the percentage of individuals in the community that falls into each category. Note that there are other traps that may emerge from reading too quickly, such as wrongly assuming that 0-10 individuals have 8 outgoing ties—a misreading that FLIPS the real reading, the idea that 8 individuals have 0-10 outgoing ties.

To make sure that you have properly read the graph visual, you might even test out a few measurements or quantities for accuracy. Look, for instance, at the 11-20 number and the light bar. Here, the light bar indicates incoming ties and rises to almost 13. The graph at this point indicates that 13 individuals have 11-20 incoming ties and aligns with the earlier reading, the idea that 8 individuals have 0-10 outgoing ties as indicated by the dark gray bar.

Part 6: Working with Visuals

After achieving this level of accuracy, you can move on to consider any larger trends that are present in the graph.

Step 2: Determine Overall Relationships

To discern a visual's overall data relationships, you will need to synthesize information in a manner that does not bring in any interpretation or extrapolation. The visual itself is all that matters. Here, return to the graph of food sharing ties from the Diagnostic Test and think about how the different quantities operate.

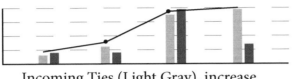

Incoming Ties (Light Gray), increase
with more individuals for more ties

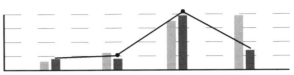

Outgoing Ties (Dark Gray), 21-30
easily the largest group, others similar
in size

Noticing trends such as these will improve comprehension, but you must also be careful to make sure that the analysis of the graph does NOT extend beyond working with evidence. For instance, the graph does not consider information about individuals with 41-50 incoming or outgoing ties. You should NEVER EXTRAPOLATE in this manner (unless a question prompt explicitly indicates that a trend will continue beyond the given data) and should avoid thinking about any quantities beyond those present in the visual (unless, again, a question prompt explicitly introduces a new and valid relationship).

Of course, there may be some cases in which trends are difficult to spot: tables that provide various pieces of information about groups, planets, substances, or other individual items may present this possibility. If you are indeed in the presence of such a collection of facts, don't panic. Simply make sure that you have read the units for the individual items properly, try to retain some information, and move on to address the questions.

Approaching the Questions

Type 1: Visuals on Their Own

Each group of questions devoted to visuals will in many cases begin with a question or two devoted to the visuals alone. Questions that ask about the visuals in the context of the passage normally follow these, and you should use the visuals-only questions to make sure that your comprehension of units and relationships is sound. In this respect, re-visit a question from the Diagnostic Test, and keep the trends in mind.

19

According to the chart, which of the following groups would represent the largest number of individuals?

A) 0-20 Incoming Ties

B) 0-20 Outgoing Ties

C) 21-30 Incoming Ties

D) 21-30 Outgoing Ties

Remember: more individuals are in the groups that have more incoming ties and in the group that has 21-30 outgoing ties

It may not be possible to predict an answer entirely, but you CAN use an efficient three-part process to work with the question.

1. Remember Overall Relationships   2. Check Answers Against Graph   3. Process of Elimination

In this case, the overall relationship indicated in Step 1 (largest numbers of individuals) should put you on the right track, but should NOT replace the second step. Check the answers as required by Step 2: A and B both combine groups, but represent fewer than 20 individuals each. C and D both represent quantities over 30, so eliminate A and B as required by Step 3. However, D (dark bar, outgoing ties) indicates more individuals than C does, so eliminate C and choose D.

Now, consider how this sort of attention to detail can help you to work with questions that call upon you to consider a passage alongside a visual.

Type 2: Visuals with the Passage

Before reaching the final few Visuals questions, you might want to formulate a general yet evidence-based idea of how the passage and the accompanying visuals relate to one another. Here are the core relationships.

- Visuals support the passage - Visuals contradict the passage - Visuals add new information on the topic

A visual that occurs with a Paired Passage set may relate to each passage in the set in a different manner, so be sensitive to this fact. Keep in mind, also, that a long reading comprehension passage will naturally address more evidence than a visual does and that you should NOT relate passage-specific evidence to a visual unless prompted to do so by the question. In fact, beyond determining a core passage-to-visual relationship, you should be careful to distinguish between the information considered in the passage and in the visual—a task that is central to the following Diagnostic Test question.

20

One of the factors that is explicitly addressed in Ready's study as described the passage but NOT in the accompanying graph is

A) a given household's incoming ties.

B) a given household's outgoing ties.

C) the role of gender in food-sharing networks.

D) the role of local political influence in food sharing networks.

Objective: find a difference between the passage and the graph

Remember: the graph considers the number of food-sharing ties (incoming and outgoing) within a community

For questions such as these, work with three-step process described above, AND bring in work with the Major Issue and Passage Details strategies as needed. Step 1 of the Visuals strategy should lead you to conclude that A and B are both wrong, since both incoming and outgoing ties are central to the graph. You are left with C and D; neither "gender" nor "political influence" is described in the graph, so figure out which one IS described in the passage. C is the correct answer, since line 55 of the passage (page 11) mentions the role of "single women" in food-sharing. The passage does indicate that some households are relatively large and wealthy, but (again, using Passage Details tactics) NEVER explicitly mentions political factors.

Part 6

Questions 1-4 are based on the following Social Studies passage and supplementary material.

This passage is adapted from "Game Corrects Children's Misreading of Emotional Faces to Tame Irritability," a 2016 Science Update article posted* by the National Institute of Mental Health.

A computer game that changes a tendency to misread ambiguous faces as angry is showing promise as a potential treatment for irritability in
Line children. The game shifts a child's judgment for
5 perceiving ambiguous faces from angry to happy. In a small pilot study, irritable children who played it experienced less irritability, accompanied by changes in activation of mood-related brain circuitry. Researchers are now following up with a
10 larger study to confirm its effectiveness.

Melissa Brotman, Ph.D., Ellen Leibenluft, M.D., Joel Stoddard, M.D., of the NIMH Emotion and Development Branch, and colleagues, reported on findings of their pilot study of
15 "interpretation bias training" for child irritability online on January 8, 2016 in the *Journal of Child and Adolescent Psychopharmacology*.

About 3 percent of youth experience chronic severe irritability. They are prone to temper
20 outbursts and are often in a grumpy mood. Parents complain of having to "walk on eggshells" to avoid unleashing verbal—and sometimes physical—outbursts. These behaviors can lead to problems with friends, with family, and at school.
25 While irritability is common in disorders such as attention deficit hyperactivity disorder (ADHD) and oppositional defiant disorder, it is a core feature of disruptive mood dysregulation disorder (DMDD), which is associated with risk
30 for developing mood and anxiety disorders—and socioeconomic underachievement later in life.

While research suggests that parent training, psychotherapy, and some medications may be helpful for severe irritability, there are no
35 established treatments for DMDD. Evidence suggests that irritable youth with DMDD tend to

misperceive emotional expressions. Compared to healthy controls, children with DMDD were more prone to rate ambiguous faces as angry. So
40 Leibenluft's team set out to test interpretation bias training (IBT), a computer game designed to diminish irritable children's tendency to view ambiguous faces as angry.

Participants rated a continuum of 15
45 ambiguous faces appearing on a computer monitor as either happy or angry. After computer training, the children shifted their ratings toward seeing some of these ambiguous faces as "happy." This effect was maintained for at least 2 weeks and was
50 associated with decreased irritability, as rated by parents and by clinicians who interviewed both parents and children.

Some of these DMDD participants also performed a face-viewing task while their brain
55 activity was being measured by functional magnetic resonance imaging (fMRI). They showed activity changes in emotional learning areas suggesting that the computer-based training may alter neural responses to emotional faces.
60 Encouraged by these findings, the researchers have launched a larger, more controlled study to learn whether IBT might be effective as a treatment. They are also testing cognitive behavioral therapy (CBT), a talk therapy that aims
65 to change behaviors in response to frustrating events. These are among the first non-drug interventions that seek to help those with DMDD.

Families with affected children can choose to receive CBT alone, IBT alone, or IBT followed
70 by CBT. Those who elect IBT will perform most computer training sessions at home, over the course of a training program which can last from 3 to 13 weeks. Participants who are interested in brain scanning will also undergo before-and-
75 after fMRI scans while they are looking at the same ambiguous faces presented in the training sessions. The researchers hope these scans will show changes in brain activity that relate to symptom improvement following treatment.
80 "The training may be calming irritability by altering circuit activity underlying interpretive biases and—hopefully—reducing anger-based reactions like outbursts," said Leibenluft.

---

*See Page 262 for the citation for this text.

174

CONTINUE

Results for 22 young people (starting on June 15, 2016) with ADHD who were subjected to an IBT recognition process for ambiguous faces

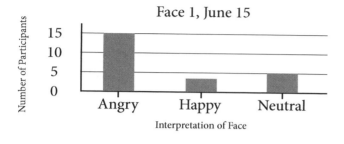

Face 1, June 15

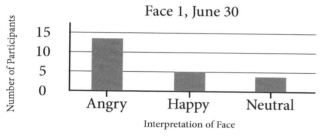

Face 1, June 30

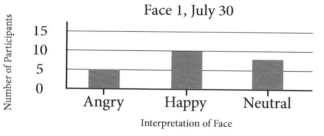

Face 1, July 30

1

As shown in the graphs, which of the following interpretation-based groups represents the largest number of participants?

A) "Neutral," June 15

B) "Happy," June 30

C) "Angry," July 30

D) "Neutral," July 30

2

The graphs could be understood as representing an unsuccessful IBT administration if "success" is defined as

A) an increased number of participants identifying the faces as happy within fifteen days.

B) a decreased number of participants identifying the faces as neutral within fifteen days.

C) a majority of participants identifying the faces as happy within fifteen days.

D) a majority of the participants identifying the faces as happy or neutral within forty-five days

3

One factor explicitly considered in the graphs but NOT in the passage is

A) a facial identification pattern for children on ADHD medication.

B) a "neutral" classification for ambiguous faces.

C) the IBT success rate after roughly two weeks.

D) IBT administration that lasts beyond four weeks.

4

Do the data present in the graphs support or contradict the ideas present in the passage?

A) Support, because effective IBT results for children with ADHD are relevant to the treatment of DMDD.

B) Support, because the graphs correlate fewer "angry" identifications with decreased irritability.

C) Contradict, because the face considered in the graphs is not one of the 15 ambiguous faces mentioned in the passage.

D) Contradict, because the graphs omit any consideration of fMRI data.

CONTINUE

Part 6

Questions 5-8 are based on the following Science passage and supplementary material.

This passage is adapted from "NIH researchers discover highly infectious vehicle for transmission of viruses among humans," a 2018 news release* from the National Institutes of Health.

Researchers have found that a group of viruses that cause severe stomach illness—including the one famous for widespread outbreaks
Line
5   on cruise ships—get transmitted to humans through membrane-cloaked "virus clusters" that exacerbate the spread and severity of disease. Previously, it was believed that these viruses only spread through individual virus particles. The discovery of these clusters, the scientists
10   say, marks a turning point in the understanding of how these viruses spread and why they are so infectious. This preliminary work could lead to the development of more effective antiviral agents than existing treatments that mainly target
15   individual particles.

The researchers studied norovirus and rotavirus—hard-to-treat viruses that are the most common causes of stomach illness, or gastroenteritis, and that afflict millions of
20   people each year. The viruses cause symptoms ranging from diarrhea to abdominal pain and can sometimes result in death, particularly among young children and the elderly. Their highly contagious nature has led to serious outbreaks in
25   crowded spaces throughout many communities, most notably in cruise ships, daycare centers, classrooms, and nursing homes. Fortunately, vaccines against rotavirus are now available and are routinely given to babies in the United States.

30   "This is a really exciting finding in the field of virology because it reveals a mode of virus spread that has not been observed among humans and animals," said study leader Nihal Altan-Bonnet, Ph.D., senior investigator and head of
35   the Laboratory of Host-Pathogen Dynamics at the National Heart, Lung, and Blood Institute

(NHLBI). "We hope that it will provide new clues to fighting a wide range of diseases involving many types of viruses, including those that cause
40   gastrointestinal illnesses, heart inflammation, certain respiratory illnesses, and even the common cold."

The study was supported in part by the Intramural Research programs of the NHLBI and
45   the National Institute of Allergy and Infectious Diseases (NIAID), both part of the National Institutes of Health. It is featured as the cover story of *Cell Host & Microbe* and appears online on August 8.

50   Until a few years ago, most scientists believed that viruses, particularly those responsible for stomach illnesses, could only behave as independent infectious agents. However, in 2015 Altan-Bonnet and her colleagues showed that
55   polioviruses could transmit themselves in packets, or membrane-bound vesicles containing multiple virus particles. The scientists compared this new model of viral transmission to a Trojan horse: a group of membrane-bound viruses arrives at a
60   host cell and deposits viruses in the cell while dodging detection by the immune system. The scientists did not know whether this system applied to animals and humans, or how effective these packets were in infecting host cells.

65   To find out, they focused on rotaviruses and noroviruses, which mainly get spread through accidental ingestion of tiny particles of an infected person's stool—through, for example, contaminated food or liquids. The
70   researchers obtained fecal samples of humans and animals (pigs and mice) and found that the viruses are shed in the stool as virus clusters inside membrane-bound packets. In addition, they found that these virus-containing vesicles
75   were significantly more infectious than the free, unbound viruses within the samples.

The researchers determined that the high level of infectiousness was likely due to the vesicles delivering many viruses at once to the target
80   tissues; protecting their viral cargo from being destroyed by prolonged exposure to enzymes; and possibly by making their viral cargo invisible to

---

*See Page 262 for the citation for this text.

CONTINUE

the antibodies that are in the stool or gut of the host. More studies are needed, but the extreme
85 potency of the virus packets, they said, has a clear consequence: it not only enhances the virus' ability to spread more aggressively; it also increases the severity of the disease it causes. Handwashing with soap and water helps prevent
90 the spread of viruses.

"Our findings indicate that vesicle-cloaked viruses are highly virulent units of fecal-oral transmission, and highlight a need for antivirals targeting vesicles and virus clustering," Altan-
95 Bonnet noted.

5

If the mortality rates present in the table are completely accurate, which of the following groups would suffer the largest number of casualties?

A) 100 infants infected with Rotavirus E

B) 1000 infants infected with Respiratory Adenovirus

C) 100 senior citizens infected with Standard Norovirus

D) 100 senior citizens infected with Standard Parainfluenza virus

Virus Type	Contexts for Occurrence	Mortality Rate (ages 0-5)	Mortality Rate (ages 65-85)	Ease of Transmission (0-10 scale)	Resistance to Vaccines (0-10 scale)
Rotavirus A	oral transmission through ingestion of infected matter	1%	3%	4	7
Rotavirus D	oral transmission through ingestion of infected matter	1%	2%	4	8
Rotavirus E	oral transmission through ingestion of infected matter	2%	2%	5	8
Standard Norovirus/ Norwalk Virus	oral transmission through ingestion of infected matter	1%	3%	4	4
Respiratory Cyncytial Virus	ingestion of infected matter, airborne infection	0.1%	0.4%	9	3
Standard Parainfluenza Virus	ingestion of infected matter, airborne infection	0.2%	0.5%	10	2
Respiratory Adenovirus	ingestion of infected matter, airborne infection	0.1%	0.5%	9	2

Note: in each 1-10 scale, 10 indicates the highest potency

CONTINUE

6

The table indicates that Standard Norovirus does NOT resemble any of the three strains of Rotavirus in terms of

A) mortality rate, ages 0-5.

B) mortality rate, ages 65-85.

C) ease of transmission.

D) resistance to vaccines.

7

The data present in the table build upon the ideas and information present in the passage by providing

A) proof that new information about virus clusters marks "a turning point" (line 10).

B) indications that norovirus and rotavirus afflict "millions of people each year" (lines 19-20).

C) statistical evidence for how often norovirus and rotavirus strains "can sometimes result in death" (lines 21-22).

D) hints about how to combat viruses that are responsible for "certain respiratory illnesses" (line 41).

8

The final three viruses represented in the table do not travel in clusters. In relation to the passage, this new information and the data in the table indicate that

A) clustered viruses typically survive for longer than non-clustered viruses.

B) virus clustering is not the only arrangement that facilitates transmission.

C) non-clustered viruses are a greater threat to senior citizens than are clustered viruses.

D) a non-clustered form can increase the vaccine resistance of a virus that is normally clustered.

Questions 9-12 are based on the following Social Studies passage and supplementary material.

This passage is adapted from Samantha Wallace, "Linking Isolated Languages: Linguistic Relationships of the Carabayo." Originally published* on EveryONE, the blog of the research site Plos One.

In 2010, English clocked in at over 360 million native speakers, and it is the third-most-commonly used native language, right behind Mandarin
Line Chinese and Spanish. While these languages
5   spread, however, other indigenous languages decline at an accelerated pace. A fraction of these enigmatic languages belong to uncontacted indigenous groups of the Amazonian rainforest, groups of people in South America who have
10 little to no interaction with societies beyond their own. Many of these groups choose to remain uncontacted by the rest of the world. Because of their isolation, not much is known about these languages beyond their existence.
15   The researchers of a recent PLOS ONE paper investigated one such language, that of the Carabayo people who live in the Colombian Amazon rainforest. Working with the relatively scarce historical data that exists for the Carabayo
20 language—only 50 words have been recorded over time—the authors identified similarities between Carabayo and Yurí and Tikuna, two known languages of South America that constitute the current language family Ticuna-Yurí. Based
25 on the correspondences, the authors posit a possible genealogical connection between these languages.
        Few resources were available to the authors in this endeavor. They analyzed historical wordlists
30 collected during the last encounter with the Carabayo people in 1969—the only linguistic data available from this group—against wordlists for the Yurí language. In addition, they sought the expertise of a native speaker of Tikuna, a linguist

*See Page 262 for the citation for this text.

CONTINUE

trained in Tikuna's many dialects. Using these
resources, the authors broke down the Carabayo
words into their foundational forms, starting with
consonants and vowels. They then compared
them to similarly deconstructed words in Yurí and
40 Tikuna.

The examination involved the evaluation of
similarities in the basic building blocks of these
words: the number of times a specific sound (or
phoneme) appeared; the composition and patterns
45 of the smallest grammatical units of a word (a
morpheme); and the meanings attached to these
words. When patterns appeared between Carabayo
and either Yurí or Tikuna, the authors considered
whether or not the languages' similarities
50 constituted stronger correspondences. They also
paid attention to the ways in which these words
would have been used by the Carabayo when the
lists were originally made many years ago.

The Yurí language was first recorded in the
55 19th century, but it is thought to have become
extinct since then. From these lists, five words
stood out: in Carabayo, ao 'father', hono 'boy',
hako 'well!', and a complex form containing
both the Yurí word from warm, noré, and the Yurí
60 word, tʃau, which corresponds in English to 'I'
or 'my'. Given the evidence, the authors contend
that the strongest link between Carabayo and Yurí
is found in the correspondence of tʃau. The study
of other languages has indicated that first-person
65 pronouns are particularly resistant to "borrowing,"
or the absorption of one language's vocabulary
into another. Therefore, the authors surmise
it is unlikely in this instance that either of the
languages absorbed tʃau from the other, but that
70 they share a genealogical link.

Similarly, the comparison of Carabayo
words to words of the living language of Tikuna
provided a high number of matches, including in
Carabayo gudda 'wait' and gu 'yes'. The matches
75 especially exhibit sound correspondences of
Carabayo g (or k) and the loss of the letter n in
certain circumstances.

Although it is possible that the Carabayo
language represents a language that had not yet
80 been documented until the time of 1969, the

results of the researchers' evaluation have led
them to conclude that Carabayo more likely
belongs to the language family of Ticuna-Yurí.

The relationship of Carabayo to Yurí and
85 Tikuna changes the structure of the Ticuna-Yurí
family by placing Carabayo on the map as a
member of that family. The Tikuna language, once
considered to be the sole surviving member of
the Ticuna-Yurí family, might now have a sibling,
90 and the identity of a barely known language has
become that much more defined.

9

Which of the following statements about words
shared by Amazonian languages can be inferred from
Figure 1?

A) Languages that use similar words to describe men
may use dissimilar words to describe women.

B) Several words that describe men are identical in
Tikuna, Yurí, and Carabayo.

C) The similarities between Tikuna and Carabayo
are most evident in words of one or two syllables.

D) Carabayo and Yurí share several pronouns but
only a few expressions of affirmation.

Figure 1: Similar Words for Three Languages

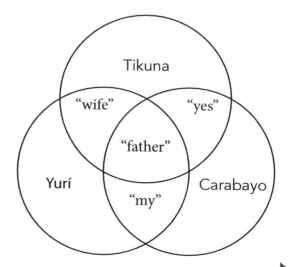

CONTINUE

Figure 2: Number of Native Speakers for Three Languages

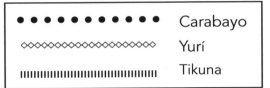

10

According to Figure 2, since 1970 the number of native speakers of Tikuna has

A) decreased as a result of the growing popularity of Yurí.

B) been consistently greater than the number of native speakers of Yurí.

C) never been greater than the number of native speakers of Carabayo.

D) exceeded the number of speakers of Carabayo by a constant margin.

11

Both the passage and Figure 1 support the idea that

A) Carabayo and Yurí have similar words for "son."

B) Carabayo and Yurí have similar words for "my."

C) Carabayo and Tikuna have similar words for "father."

D) Carabayo and Tikuna have large numbers of similar pronouns.

12

A student notices that Figure 2 does not present information from before 1970 in its data on the Carabayo language. The passage indicates that this absence of information may be due to the fact that

A) most speakers of Carabayo were necessarily bilingual.

B) Carabayo and Yurí were once assumed to be identical.

C) researchers did not make contact with the Carabayo people before 1969.

D) the Carabayo wordlists from before 1969 were proven to be inaccurate.

CONTINUE

Questions 13-16 are based on the following Science passages and supplementary material.

Passage 1 is adapted from "New 3D Measurements Improve Understanding of Geomagnetic Storm Hazards," while Passage 2 is adapted from "Preparing the Nation for Intense Space Weather." Both passages are news releases* from the U.S. Geological Survey.

Passage 1

Space weather events such as geomagnetic storms can disturb the earth's magnetic field, interfering with electric power grids,
Line radio communication, GPS systems, satellite
5 operations, oil and gas drilling, and air travel. Scientists use models of the earth's structure and measurements of Earth's magnetic field taken at USGS observatories to determine which sections of the electrical grid might lose power during a
10 geomagnetic storm.

In a new U.S. Geological Survey study, scientists calculated voltages along power lines in the mid-Atlantic region of the U.S. using 3D data of the earth. These data, taken at Earth's surface,
15 reflect the complex structure of the earth below the measurement sites and were collected during the National Science Foundation EarthScope USArray project. The scientists found that for many locations, the voltages they calculated
20 were significantly different from those based on previous 1D calculations, with the 3D data producing the most precise results.

"Using the most accurate data available to determine vulnerable areas of the power grid
25 can help maintain life-saving communications and protect national security during severe geomagnetic storms," said Greg Lucas, a USGS scientist and the lead author of the study. "Our study suggests that 3D data of the earth should be
30 used whenever they are available."

Electric currents from a March 1989 geomagnetic storm caused a blackout in Québec and numerous glitches in the U.S. power grid. In past studies, scientists using simple 1D models of
35 the earth would have found that 16 high-voltage electrical transmission lines were disturbed in the mid-Atlantic region during the storm, resulting in the blackout. However, by using realistic 3D data to calculate the 1989 scenario, the new study
40 found that there might have actually been 62 vulnerable lines.

"This discrepancy between 1D- and 3D-based calculations of the 1989 storm demonstrates the importance of realistic data, rather than relying on
45 previous 1D models, to determine the impact that a geomagnetic storm has on power grids," Lucas said.

Passage 2

The entire Canadian province of Québec, which covers twice as much area as the State of
50 Texas, was plunged into darkness on the morning of March 13, 1989. An intense geomagnetic storm seized Québec's power-grid system, tripping relays, damaging high-voltage transformers, and causing a blackout.

55 This geomagnetic storm's impact on Québec pales in comparison to what could happen in the future. A report by the National Academy of Sciences suggests that a rare but powerful magnetic superstorm could cause continent-
60 wide loss of electricity and substantial damage to power-grid infrastructure that could persist for months and cost the Nation in excess of $1 trillion.

"Utility groups rely on historical data collected
65 by long-running USGS (U.S. Geological Survey) magnetic observatories to see what a worst-case scenario could look like," said Mark Olson, a standards developer with the North American Electric Reliability Corporation (NERC).
70 "These data help NERC draft standards aimed at maintaining reliable operations of the North American power grid."

When a large sunspot emerges, the likelihood of an abrupt emission of radiation and an intense
75 solar wind becomes greater. When these winds reach the Earth, electrically charged particles enter the Earth's magnetosphere, ionosphere, and interior, inducing a geomagnetic storm.

---

*See Page 263 for the citations for these texts.

CONTINUE

Part 6

Cost of Damage Caused by Four Geomagnetic Storms

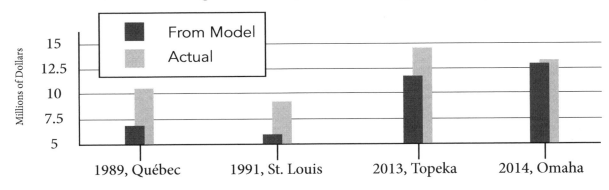

13

The chart as a whole indicates that

A) the damage dealt by geomagnetic storms has increased steadily over a 15-year period.

B) more precise modeling can minimize the financial liabilities posed by a geomagnetic storm.

C) 3D modeling enables more accurate damage estimates than are possible with 1D modeling.

D) modeling may have a tendency to underestimate the severity of geomagnetic storms.

14

Based on the chart, which of the following is true of the geomagnetic storm that struck Topeka in 2013?

A) It caused more dollars worth of damage than any other storm measured.

B) It was easy to study because of its large impact.

C) It was twice as deadly as the Québec storm.

D) It remains the most powerful geomagnetic storm on record.

15

What information would be most helpful in an assessment of the data in the chart alongside Greg Lucas's claims in Passage 1?

A) Whether Lucas was present for the Québec storm

B) When 1D superstorm models began to be replaced by 3D models

C) How large the area affected by each superstorm was

D) Why Lucas began to study geomagnetic storms

16

In relation to Passage 2, the chart primarily provides

A) a specific measure of the damage associated with one "geomagnetic storm's impact" (line 55).

B) "historical data" (line 64) that has helped researchers to reach a consensus.

C) a suggestion of the size of the "North American power grid" (lines 71-72).

D) statistics for the damage caused by the typical "geomagnetic storm" (line 78).

STOP

**After you have finished the questions, consult the relevant answers on Page 184.
Do not turn to any other section.**

Answer Key on the Next Page

Answer Key
Visual Evidence

Passage 1		Passage 2		Passage 3		Passage 4	
1.	D	5.	C	9.	A	13.	D
2.	C	6.	D	10.	B	14.	A
3.	B	7.	C	11.	B	15.	B
4.	A	8.	B	12.	C	16.	A

For detailed answer explanations for this practice section please visit **prepvantagetutoring.com/reading**.

Part 7

Practice Tests
Full Reading Sections

Reading Test

65 MINUTES, 52 QUESTIONS

Turn to Section 1 of your answer sheet to answer the questions in this section.

Each passage or pair of passages below is followed by a number of questions. After reading each passage or pair, choose the best answer to each question based on what is stated or implied in the passage or passages and in any accompanying graphics (such as a table or graph).

Questions 1-10 are based on the following passage.

This passage is adapted from Kenneth Mulmerton, "Magic Lantern Snow," a short story that first appeared in 2008.

If you visit the town where I grew up, one of the first things you will notice—notice, that is, after you turn off the highway, locate the
Line main street, and drive past a pet hospital, a fire
5 station, a small lending library with a fearsome gabled roof, and a self-important wooden sign that says "Bramble Creek Welcomes You"—is a barbershop. This barbershop looks rather like an oversized shed. And where it is situated, you can
10 even find a few of the rocks and trees and hills that the people of Bramble Creek have spent so much of their town's lifetime trying to landscape out of existence. Normally, a somewhat rusticated location would hurt a business like this, mostly
15 by keeping it from being readily visible. But you will notice this barbershop. Certainly. You see, out in front, there is a huge sign with gold letters on a dark red background. "Vic's Haircuts for Men" reads the great gilded script, with the especially

20 tremendous characters of "Vic's" given a line all to themselves. Now, what is rather curious about this is that nobody affiliated with Vic's (established 1963) was ever named Vic. To date, nobody has discovered who Vic is, or was, or
25 whether he even exists. Not even the Bramble Creek boys of nine and ten who were Vic's (the institution's, not the man's) most reliable customers were able to figure it out.

Looking back, I am a little puzzled by this.
30 For a boy of nine or ten, anything that carries the slightest air of the mysterious—from the construction site across the street to the old mayoral campaign buttons in the basement—any such trifle may well become the first ingredient
35 in a line of schemes and speculations that spans days, weeks, or (in the case of especially dogged imaginations) months. Yet the air in Vic's is the air of routine—a gruesome haze concocted from lingering cigar smoke and musty packing papers.
40 An air in which mystery and imagination cough, splutter, and die.

Today, Vic's is just like it was when I was younger. It still has the same barber—the barber with the 19th-century sideburns, a big
45 stout fellow who lazily snips a piece here, a piece

CONTINUE

there off the head of the sensitive lad in the seat by the window—a lad who spends his whole visit blinking and wriggling and squinting and fidgeting and looking very much like a royal
50 infant enthroned upon some ancient medical apparatus. Nevertheless, all those pieces snipped here and there over the space of twenty minutes always add up to the same "little boy's cut." From time to time the little boy's father will glance
55 over his newspaper and nod his approval as the familiar contours of the "little boy's cut" gradually emerge. But what is this "little boy's cut," as that barber condescendingly calls it when he thinks that none of the little boys can hear him? Well, let
60 me just say that all you need to create something comparable to the "little boy's cut" are clear eyes, a steady hand, an unflinching determination to humiliate the "little boy" in question, a pair of garden clippers, and about a minute and a half.
65 Alas, you will see almost every boy in Bramble Creek adorned with this "little boy's cut," since just about every boy in Bramble Creek goes to Vic's (as I'm pretty sure I've mentioned, though I might as well return to the point for emphasis).
70 And yes, I too have worn my share of "little boy's cuts." Surely there are more humiliating hairstyles. Though not many.

`1`

The narrator of the passage primarily describes

A) a series of needless changes that led to the decline of a community.

B) a set of ongoing conditions that were present in his own youth.

C) an event that marked his entry into a new period of maturity.

D) instances of misunderstanding that involve different generations

`2`

Over the course of the passage, the narration shifts in focus from

A) a group of pleasant reflections to a scene that the narrator finds offensive.

B) a broad account of a community to an investigation of that community's ideology.

C) a description of a setting to a typical incident within that setting.

D) a variety of unresolved questions to an analysis that promotes nonconformity.

`3`

As used in line 9, "situated" most nearly means

A) referenced.

B) committed.

C) contextualized.

D) positioned.

`4`

According to the narrator, Vic's barbershop can be located easily on account of its

A) connection with rustic life.

B) proximity to important town institutions.

C) accessibility from a highway.

D) large and obtrusive sign.

CONTINUE

5

How does the parenthetical phrase in line 27 differ from the parenthetical phrase in lines 68-69?

A) The first offers a distinction; the second calls attention to the narrator himself.

B) The first reiterates an important point; the second offers a new perspective.

C) The first refers to a point of uncertainty; the second helps to resolve that same uncertainty.

D) The first is informed by a tone of sarcasm; the second conveys the narrator's desire for sympathy.

6

The narrator primarily characterizes the interior of Vic's barbershop as

A) predictable and oppressive.

B) disorderly and absurd.

C) evocative of nostalgia.

D) a source of mystery.

7

Which choice provides the best evidence for the answer to the previous question?

A) Lines 13-15 ("Normally . . . visible")

B) Lines 23-25 ("To date . . . exists")

C) Lines 37-39 ("Yet the . . . papers")

D) Lines 42-43 ("Today . . . younger")

8

As used in line 53, "add up to" most nearly means

A) congregate for.

B) result in.

C) make an estimate of.

D) compete with.

9

Which of the following is most similar to the situation described in lines 53-57 ("From . . . emerge")?

A) A coach offers reassurance to a team that has lost confidence in its own abilities.

B) A traveler arrives at an important landmark and is reminded of a series of events from his childhood.

C) A concert-goer experiences moments of satisfaction while listening to a symphony that he knows well.

D) A writer uses an ironic and detached tone to describe an experience that had once been a source of strong emotion.

10

Which choice provides the best evidence that the narrator regards the "little boy's cut" with disapproval?

A) Lines 43-47 ("They . . . window")

B) Lines 57-59 ("But . . . him")

C) Lines 59-64 ("Well . . . half")

D) Lines 70-71 ("And . . . cuts")

CONTINUE

Questions 11-20 are based on the following passage.

This passage is adapted from "Of the Origin of Government" by David Hume, an essay first published in 1777.

All men are sensible of the necessity of justice to maintain peace and order; and all men are sensible of the necessity of peace and order for the
Line maintenance of society. Yet, notwithstanding this
5 strong and obvious necessity, such is the frailty or perverseness of our nature! It is impossible to keep men faithfully and unerringly in the paths of justice. Some extraordinary circumstances may happen, in which a man finds his interests to be
10 more promoted by fraud or rapine, than hurt by the breach which his injustice makes in the social union. But much more frequently he is seduced from his great and important, but distant interests, by the allurement of present, though often very
15 frivolous temptations. This great weakness is incurable in human nature.
    Men must, therefore, endeavour to palliate what they cannot cure. They must institute some person under the appellation of the magistrate,
20 whose peculiar office it is to point out the decrees of equity, to punish transgressors, to correct fraud and violence, and to oblige men, however reluctant, to consult their own real and permanent interests. In a word, obedience is a new duty
25 which must be invented to support that of justice, and the ties of equity must be corroborated by those of allegiance.
    But still, viewing matters in an abstract light, it may be thought that nothing is gained by this
30 alliance, and that the factitious duty of obedience, from its very nature, lays as feeble a hold of the human mind, as the primitive and natural duty of justice. Peculiar interests and present temptations may overcome the one as well as the other. They
35 are equally exposed to the same inconvenience; and the man who is inclined to be a bad neighbour, must be led by the same motives, well or ill understood, to be a bad citizen or subject.

Not to mention, that the magistrate himself may
40 often be negligent, or partial, or unjust in his administration.
    Experience, however, proves that there is a great difference between the cases. Order in society, we find, is much better maintained
45 by means of government; and our duty to the magistrate is more strictly guarded by the principles of human nature, than our duty to our fellow-citizens. The love of dominion, is so strong in the breast of man, that many not only
50 submit to, but court all the dangers, and fatigues, and cares of government; and men, once raised to that station, though often led astray by private passions, find, in ordinary cases, a visible interest in the impartial administration of justice. The
55 persons who first attain this distinction, by the consent, tacit or express, of the people, must be endowed with superior personal qualities of valour, force, integrity, or prudence, which command respect and confidence; and, after
60 government is established, a regard to birth, rank, and station, has a mighty influence over men, and enforces the decrees of the magistrate. The prince or leader exclaims against every disorder which disturbs his society. He summons all his partisans
65 and all men of probity to aid him in correcting and redressing it, and he is readily followed by all indifferent persons in the execution of his office. . .
    But though this progress of human affairs
70 may appear certain and inevitable, and though the support which allegiance brings to justice be founded on obvious principles of human nature, it cannot be expected that men should beforehand be able to discover them, or foresee their operation.
75 Government commences more casually and more imperfectly. It is probable, that the first ascendent of one man over multitudes began during a state of war; where the superiority of courage and of genius discovers itself most visibly, where
80 unanimity and concert are most requisite, and where the pernicious effects of disorder are most sensibly felt. The long continuance of that state, an incident common among savage tribes, inured the people to submission; and if the chieftain

CONTINUE →

85 possessed as much equity as prudence and valour, he became, even during peace, the arbiter of all differences, and could gradually, by a mixture of force and consent, establish his authority.

11

The main purpose of the passage is to

A) articulate a series of distinctions between desirable and oppressive governments.

B) revisit and modernize traditional ideas about the origins of government.

C) draw meaningful connections between human psychology and the structure of government.

D) promote a spirit of civic participation by emphasizing the necessity of government.

12

One of the central ideas of the passage is that

A) government institutions should be consistently scrutinized and reformed.

B) the centralization of authority can prevent social disorder.

C) punishing lawbreakers is a government's most significant function.

D) successful governments tend to create permanent aristocracies.

13

As used in line 10, "promoted" most nearly means

A) honored.

B) publicized.

C) served.

D) defined.

14

Which choice best supports Hume's idea that all people are guided by some of the same fundamental ideals?

A) Lines 1-4 ("All men . . . society")

B) Lines 12-15 ("But much . . . temptations")

C) Lines 28-33 ("But still . . . justice")

D) Lines 33-34 ("Peculiar . . . other")

15

Hume's statement in lines 17-18 ("Men . . . cure") is best understood as

A) a recommendation for how to address an inherently problematic situation.

B) an acknowledgment of a few of the logical shortcomings of his proposals.

C) a paraphrase of one of the arguments of Hume's ideological opponents.

D) a reference to a hypothetical situation that Hume declines to examine.

16

As characterized in the passage, the "man" mentioned in line 36 would be notable for his

A) status as an outcast within his own community.

B) belief that all forms of government are equally oppressive.

C) acts of violent and irresponsible protest.

D) blatant disrespect for his government and its laws.

CONTINUE

17

As used in line 54, "impartial" most nearly means

A) equitable.

B) accepting.

C) dismissive.

D) basic.

18

According to Hume, the "state of war" (lines 77-78) is significant because

A) its similarity to perceived states of peace and prosperity has generally been underestimated.

B) it provided conditions under which individual leaders could demonstrate a suitability for governance.

C) its prevalence forced societies that had formed democratic and de-centralized governments to adopt new institutions.

D) it persists among societies that are relatively small and that have remained in isolation.

19

Hume argues that the "magistrate" first introduced in line 19 is

A) valuable as a theoretical construct but not representative of any real individual.

B) directly analogous to the leader of a unified tribal community.

C) obeyed by a society's less powerful citizens more as the result of fear than of loyalty.

D) aided in enforcing social order by humanity's respect for status and hierarchy.

20

Which choice provides the best evidence for the answer to the previous question?

A) Lines 39-41 ("Not . . . administration")

B) Lines 45-48 ("and our . . . fellow-citizens")

C) Lines 59-62 ("After . . . magistrate")

D) Lines 82-84 ("The long . . . submission")

CONTINUE

Questions 21-31 are based on the following passages.

Passage 1 is adapted from the PLOS EveryOne Online article* "Sharing Was Caring for Ancient Humans and Their Prehistoric Pups" (2013) by Michelle Dohm. Passage 2 is adapted from the PLOS One journal article* "Ancient DNA Analysis of the Oldest Canid Species from the Siberian Arctic and Genetic Contribution to the Domestic Dog" (2015) by Esther J. Lee et al.

Passage 1

While the tale of how man's best friend came to be (i.e., domestication) is still slowly unfolding, a recently published study in PLOS ONE may
Line provide a little context—or justification?—for
5 dog lovers everywhere. It turns out that even thousands of years ago, humans loved to share food with, play with, and dress up their furry friends.

In the study titled "Burying Dogs in Ancient
10 Cis-Baikal, Siberia: Temporal Trends and Relationships with Human Diet and Subsistence Practices," biologists, anthropologists, and archaeologists joined forces to investigate the nature of the ancient human-dog relationship by
15 analyzing previously excavated canid remains worldwide, with a large portion of specimens in modern-day Eastern Siberia, Russia. The authors performed genetic analysis and skull comparisons to establish that the canid specimens
20 were most likely dogs, not wolves, which was an unsurprising but important distinction when investigating the human-canine bond. The canid skulls from the Cis-Baikal region most closely resembled those of large Siberian huskies, or sled
25 dogs. Radiocarbon dating from previous studies also provided information regarding the dates of death and other contextual information at the burial sites.

The researchers found that the dogs buried in
30 Siberia, many during the Early Neolithic period 7,000-8,000 years ago, were only found at burial sites shared with foraging humans. Dogs were

found buried in resting positions, or immediately next to humans at these sites, and their graves
35 often included various items or tools seemingly meant for the dogs. One dog in particular was adorned with a red deer tooth necklace around its neck and deer remnants by its side, and another was buried with what appears to be a pebble or
40 toy in its mouth.

By analyzing the carbon and nitrogen in human and dog specimens in this region, the researchers were able to determine similarities in human and dog diets, both of which were rich in fish. This
45 finding may be somewhat surprising because one might assume that dogs helped humans hunt terrestrial game, and would consequently be less likely found among humans that ate primarily fish.

The authors speculate that dogs were
50 considered spiritually similar to humans, and were therefore buried at the same time in the same graves. The nature of the burials and the similarities in diet also point toward an intimate and personal relationship, both emotional and
55 social, between humans and their dogs—one that involved sharing food and giving dogs the same burial rites as the humans they lived among. Ancient dogs weren't just work animals or hunters, the authors suggest, but important
60 companion animals and friends as well.

Passage 2

It is widely accepted that the domestic dog (Canis lupus familiaris) descended from the gray wolf (Canis lupus), but the process of domestication as well as geographical origin
65 and approximate date of first domestication is still debated. Genetic studies of modern dog and wolf populations have shown divergent views, from a single origin in East/South Asia or the Near East to multiple areas of
70 domestication and/or hybridization with regional wolf breeds. Furthermore, the possibility of admixture with other canid species has also been previously suggested. On the other hand, recent mitochondrial genome analysis of ancient
75 canids has suggested a European origin of domestic dogs. Archaeological evidence is not

*See Page 217 for the citations for these texts.

CONTINUE

always straightforward for the morphological
identification of domestic dogs, especially as the
earliest dogs were essentially the same size as
80   wolves, but advanced morphometric analyses
have improved the efforts. . .
     Archaeological and paleontological research
conducted in the Arctic Siberia within past couple
of decades has yielded a large amount of bone
85   material suitable for genetic studies, as such
material mostly comes from permafrost deposits
that are common in the area. Many ancient DNA
studies have focused on extinct Pleistocene or
wild species that occupied Siberia, but here we
90   focus on the oldest domesticated species Canis.
Different Canidae species, such as the arctic fox
and wolf, were among the Pleistocene arctic
fauna that continued into the present. Within the
region, studies have claimed the presence of dogs
95   in the Russian Plain and Kamchatka by 13,000
BC. A recent study has suggested the presence of
a domestic dog in southern Siberia dated to ca.
33,300 BC, which predates the oldest evidence
from western Europe and the Near East. However,
100 the Siberian canid remain was morphologically
most similar to dogs from Greenland and unlike
ancient and modern wolves and putative dogs
from central Russia.

21

Which of the following choices best supports the
claim that the author sets forward in lines 5-8 ("It
turns . . . friends")?

A) Lines 9-17 ("In the . . . Russia")

B) Lines 17-20 ("The authors . . . wolves")

C) Lines 25-28 ("Radiocarbon . . . sites")

D) Lines 36-40 ("One . . . mouth")

22

The statements in lines 29-40 of Passage 1 would be
most clearly contradicted by the discovery that

A) the functions of some of the items found with
buried dogs have not been firmly identified.

B) dogs in Greenland were routinely buried with
toys and other trinkets.

C) the diets of Siberian dogs were not identical to
the diets of humans in Siberia.

D) some Siberian dogs were buried at locations far
from human burial sites.

23

As used in line 53, "intimate" most nearly means

A) vulnerable.

B) secret.

C) routine.

D) close.

24

The final sentence of Passage 1 mainly serves to

A) return to and re-affirm a claim presented earlier.

B) summarize and endorse a specific methodology.

C) clarify a point in a manner meant to win over
skeptical readers.

D) re-state a finding that the authors of the study
found surprising.

CONTINUE

Test 1

25

The primary purpose of Passage 2 is to

A) present the debate inspired by a specific study.

B) discuss challenges and uncertainties that recent research may help to address.

C) explain a new consensus in a field that has often been confronted with uncertainty.

D) underscore the flaws in an archaeological theory.

26

As used in line 67, "divergent" most nearly means

A) aberrant.

B) unfamiliar.

C) various.

D) indefinite.

27

The authors of Passage 2 indicate that wolves

A) posed a threat to early hunting communities.

B) are somewhat similar to early domestic dogs.

C) were typically larger than early domestic dogs.

D) were highly resistant to domestication attempts.

28

In analyzing the domestication of dogs, both passages consider information derived from

A) genetic analysis.

B) digital modeling.

C) radiocarbon dating.

D) dietary investigation.

29

The authors of Passage 2 would argue that the "burial sites" (lines 31-32) mentioned in Passage 1

A) offer evidence that contradicts the public's understanding of the domestication of dogs.

B) complicate the idea that early dogs resembled modern wolves.

C) do not provide earliest prospective evidence of the domestication of dogs.

D) suggest an attitude towards dogs that probably did not extend beyond Siberia.

30

Which choice provides the best evidence for the answer to the previous question?

A) Lines 71-73 ("Furthermore . . . suggested")

B) Lines 76-78 ("Archaeological . . . dogs")

C) Lines 87-90 ("Many . . . Canis")

D) Lines 96-99 ("A recent . . . Near East")

31

In contrast to Passage 2, Passage 1 places a strong focus on the investigation of

A) the work of "biologists, anthropologists, and archaeologists" (lines 12-13).

B) the specific "nature of the ancient human-dog relationship" (line 14).

C) specific groups of "canid specimens" (line 19).

D) research involving animal remains found "in Siberia" (lines 29-30).

CONTINUE

Questions 32-42 are based on the following passage and supplementary material.

This passage is an excerpt from "Can Public Transit and Ride-Share Companies Get Along?" by Kyle Shelton. Originally published* in 2016 by The Conversation.

In Centennial, Colorado and Altamonte Springs, Florida, residents and visitors can now get subsidized rides to the nearest train station. In
Line both cases the cities foot the bill, or at least part
5 of it, but it's not a public bus that makes the trip. Rather, it's a car driven by someone working for ride-sharing companies Lyft and Uber.

There are potential public benefits—the hope of increased ridership, better service for hard-to-
10 serve areas, and cost and equipment efficiencies. Competition could push sometimes slow-moving transit agencies to innovate and improve. There are also risks. Ride-sharing companies have devastated the private taxi market, effectively
15 undercutting the entire industry in some cities. Mobility rights advocates and transit employees fear that the same thing could happen to public transit, remaking, under private ownership, the way millions of Americans get around every day.
20 To maximize the benefits while minimizing the risks, we need to know how ride-share companies will affect public transportation. Might public transit agencies come to regret entering into agreements with private-sector competitors?
25 Can the new arrangements improve service for customers, save agencies money, and make a profit for the companies?

With numerous pilot projects similar to Centennial and Altamonte Springs just getting
30 underway, there is little existing research into the effects that cooperating with ride-sharing companies will have on public transit operators.

But the role that ride-sharing companies are now playing is not a new one. Private companies
35 have long found ways to fill transportation needs for people who do not own cars or who live in places where public transit does not reach—such

as Baltimore's hack cabs or New York City's "dollar vans."
40 A ride-share company's smartphone app may be more formalized, but Uber and Lyft have tapped into a similar market as these informal transit systems. The companies serve users unhappy with existing options—either because
45 public transit failed to serve them, other options cost too much or they deemed transit vehicles uncomfortable or unsafe.

A future in which ride-sharing companies fully replace mass transit is unlikely. There are
50 too many advantages built into existing systems. Buses and trains carry more people than cars and vans. The benefits of fixed transit lines— structured and stable development corridors and dedicated rights-of-way—are simply not
55 replicable by ride-sharing companies. While Uber and Lyft will likely continue to grow, they are unlikely to draw riders off well-functioning transit lines. But they can complement them.

A likely outcome of ride-share and authority
60 interaction is more of what is already taking shape in Colorado, Florida, and many other locales— small-scale, replicable cooperation. Centennial and Altamonte Springs are attempting to address what is known in the transportation sector as the
65 "first mile/last mile" problem. The idea is that many potential transit riders don't use the service because it's too far from either the beginning or end of a given trip. Offering ride-sharing as a way to connect from the doorway to the transit stop
70 may help overcome this issue.

Bridj, a newer player to the ride-sharing world that styles itself as "pop-up" microtransit, is running a pilot project in Kansas City that intends to augment existing public transit service by
75 making connections in ways existing buses do not. The company contracted with the Kansas City Area Transportation Authority in March 2016 to run on-demand shuttles between the downtown area and a pocket of residential areas southwest of
80 the city during peak hours.

While both areas are served by regular KCATA bus routes, they are not directly connected, so private vehicles are much faster. Instead of

---

*See Page 217 for the citation for this text.

CONTINUE

changing the existing bus routes or adding new
85 ones, KCATA is hoping Bridj service can more
cheaply cover the gap.

    The biggest question about these new
relationships is how well they meet riders' needs
over time. Disability rights advocates have already
90 warned that substituting ride-share services for
existing agency-run paratransit programs—on-
demand rides for users with disabilities—may be
a violation of the Americans with Disabilities Act.
Public agencies and most private transportation
95 companies are bound to provide these services to
all users, but it's not yet clear whether newer ride-
sharing companies must also—or how contracting
with a government agency might require it.

32

The author characterizes the "subsidized rides"
project mentioned in the first paragraph as

A) comparable to other recent endeavors designed to
   improve transit practices.

B) an unfortunate yet inevitable concession to
   ride-sharing companies.

C) popular among commuters despite researchers'
   uncertainty about the virtues of ride-sharing.

D) the natural outcome of questionable strategic
   decisions by taxi companies.

Four Transportation Methods in the Boston Metro Area

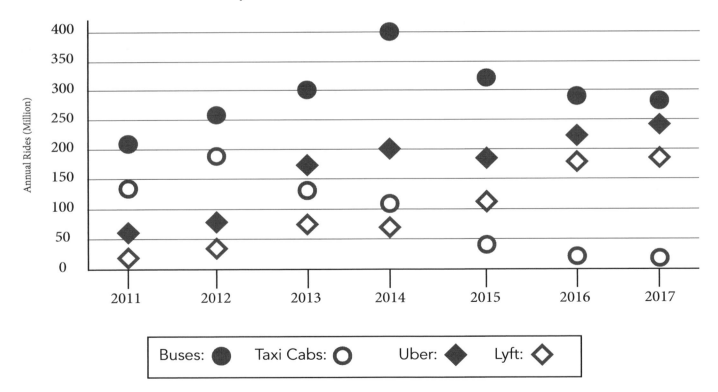

CONTINUE

33

Which choice provides the best evidence for the answer to the previous question?

A) Lines 6-7 ("Rather . . . Uber")

B) Lines 13-15 ("Ride-sharing . . . cities")

C) Lines 22-24 ("Might . . . competitors?")

D) Lines 28-32 ("With . . . operators")

34

As used in line 11, "push" most nearly means

A) publicize.

B) sideline.

C) build up.

D) motivate.

35

Which of the following situations illustrates both "benefits" and "risks" as described in the second paragraph (lines 8-19)?

A) A ride-sharing service offers discounted rides that lead to falling earnings and mass layoffs for a local cab company.

B) A company that initially operated a ride-sharing app expands its operations into the management of train lines.

C) A for-profit company that operates a fleet of city buses faces negative publicity in relation to its hiring practices.

D) The presence of multiple ride-sharing companies in a city forces a taxi company to revise its business model.

36

As used in line 35, "fill" most nearly means

A) replace.

B) overcome.

C) accompany.

D) satisfy.

37

On the basis of the passage, ride-sharing companies would be more likely to entirely replace public transportation if these companies were to

A) build transit stations that could gradually replace similar city-operated locations.

B) implement more rigorous safety measures.

C) independently operate mass transit lines of their own.

D) enlarge their fleets of privately-operated vehicles.

38

Which choice provides the best evidence for the answer to the previous question?

A) Lines 43-47 ("The companies . . . unsafe")

B) Lines 55-58 ("While . . . lines")

C) Lines 68-70 ("Offering . . . issue")

D) Lines 71-76 ("Bridj . . . not")

CONTINUE

39

The final paragraph of the passage serves primarily to

A) urge the resolution of a debate.

B) cast doubt on the value of an innovation.

C) examine the motives of a single group.

D) note various points of uncertainty.

40

According to the chart, in what year did the combined number of Uber and Lyft rides first overtake the number of taxi cab rides in the Boston Metro Area?

A) 2012

B) 2013

C) 2014

D) 2015

41

Which of the following represents the greatest disparity, as represented in the chart?

A) Taxi cab rides and Uber rides, 2011

B) Bus rides and Uber rides, 2013

C) Lyft rides and Uber rides, 2015

D) Uber rides and taxi cab rides, 2017

42

The author of the passage would regard the data in the chart as

A) of limited use in determining whether ride-sharing companies have "devastated the private taxi market" (line 14).

B) helpful in demonstrating that transit agencies should regret "agreements with private-sector competitors" (line 24).

C) reliably suggestive that Uber and Lyft "will likely continue to grow" (line 56).

D) contradicting the idea that "private vehicles are much faster" (line 83) than standard public transportation.

CONTINUE

Questions 43-52 are based on the following passage and supplementary material.

This passage is adapted from "The Nose Knows: Oriental Honey Buzzards Use Nose and Eyes to Forage for Sweet Treats" by Charlotte Bhaskar. Originally published* by EveryOne, the PlosOne community blog.

Winnie the . . . Buzzard? The Oriental honey buzzard *Pernis orientalis* feeds primarily on honey and bee or wasp larvae. But how do they
Line find their food?
5   In the winter, thousands of Oriental honey buzzards migrate to Taiwan to forage. These migrating honey buzzards especially target apiaries for a tasty treat not found in nature: "pollen dough." Beekeepers make softball-sized
10   balls of pollen dough from pollen, soybeans, and sugar to feed their bees in winter when flowers are scarce.
       The unusual appearance of pollen dough (bright yellow, perfectly round, and very unlike
15   honeycombs or bee larvae) led PLOS ONE authors to hypothesize that the honey buzzards might be using their noses (olfaction) in addition to visual sightings to identify the dough as food. Olfaction doesn't appear to be very ecologically
20   important to other raptor species, so the possibility that honey buzzards use their sense of smell as well as vision to find food is exciting.
       Specifically, the authors asked:

1.   Can honey buzzards distinguish between
25   visually identical doughs missing a specific food ingredient (pollen, sugar, or soybeans)?
2.   Are buzzards influenced by the pollen dough's color?

30   To test these hypotheses, the authors ran a series of field experiments. In their first experiment, the authors focused on the buzzards' ability to smell specific ingredients in the pollen

dough—specifically pollen, one of their sources of
35   nutrition in the wild. To do so, the authors varied the pollen, soybean, or sugar content between two dough samples, but kept the appearance of both samples identical in terms of texture, brightness, and color (yellow).
40   In the second experiment, the authors examined the buzzards' reliance on visual cues by varying the colors of two potential dough samples between yellow, black, and green. They kept the ingredients of both dough samples the same.
45   The third and final experiment was a variation on the first experiment, in which the dough was dyed black instead of yellow. The results from experiment 1 revealed that buzzards strongly preferred pollen-containing doughs. In the second
50   experiment, all buzzards exclusively chose to eat yellow dough instead of black or green dough. The results from the third experiment backed up experiment 1's results, with buzzards again preferring to eat pollen-containing dough over
55   non-pollen-containing dough, even though it was dyed black.
       Based on the results from experiments 1 and 3, the authors posit that honey buzzards prefer pollen-containing dough over dough with no
60   pollen added. It seems probable that the ability to select between two visually identical samples is based on the buzzards' ability to smell the differences.
       The authors also looked at the olfactory
65   receptor (OR) gene repertoire size in the honey buzzard's genome. The number of different scents a species can distinguish is linked to its number of OR genes. Their gene analysis showed that the Oriental honey buzzard has the largest OR
70   gene repertoire of the diurnal raptors—almost five times as large as the OR gene repertoire of peregrine falcons or golden eagles!
       Taken together, these results suggest that the Oriental honey buzzard uses both olfaction and
75   color vision when foraging for food. Additionally, the results of experiment 3 (where all dough samples were colored black) suggest that olfaction might predominate over vision in cases where the two senses seem to conflict.

---

*See Page 217 for the citation for this text.

CONTINUE ➤

80   While more work still needs to be done to discover the extent of the role olfaction plays in Oriental honey buzzards' feeding strategy, it seems clear that in this case the nose (or beak!) knows.

43

The author's purpose in writing this passage is to describe

A) fieldwork from different research teams that yielded surprisingly similar results.

B) popular beliefs that were overturned in the course of a single study.

C) experiments dedicated to different factors as part of a single coordinated inquiry.

D) different hypotheses that are individually convincing yet ultimately incompatible.

44

In lines 14-15 and 26-27, the author of the passage uses parenthetical phrases in order to

A) address apparent misconceptions that surround a research project.

B) clarify some of the concepts or properties behind specific terms.

C) paraphrase testimonies from specialists in animal biology.

D) lend an approachable and easygoing tone to the discussion.

Results of a 2012 Study of Oriental Honey Buzzard Reactions to Dough Samples (Varying Scents from Varying Pollen Content; Varying Color from Artificial Dyes)

Buzzard Age	Preferred Scented	Preferred Unscented	Preferred Yellow	Preferred Black
3-8 years	35	0	35	0
10-12 years	40	0	27	13
14-18 years	20	0	11	9
	Same Color		Same Scent	

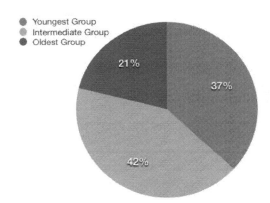

● Youngest Group
● Intermediate Group
● Oldest Group

21%
37%
42%

CONTINUE

45

As used in line 22, "exciting" most nearly means

A) intriguing.

B) unnerving.

C) entertaining.

D) unpredictable.

46

In what respect did the third experiment performed by the researchers differ from the first experiment?

A) The first experiment did not consider variations in dough composition.

B) The first experiment did not consider variations in dough color.

C) The first experiment involved a larger sample of buzzards.

D) The first experiment involved a smaller sample of buzzards.

47

As used in lines 50, "exclusively" most nearly means

A) unthinkingly.

B) sophisticatedly.

C) prejudicially.

D) consistently.

48

According to the passage, Oriental honey buzzards possess a sense of smell that

A) plays a crucial role in enabling them to hunt live prey.

B) is comparable in intensity to the sense of smell in related raptor species.

C) may override visual information about food sources.

D) becomes more powerful as the buzzards grow older.

49

Which choice provides the best evidence for the answer to the previous question?

A) Lines 5-9 ("In the winter . . . dough")

B) Lines 19-22 ("Olfaction . . . exciting")

C) Lines 64-68 ("The authors . . . OR genes")

D) Lines 75-79 ("Additionally . . . conflict")

50

Which choice most effectively suggests that the researchers described in the passage gathered conclusive evidence that is relevant to Question 2 (lines 28-29)?

A) Lines 31-35 ("In their first . . . wild")

B) Lines 40-43 ("In the second . . . green")

C) Lines 49-51 ("In the . . . dough")

D) Lines 68-70 ("Their gene . . . raptors")

CONTINUE

51

Together, the table and the graph indicate that

A) younger honey buzzards do not use visual clues to distinguish between food sources.

B) younger honey buzzards distinguish between food sources more rapidly than do older honey buzzards.

C) older honey buzzards respond to scents more strongly than they respond to visual clues.

D) older honey buzzards typically survive without relying on visual clues.

52

What might explain the disparity between the honey buzzard responses indicated by the table and the graph and the findings recorded in the passage?

A) The passage most likely presents information that pre-dates the information gathered in the table and the graph.

B) The researchers mentioned in the passage considered a sample population much smaller than that considered for the table and the graph.

C) The researchers mentioned in the passage might have tested honey buzzards from the youngest age group indicated in the chart.

D) The researchers mentioned in the passage intentionally tested birds other than honey buzzards as part of their study.

STOP
If you finish before time is called, you may check your work on this section only.
Do not turn to any other section.

Answer Key on the Next Page

Answer Key: Test 1

Passage 1	Passage 2	Passage 3	Passage 4	Passage 5
1. B	11. C	21. D	32. A	43. C
2. C	12. B	22. D	33. D	44. B
3. D	13. C	23. D	34. D	45. A
4. D	14. A	24. A	35. A	46. B
5. A	15. A	25. B	36. D	47. D
6. A	16. D	26. C	37. C	48. C
7. C	17. A	27. B	38. B	49. D
8. B	18. B	28. A	39. D	50. C
9. C	19. D	29. C	40. B	51. C
10. C	20. C	30. D	41. D	52. C
		31. B	42. A	

Question Types

Major Issue
1-2, 11-12, 25, 43

Passage Details
4-5, 9, 15-16, 18, 22, 24, 27, 35, 39, 44, 46

Command of Evidence
6-7, 10, 14, 19-20, 21, 32-33, 37-38, 48-50

Word in Context
3, 8, 13, 17, 23, 26, 34, 36, 45, 47

Graphics and Visuals
40-42, 51-52

Passage Comparison
28-31

Self-Evaluation
Checklist for Test 1

Passage Types

- Hardest Readings _____ ; _____
- Easiest Readings _____ ; _____

Sources of Difficulty   _____ Comprehending Main Idea (Passages ___, ___, ___)
(Check all that apply.)   _____ Remembering Passage Details (Passages ___, ___, ___)
                               _____ Working with Style and Vocabulary (Passages ___, ___, ___)

Question Types

- Major Issue: Incorrect _____   Tossup _____   Challenges: _____
- Passage Details: Incorrect _____   Tossup _____   Challenges: _____
- CoE: Incorrect _____   Tossup _____   Challenges: _____
- Word in Context: Incorrect _____   Tossup _____   Challenges: _____

Sources of Difficulty   _____ Understanding the Question   _____ Locating or Analyzing Evidence
(Check all that apply.)   _____ Predicting the Answers   _____ Eliminating False Answers

Vocabulary

- New Words: _____
- Total Questions with Advanced Vocabulary _____   Number Right _____   Number Wrong _____

Overall Strategy

- Time Per Passage (Estimate): 1 _____   2 _____   3 _____   4 _____   5 _____
- Total Time for the Test _____   Time Left Over _____   OR Time Needed Beyond 65 Minutes _____
- Passages with Note-Taking _____   Questions Right for These _____   Questions Wrong for These _____
- Passages with NO Notes _____   Questions Right for These _____   Questions Wrong for These _____

Sources of Difficulty   _____ Slow Reading or Rereading   _____ Complicated or Time-Consuming Notes
(Check all that apply.)   _____ Inaccurate Annotations   _____ Rushed Through Passages or Questions

Answer Explanations
Test 1, Pages 186-202

Passage 1, Pages 186-188

1. <u>B</u> is the correct answer.

The passage focuses on the narrator's account of a barbershop that he recalls from his childhood, and which continues to exist: "Today, Vic's is just like it was when I was younger" (42-43). Choose B to reflect this content; be careful not to choose C, since the narrator's experience with Vic's does NOT focus on a single specific incident that carries a positive tone. A and D can both be eliminated as illogical and overly extreme negatives since the passage does not discuss generational conflict (even though the adult barber is presented as a negative figure) or damaging changes (even though the changes to the town meet with the narrator's disapproval).

2. <u>C</u> is the correct answer.

The passage begins with a general discussion of Vic's barbershop and then gradually narrows in focus to consider a particular type of hair-cutting: the "little boy's cut." Choose C to reflect this content. A is a trap answer, since while the narrator's tone in describing the little boy's cut is not entirely positive, it is outside of the scope of the passage to know whether he finds this practice offensive (as opposed to ridiculous). B and D can both be eliminated, since the passage does NOT contain enough detailed analysis to determine whether the narrator is interested in exploring ideology or questions of non-conformity, as opposed to being interested in portraying a community in considerable detail.

3. <u>D</u> is the correct answer.

In line 9, "situated" refers to the physical location of the barbershop; choose answer D to reflect this content. Be careful not to choose C, since "contextualized" refers to how meaning is constructed but not to the physical position of an object or a location. A (indicating an explanation or allusion) and B (indicating purpose or devotion) both raise contexts that are inappropriate to a straightforward description of a physical location.

4. <u>D</u> is the correct answer.

The narrator indicates that it is impossible to miss the barbershop--"But you will notice this barbershop. Certainly" (lines 15-16)--and attributes this situation to "a huge sign with gold letters on a dark red background" (lines 17-18). Choose answer D to support this content. B and C can be dismissed since the barbershop is NOT described as being particularly close to either the highway or major town institutions. A should be eliminated since the shop's problematic connection to rustic life would NOT influence whether it is or is not easy to locate.

5. <u>A</u> is the correct answer.

In line 27, the parenthetical comment offers clarification by helping the reader to see a distinction between the shop and the hypothetical owner; in lines 68-69, the comment draws attention to the narrator as the individual who is controlling what information is provided to the reader. Choose A to support this content. D can be eliminated, since neither parenthetical comment offers a clear tone; B can be dismissed as illogical, since the second parenthetical comment reiterates information rather than introducing new information. C can also be dismissed since the two comments refer to entirely different content.

6. <u>A</u> is the correct answer.

In lines 37-39, the narrator describes how the shop has a distinctive and unpleasant smell resulting from routine activities occurring over and over. This content best supports A. Be careful not to choose C, since nostalgia implies recollections that are positive, and while the barbershop triggers vivid memories for the narrator, those memories are NOT necessarily positive. B can be dismissed since nothing in the description of the shop as predictable indicates that the shop is disorderly, and D mistakenly appears to reference the name of the barbershop (which IS a source of mystery) instead of the "interior," which is not mysterious and is in fact well-known to the narrator.

7. <u>C</u> is the correct answer.

See the previous answer explanation for analysis of the correct line reference. A focuses on what conditions would likely affect a business located in the same place as the barbershop; B discusses the why the name of the shop is unusual. D suggests that the shop has remained the same for a long stretch of time. None of these other answers give a relevant description of the nature of the shop's interior, and therefore all should be rejected.

8. <u>B</u> is the correct answer.

In line 53, "add up to" refers to the haircut that results from the barber's actions, so that this phrase means "lead to" or "result in" in the context of the barber's cumulative work. Choose B to reflect this meaning. A wrongly refers to a group of people coming together, C wrongly refers to measurement, and D wrongly refers to a scenario involving conflict or competition, so that none of these answers properly convey the idea of a result or outcome.

9. <u>C</u> is the correct answer.

Lines 53-57 describe how a father casually acknowledges the process of his son's haircut because he is already familiar with what the resulting style is going to be. This is most comparable to someone listening to a symphony that he knows well; choose C to reflect this content. A can be dismissed since the father is not represented as reassuring or even engaging with his child; B (which wrongly assumes a sense of deep personal attachment for the father) and D (which assumes disinterest) can also both be rejected since they require assumptions about the father's emotional state as he watches the haircut progress, when the father is depicted mostly as an approving OBSERVER of the emotions of other characters.

10. <u>C</u> is the correct answer.

In lines 59-64, the narrator notes with disapproval that there is no skill or aesthetic taste involved in executing the "little boy's cut," and that the cut is likely to result in humiliation for the child. This content suggests that the narrator disapproves of the cut; choose C. A gives a description of the barber and of how he approaches his work; B describes the condescending term that is used to describe the particular hairstyle. D acknowledges that the narrator has personally experienced wearing this hairstyle. None of these other answers convey disapproval of the hairstyle, and all should be eliminated.

Passage 2, Pages 189-191

11. <u>C</u> is the correct answer.

Throughout the passage, Hume describes aspects of human psychology, such as the "incurable" draw toward "frivolous temptations" (lines 15-16) and in turn describes the corresponding offices of government. Choose C to reflect this content. A is wrong because the passage only makes brief reference to the potential of governments to oppress. Eliminate B because the passage does not discuss historical ideas about government, although it does mention the possible origins of a prince or leader. D can be ruled out, since the passage is persuasive regarding the simple necessity of government, but not regarding PARTICIPATION in government.

12. <u>B</u> is the correct answer.

With respect to innate antisocial and destructive impulses, Hume says, "Men must, therefore, endeavor to palliate what they cannot cure" (lines 17-18). B correctly identifies the major thesis that government can curb social disorder. Eliminate A, which wrongly focuses on the topic of reform of government, when the passage is mostly devoted to the motives and reasoning behind the CREATION of civil government. C should be ruled out because punishment is only one item within a larger list of government duties, while D is wrong because the passage is concerned with governance, NOT with matters of class.

13. <u>C</u> is the correct answer.

The word "promoted" in this context refers to the advancement of one's interests, so choose C. A is wrong because this meaning of "promoted" refers more to a benefit or duty bestowed upon someone. B is an irrelevant meaning in the present context, as it refers to the promulgation of information. D calls attention to the idea of clarifying a concept (NOT to actions that take place) and should thus be ruled out.

14. <u>A</u> is the correct answer.

Lines 1-4 offer a universal statement about human behavior, which Hume devotes the rest of the passage to proving, so that A is the best answer. B is wrong because, although it does describe a generality, it is less about ideals and more about vices. C and D can be eliminated because they are both hypothetical statements that describe potential objections to or nuances of Hume's arguments, NOT statements that specify the ideals that guide all people.

15. <u>A</u> is the correct answer.

Lines 17-18 declare that an intractable problem must at least be mitigated, so that A is the best answer. Eliminate B, because this statement is a significant part of Hume's thesis, NOT a weakness of it. C describes these lines inaccurately, because they present Hume's argument, NOT his opponents' ideas, while D is wrong because these lines are not hypothetical and Hume examines their premise for much of the passage.

16. <u>D</u> is the correct answer.

Line 36 describes a man who is both a bad neighbor and a bad citizen—someone unconcerned with the rules of community or the laws of larger society. Choose D as the best answer. A draws too extreme a conclusion; the man's community's perception of him is never described. B is baseless speculation about the man's inner state, so it is wrong, while C overstates the negative aspects of the behavior of the man, since this individual is an undesirable neighbor and subject but is NOT an explicitly violent one.

17. <u>A</u> is the correct answer.

In this context, "impartial" describes the way that justice should be administered, a topic which many men are naturally interested in. The best answer is A, "equitable," because this usage refers to fairness. Rule out B and C, which would better refer to a personal quality than to an abstract or social concept. D is most relevant to something simple or fundamental, NOT to the administration of justice, and is thus out of context.

18. <u>B</u> is the correct answer.

Hume presents the belief that the "state of war" described in lines 77-78 most likely led to the emergence of the social function of the leader. B is correct, while A is incorrect because Hume's claim is not that peace and war are similar, but that wartime leadership eventually became peacetime leadership. C is wrong because democracy is not a characteristic of the posited early society. Eliminate D as an answer that mistakes Hume's idea that the "state of war" persists among small savage groups for the very different idea that such a state is present in small and isolated, but still organized, societies.

19. <u>D</u> is the correct answer.

About the magistrate, Hume says, ". . . after government is established, a regard to birth, rank, and station, has a mighty influence over men, and enforces the decrees of the magistrate . . ." (lines 59-62). These lines clearly describe a relationship between respect for authority and the efficacy of the magistrate. Choose D as a reflection of this content. Eliminate A, since the magistrate is an abstract office but is filled by real people. B is incorrect because the magistrate is a separate role from that of the leader, even if both are important. C is incorrect because the passage discusses not fear but respect as the reason for the magistrate's power.

20. <u>C</u> is the correct answer.

See the previous answer explanation for analysis of the correct line reference. A is wrong because it describes flaws of specific magistrates and does not closely relate to the overall office. B can be ruled out because while it does introduce the idea that allegiance to authority is innate, the relevant line reference involves more of a general statement, while D is wrong because it relates not to magistrates but to the leader or prince.

Passage 3, Pages 192-194

21. <u>D</u> is the correct answer.

Lines 36-40 describe dogs who were buried with decorative, meaningful items: a necklace and possibly a toy. Because of the degree of care implied by these findings, D best supports the proposition in lines 5-8. A, B, and C describe the background and methods of the study, rather than its specific findings, so eliminate these options.

22. <u>D</u> is the correct answer.

Lines 29-40 explain the age, species, characteristics, and context of the archaeological evidence under consideration in the study. The relevant claim would be therefore best contradicted by archaeological findings of the same type of canid remains but in a setting different enough to render conclusions impossible to draw. Choose D. Eliminate A, since it would contradict conclusions about the objects found, but not the fact of their existence. B is incorrect, because discovering similar sites would REINFORCE the authors' conclusions. Eliminate C because the findings about the dogs' diets are not mentioned in these lines.

23. <u>D</u> is the correct answer.

In this context, "intimate" is parallel to "personal" and describes the "relationship" of the people and their dogs. Choose D, which is the meaning most in line with "personal." Rule out A, which is similar in meaning but introduces an inappropriate negative tone. B is likewise too extreme a meaning and can be eliminated since it wrongly indicates a context of hidden information or of something unknown. C, "routine," wrongly introduces the context of repetition rather than calling attention to a close relationship.

24. <u>A</u> is the correct answer.

The final sentence of Passage 1 summarizes of the authors' conclusion about the relationship of ancient humans and dogs, a conclusion which is briefly explained in the first paragraph. Choose A and rule out B because this is not a methodological claim. C is incorrect because it is not a clarification, but a conclusion. D is also incorrect because, while it is a restatement of lines 5-8, there is no strong indication that the authors regarded a finding as surprising, but simply that a specific finding is their major takeaway.

25. <u>B</u> is the correct answer.

Passage 2 presents the obstacles that arise in relation to attempts to pinpoint the origin of domestic dogs and mentions recent work that clarifies some complex issues. Choose B to reflect this content. A is wrong because the authors describe not a new debate but overarching problems faced within a field of study. C is wrong because while the authors do appear hopeful for some certainty, they make no claims to settle all the issues of continued research in the field. D is wrong because it is too specific; the passage identifies conflicting hypotheses but does NOT eliminate one or another on the basis of faulty reasoning.

26. <u>C</u> is the correct answer.

"Divergent" in this context refers to the variety of perspectives that researchers have shared regarding the origins of the domestic dog. Choose C, which fits the situation of numerous, differing viewpoints. Rule out A, which is an extreme and highly negative meaning of "divergent." B and D would both indicate that the perspectives considered in the passage are unclear or difficult to define, so that these answers introduce inappropriate negatives as well.

27. <u>D</u> is the correct answer.

Passage 2 emphasizes the similarity of wolves and domestic dogs, with the authors stating in lines 78-80 that early dogs were the same size as wolves were. Choose B and eliminate A, which applies a faulty negative tone to a passage that primarily presents wolves as a point of comparison for domesticated dogs, NOT as a threat to humans. C contradicts the text in lines 78-80, so rule it out. D is also not discussed by the text, since the author focuses on domesticated dog species that resembled wolves, NOT on the domestication of actual wolves.

28. <u>A</u> is the correct answer.

Passage 1 discusses genetic analysis (line 18, A), radiocarbon dating (line 25, C), and dietary analysis (lines 41-44, D). Passage 2 explicitly discusses only genetic analysis (line 18), but even if other methods (such as digital modeling, B) underly the discussion, they are never mentioned. Therefore, A is correct.

29. C is the correct answer.

The authors of Passage 2 are most concerned with establishing an earliest possible date and location for the domestication of dogs. As they state in lines 96-98, "A recent study has suggested the presence of a domestic dog in Siberia dated to ca. 33,000 BC, which predates the oldest evidence from Western Europe and the Near East." Therefore, choose C, since the authors are considering evidence much older than is presented in Passage 1. A can be eliminated, since it involves speculation about the perspective of "the public." B is irrelevant because the burial sites describe human attitudes toward dogs and the authors are not, in those lines, describing the physiology of the canid skeletons. D is wrong because it mistakes the geographic focus on Siberia in Passage 2 for an argument that a group of research findings (which may in fact have broad implications not mentioned in the passage) are not applicable beyond Siberia.

30. D is the correct answer.

See the previous answer explanation for analysis of the correct line reference. A is incorrect because it is not relevant to the main claim of Passage 1. B is only tangentially related to dating samples, the concern of Passage 2, and since the authors of Passage 1 are certain about the identification of the canids as dogs, not wolves, this answer can be eliminated. C is not an item of evidence, but instead a general statement about the longevity of several species, so that it is wrong.

31. B is the correct answer.

Passage 1 mostly analyzes the relationship between humans and dogs, whereas Passage 2 is mostly concerned with summarizing and drawing conclusions from large-scale findings. B is correct. A is not an effective answer because it names experts who would be of interest to the authors of BOTH passages and thus contradicts the question prompt. C introduces a similar problem since almost all of the archaeological evidence discussed by each passage deals with "canid specimens," while D is incorrect because both passages involve evidence found in Siberia.

Passage 4, Pages 195-198

32. A is the correct answer.

In lines 28-32, the author refers back to the subsidized ride projects mentioned in the first paragraph and indicates that there are "numerous pilot projects" similar to these endeavors. This information supports A. B wrongly applies a strongly negative tone to the effects of ride-sharing companies, while the author in fact calls attention to both positive and negative effects in the passage. C mistakes this combination of clear positives and negatives for "uncertainty" on the part of researchers (who are not mentioned in any accompanying line reference) while D criticizes the business practices of taxi companies (which are facing problems due to the efficiency of ride-sharing companies, NOT due necessarily due to their own poor choices).

33. D is the correct answer.

See the previous answer explanation for analysis of the correct line reference. A indicates that Uber and Lyft are participating in "subsidized rides" projects, B notes the ability of ride-sharing companies to pose a threat to taxi companies, and C calls attention to a possible liability of collaboration between ride-sharing companies and public transit options. Although all of these choices relate to ride-sharing, none of them align with answers to the previous question, though make sure not to wrongly align B with Question 32 D.

34. D is the correct answer.

In line 11, "push" indicates an action related to the kind of increased competition that will cause or "motivate" transit agencies to "innovate and improve" (line 12). Choose D to reflect this context of outcomes and this positive tone. A (context of spreading news), B (wrongly negative), and C (best for a context of support or physical accumulation) all introduce faulty meanings or connotations and should thus be eliminated.

35. A is the correct answer.

In requiring a scenario that involves "benefits" and "risks" related to the presence of ride-sharing in the context of public transportation, the question calls for an answer that combines positive and negative elements. The pairing of "discounted rides" (positive) with "falling earnings and massive layoffs" (negative) makes A an appropriate answer. Eliminate B and D as not presenting any clear negative consequences for public transit or taxi services as outlined in the paragraph, and eliminate C as placing emphasis on negatives (NOT positives, as the paragraph necessitates) for a ride-sharing company.

36. D is the correct answer.

In line 35, "fill" refers to the "transportation needs" that private companies are designed to address in an effective manner, or to "satisfy." Choose D and eliminate A and B, which would indicate that the "transportation needs" have disappeared or are no longer important, NOT that the needs are being met by valued companies. C raises the context of people or items being placed together, NOT the context of a need fulfilled by a service or company.

37. C is the correct answer.

In lines 55-58, the author discusses one of the limitations that faces companies such as Uber and Lyft: these companies cannot draw commuters off of transit lines, and naturally do not own such transit lines themselves. This observation of an advantage that ride-sharing companies do NOT have occurs in the context of a discussion of why it is "unlikely" (line 49) that ride-sharing will replace mass transit, so that C indicates a situation that, if it were possible, might benefit ride-sharing companies. A only calls attention to transit stations (not to transit lines overall), while B and D call attention to tactics that might help ride-sharing companies but that are NOT directly related in the passage the elimination of public transportation.

38. <u>B</u> is the correct answer.

See the previous answer explanation for analysis of the correct line reference. A calls attention to sources of dissatisfaction with public transportation, C broadly indicates that ride-sharing can co-exist with public transit (NOT replace it), and D explains one initiative that links a ride-sharing company to public transit services. Only A effectively indicates that ride-sharing is superior to public transit in some respects, but does not raise any possibilities for how ride-sharing would completely replace public transit options.

39. <u>D</u> is the correct answer.

The final paragraph raises a "question" (line 87) about new relationships and notes a situation related to ride-sharing companies that is "not yet clear" (line 96). This paragraph thus raises a few different points of uncertainty as described in D. Choose this answer and eliminate A (which indicates certainty and resolution instead) and B (which is strongly negative, NOT uncertain). C mistakes the paragraph's analysis of possibilities for an examination of desires or "motives," and wrongly references "a single group" when in fact multiple groups (riders, disability advocates, agencies, and companies) are mentioned.

40. <u>B</u> is the correct answer.

In 2012, there were almost 200 million cab rides in the Boston Metro Area, while there were fewer than 100 million Uber rides and fewer than 50 million Lyft rides. However, the number of Uber rides alone exceeded the number of cab rides in 2013. For this reason, eliminate A and choose B as indicating the FIRST year to fulfill the requirement of more Uber and Lyft rides (combined) than cab rides. C and D both indicate years in which Uber rides alone CONTINUED to exceed cab rides.

41. <u>D</u> is the correct answer.

Consider the differences represented by each pairing: A represents a difference of less than 100 million, B represents a difference of just over 100 million, C represents a difference of roughly 50 million, and D represents a difference of well over 150 million. On the basis of this evidence, D is the best answer.

42. <u>A</u> is the correct answer.

Although the chart indicates that the ride-sharing companies Uber and Lyft grew to provide more rides than taxi companies did in the Boston Metro Area, the chart does not consider other areas of the country or provide financial information (as the passage does). Thus, the chart would be of limited use in assessing the effect of ride-sharing companies on taxi companies, as indicated in A. Choose this answer and eliminate B (agreements between groups) and D (vehicle speed) as answers that wrongly offer strong statements based on factors that are NOT considered in the chart. C relies on a faulty extrapolation beyond the years explicitly given in the chart, which are the only years that can be analyzed here, since the growth in rides for Uber and Lyft up to 2017 does NOT necessarily indicate that these companies will offer more rides in the future.

Passage 5, Pages 199-202

43. <u>C</u> is the correct answer.

The passage describes how researchers tried to determine whether or not honey buzzards used smell as a way of finding food (a single inquiry) and the three distinct experiments utilized in the process of answering this question. Choose C to reflect this content. A can be dismissed since the fieldwork was all conducted by a single research team, while B can be rejected since the passage's most conversational and accessible segments (such as the first paragraph) should not be mistaken for expressions of popular beliefs held at the start of the study. D can also be rejected since the study began with a SINGLE hypothesis that was subsequently investigated under a series of coordinated studies.

44. <u>B</u> is the correct answer.

In lines 15-16 and 26-27, the author of the passage uses parenthetical phrases to offer clarifying information such as definitions or examples, explaining (respectively) the appearance of pollen dough and the nature of various food ingredients. Choose B to support this content. A can be eliminated since the phrases only offer objective information, not persuasive rhetoric designed to address misconceptions, while C can be rejected since the phrases do NOT immediately follow statements from specialists. D can be rejected since the phrases convey information rather than serving stylistic functions.

45. <u>A</u> is the correct answer.

In line 22, "exciting" refers to a possibility that could be intellectually engaging or interesting since, from a research perspective, this possibility could be an important way of distinguishing honey buzzards from other bird species. Choose A to reflect this meaning. B (inappropriately implying something that is worrying or alarming), C (inappropriately implying something that merely provides pleasure or amusement), and D (inappropriately implying something that is unstable or uncertain) all introduce improper contexts and should thus be eliminated.

46. <u>B</u> is the correct answer.

In both the first and third experiments, different dough samples with varying ingredients were used, but in the third experiment, the dough was dyed black. This, the first experiment did not test for variations in dough color: choose B to support this content. A can be eliminated since both experiments involved variations in dough composition, while C and D can be eliminated since the passage gives no indication that the number of buzzards varied in either experiment.

47. <u>D</u> is the correct answer.

In line 50, "exclusively" refers to a behavior (here, buzzards reliably choosing to eat a certain kind of food) that is repeated in every case. Choose D to reflect this meaning. A (inappropriately implying that a behavior was repeated without reflection or consideration), B (inappropriately implying that a behavior was an indication of intelligence or progress), and C (inappropriately implying that a behavior was an indication of bias) all introduce improper contexts and should thus be eliminated.

48. C is the correct answer.

In lines 75-79, the author explains that buzzards might rely on their sense of smell more than on their sense of sight in the process of determining what to eat. Choose C to reflect this content. A can be rejected since the discussion of how buzzards use their sense of smell is limited to the context of eating pollen dough, NOT the context of eating live prey. B can be rejected since the power of the sense of smell is not contrasted between raptor species, and D can be rejected since there is no discussion of how smell might change as buzzards age.

49. D is the correct answer.

See the previous answer explanation for analysis of the correct line reference. A explains a particular food source that is popular with honey buzzards, while B explains why a particular hypothesis was intriguing to researchers. C explains how genetic analysis was used to complement the fieldwork studies. None of these line references explain that buzzards might favor olfactory information over visual information about food sources, and they should all therefore be rejected.

50. C is the correct answer.

Lines 28-29 identify a central research question: whether or not buzzards are influenced by the color of pollen dough. In lines 49-51, the author indicates that experiments showed all buzzards consistently choosing to eat yellow dough, rather than dough which had been artificially colored. This finding offers a strong answer to the research question posed at the beginning of the study, so choose C to support this content. A describes the goal of the first experiment, which reflected a different research question, while B describes how the experiment designed to test buzzards' response to visual cues was set up. D describes an apparent genetic difference between honey buzzards and other similar bird species. None of these answers present a finding that addresses the second research question, and they should therefore all be eliminated.

51. C is the correct answer.

The table and the graph indicate that the oldest group of buzzards represents the smallest portion of the overall buzzard population involved in the study, that these older buzzards showed an exclusive preference for scented over unscented dough, and that these buzzards exhibited a mild preference for yellow over black dough. This data suggests that older buzzards display a stronger response to variation in scent cues than they do to variation in color cues; choose C to reflect this content. A can be eliminated since the youngest buzzards showed the strongest preference for yellow dough, indicating that these buzzards rely strongly on visual cues, while B can be eliminated since the graphs do not give any indication of how long it took buzzards to respond to either visual or scent cues. D can be eliminated since it makes an overly broad assumption about the issue of how buzzards survive, NOT about how buzzards react to a few food sources as noted in the table.

52. C is the correct answer.

The table and the graph indicate findings for three different groups of buzzards, and for the youngest group of buzzards, the findings from the 2012 study represented in the table are consistent with the findings recorded in the passage. This situation suggests that the buzzards studied in the research described in the passage might have been from the youngest age group. Choose C to reflect this content. A can be rejected since there is nothing to indicate that the different findings would be tied to different dates, while B can be rejected since a smaller population does NOT necessarily imply inconsistent results. D can also be rejected, since nothing in the passage indicates that researchers would have had reason to test birds other than honey buzzards.

NOTES

- The first reading for Passage 3 on Page 192, "Sharing Was Caring for Ancient Humans and Their Prehistoric Pups," is adapted from the article of the same name published by EveryOne, the PLOS One community blog. 28 May 2013, PLOS One. https://blogs.plos.org/everyone/2013/05/28/sharing-was-caring-for-ancient-humans-and-their-prehistoric-pups/. Accessed 7 January 2019.

- The second reading for Passage 3 on Pages 192-193, "Ancient DNA Analysis of the Oldest Canid Species from the Siberian Arctic and Genetic Contribution to the Domestic Dog," is adapted from the article of the same name published as a PLOS One journal article. 27 May 2015, PLOS One. https://journals.plos.org/plosone/article?id=10.1371/journal.pone.0125759#abstract0. Accessed 7 January 2019.

- Passage 4 on Pages 195-196, "Can Public Transit and Ride-Share Companies Get Along?," is adapted from the article of the same name published by The Conversation. 22 September 2016, The Conversation online. https://theconversation.com/can-public-transit-and-ride-share-companies-get-along-64269. Accessed 7 January 2019.

- Passage 5 on Pages 199-200, "The Nose Knows: Oriental Honey Buzzards Use Nose and Eyes to Forage for Sweet Treats," is adapted from the article of the same name published by EveryOne, the PLOS One community blog. 11 September 2016, PLOS One. https://blogs.plos.org/everyone/2015/09/11/the-nose-knows-oriental-honey-buzzards-use-nose-and-eyes-to-forage-for-sweet-treats/. Accessed 7 January 2019.

Test 2

Reading Test

65 MINUTES, 52 QUESTIONS

Turn to Section 1 of your answer sheet to answer the questions in this section.

Questions 1-10 are based on the following passage.

This passage is an excerpt from "A Death in the Desert" (1903) by Willa Cather.

Everett Hilgarde was conscious that the man in the seat across the aisle was looking at him intently. He was a large, florid man, wore
Line a conspicuous diamond solitaire upon his third
5 finger, and Everett judged him to be a traveling salesman of some sort. He had the air of an adaptable fellow who had been about the world and who could keep cool and clean under almost any circumstances.
10 The "High Line Flyer," as this train was derisively called among railroad men, was jerking along through the hot afternoon over the monotonous country between Holdridge and Cheyenne. Besides the blond man and himself
15 the only occupants of the car were two dusty, bedraggled-looking girls who had been to the Exposition at Chicago, and who were earnestly discussing the cost of their first trip out of Colorado. The four uncomfortable passengers
20 were covered with a sediment of fine, yellow dust which clung to their hair and eyebrows like gold powder. It blew up in clouds from the bleak, lifeless country through which they passed, until they were one color with the sagebrush and
25 sandhills. The gray-and-yellow desert was varied only by occasional ruins of deserted towns, and the little red boxes of station houses, where the spindling trees and sickly vines in the bluegrass yards made little green reserves fenced off in that
30 confusing wilderness of sand. . . .
The blonde gentleman had seemed interested in Everett since they had boarded the train at Holdridge, and kept glancing at him curiously and then looking reflectively out of the window,
35 as though he were trying to recall something. But wherever Everett went someone was almost sure to look at him with that curious interest, and it had ceased to embarrass or annoy him. Presently the stranger, seeming satisfied with his observation,
40 leaned back in his seat, half-closed his eyes, and began softly to whistle the "Spring Song" from *Proserpine*, the cantata that a dozen years before had made its young composer famous in a night. Everett had heard that air on guitars in Old
45 Mexico, on mandolins at college glees, on cottage organs in New England hamlets, and only two

CONTINUE ➡

weeks ago he had heard it played on sleighbells at a variety theater in Denver. There was literally no way of escaping his brother's precocity. Adriance
50 could live on the other side of the Atlantic, where his youthful indiscretions were forgotten in his mature achievements, but his brother had never been able to outrun *Proserpine*, and here he found it again in the Colorado sand hills. Not that
55 Everett was exactly ashamed of *Proserpine*; only a man of genius could have written it, but it was the sort of thing that a man of genius outgrows as soon as he can.

Everett unbent a trifle and smiled at his
60 neighbor across the aisle. Immediately the large man rose and, coming over, dropped into the seat facing Hilgarde, extending his card.

"Dusty ride, isn't it? I don't mind it myself; I'm used to it. . . I've been trying to place you for
65 a long time; I think I must have met you before."

"Thank you," said Everett, taking the card; "my name is Hilgarde. You've probably met my brother, Adriance; people often mistake me for him."

70 The traveling man brought his hand down upon his knee with such vehemence that the solitaire blazed.

"So I was right after all, and if you're not Adriance Hilgarde, you're his double. I thought I
75 couldn't be mistaken. Seen him? Well, I guess! I never missed one of his recitals at the Auditorium, and he played the piano score of *Proserpine* through to us once at the Chicago Press Club. I used to be on the Commercial there before I began
80 to travel for the publishing department of the concern. So you're Hilgarde's brother, and here I've run into you at the jumping-off place. Sounds like a newspaper yarn, doesn't it?"

The traveling man laughed and offered Everett
85 a cigar, and plied him with questions on the only subject that people ever seemed to care to talk to Everett about.

1

The main purpose of the passage is to demonstrate

A) how one character's pessimistic outlook can be explained by another character's success.

B) how one character uses conversation to distract himself from unpleasant events.

C) how two characters strike up a friendship despite apparent differences of opinion.

D) how two characters react to one another in the course of a chance encounter.

2

Which choice best describes a technique that the narrator uses to develop Everett as a character?

A) Illustrating Everett's attitude towards both *Proserpine* and his brother by presenting a few of Everett's thoughts and memories

B) Implying that Everett is eager for change by contrasting details from Everett's past and present

C) Hinting at Everett's motives by creating a parallel between Everett's distance from his brother and Everett's misunderstanding of *Proserpine*

D) Defining Everett's background by contrasting Everett's comments and gestures with those of the traveling man

3

In context, the name of the train on which Everett is a passenger is best understood as

A) unlucky.

B) ironic.

C) endearing.

D) puzzling.

4

The description that appears in lines 25-30 ("The gray-and-yellow . . . sand") serves mainly to

A) complement Everett's state of personal discontent.

B) suggest that Everett's destination will be remote and unpleasant.

C) introduce a culture that is unfamiliar to the major characters.

D) expand upon a previous characterization of a landscape.

5

Which choice does NOT effectively indicate that the meeting described in the passage resembles earlier meetings in Everett's life?

A) Lines 35-38 ("But . . . him")

B) Lines 59-62 ("Everett . . . card")

C) Lines 66-68 ("Thank you . . . him")

D) Lines 84-87 ("The traveling . . . about")

6

On the basis of the passage, Everett would mostly likely agree that *Proserpine* is

A) likely to increase in popularity despite its stylistic flaws.

B) a manifestation of his brother's talent as a composer.

C) a reflection of his brother's difficult yet intriguing personality.

D) consistently pleasing regardless of the style in which it is played.

7

Which choice provides the best evidence for the answer to the previous question?

A) Lines 44-48 ("Everett . . . Denver")

B) Lines 49-52 ("Adriance . . . achievements")

C) Lines 52-54 ("his brother . . . hills")

D) Lines 54-58 ("Not that . . . can")

8

Upon learning that he has mistaken Everett for Adriance, the traveling man reacts by

A) treating Everett in the same admiring manner in which he would have treated Adriance.

B) asking Everett to attempt to contact Adriance.

C) acknowledging his error but conveying his delight in meeting Everett.

D) analyzing *Proserpine* in a manner that is meant to appeal to Everett.

9

As used in line 71, "vehemence" most nearly means

A) unbounded passion.

B) unwavering devotion.

C) persuasive tact.

D) physical force.

10

As used in line 81, "concern" most nearly means

A) coverage.

B) circumstance.

C) corporation.

D) calling.

CONTINUE

Questions 11-21 are based on the following passages.

Passage 1 is adapted from Emma Goldman, "Marriage and Love" (1911). Passage 2 is adapted from Ida Tarbell, *The Business of Being a Woman* (1921).

Passage 1

The woman considers her position as worker transitory, to be thrown aside for the first bidder. That is why it is infinitely harder to organize
Line women than men. "Why should I join a union?
5 I am going to get married, to have a home." Has she not been taught from infancy to look upon that as her ultimate calling? She learns soon enough that the home, though not so large a prison as the factory, has more solid doors and bars. It has
10 a keeper so faithful that naught can escape him. The most tragic part, however, is that the home no longer frees her from wage slavery; it only increases her task.

According to the latest statistics submitted
15 before a Committee "on labor and wages, and congestion of population," ten per cent. of the wage workers in New York City alone are married, yet they must continue to work at the most poorly paid labor in the world. Add to this
20 horrible aspect the drudgery of housework, and what remains of the protection and glory of the home? As a matter of fact, even the middle-class girl in marriage can not speak of her home, since it is the man who creates her sphere. It is
25 not important whether the husband is a brute or a darling. What I wish to prove is that marriage guarantees woman a home only by the grace of her husband. There she moves about in HIS home, year after year, until her aspect of life and human
30 affairs becomes as flat, narrow, and drab as her surroundings. Small wonder if she becomes a nag, petty, quarrelsome, gossipy, unbearable, thus driving the man from the house. She could not go, if she wanted to; there is no place to go. Besides, a
35 short period of married life, of complete surrender

of all faculties, absolutely incapacitates the average woman for the outside world.

Passage 2

Every night they draw to their shelter millions of men who have toiled since morning to earn
40 the money to build and keep them running. All day they shelter millions of women who toil from dawn to dark to put meaning into them. To shelter two people and the children that come to them, to provide them a place in which to eat and sleep, is
45 that the only function of these homes? If that were all, few homes would be built. When that becomes all, the home is no more! To furnish a body for a soul, that is the physical function of the home.

There are certain people who cry out that for a
50 woman this undertaking has no meaning—that for her it is a cook stove and a dustpan, a childbed, and a man who regards her as his servant. One might with equal justice say that for the man it is made up of ten, twelve, or more hours, at
55 the plow, the engine, the counter, or the pen for the sake of supporting a woman and children whom he rarely sees! Unhappily, there are such combinations; they are not homes! They are deplorable failures of people who have tried to
60 make homes. To insist that they are anything else is to overlook the facts of life, to doubt the sanity of mankind which hopefully and courageously goes on building, building, building, sacrificing, binding itself forever and ever to what?—a shell?
65 No, to the institution which its observation and experience tell it is the one out of which men and women have gotten the most hope, dignity, and joy—the place through which, whatever its failures and illusions, they get the fullest
70 development and the opportunity to render the most useful social service.

It is this grounded conviction that the home takes first rank among social institutions which gives its tremendous seriousness to the Business
75 of Being a Woman. She is the one who must sit always at its center, the one who holds a strategic position for dealing directly with its problems.

CONTINUE

Far from these problems being purely of a menial nature, as some would have us believe, they are
80 of the most delicate social and spiritual import. A woman in reality is at the head of a social laboratory where all the problems are of primary, not secondary, importance, since they all deal directly with human life.

11

In Passage 1, Goldman argues that men

A) refuse to acknowledge the negative repercussions of social expectations for women.

B) suppress women's natural inquisitiveness in a gradual and methodical manner.

C) dominate domestic life in a manner that undermines women's independence.

D) are unappreciative of women regardless of women's personal attributes.

12

Which choice provides the best evidence for the answer to the previous question?

A) Lines 5-7 ("Has . . . calling?")

B) Lines 19-20 ("Add . . . home?")

C) Lines 28-31 ("There . . . surroundings")

D) Lines 34-37 ("Besides . . . world")

13

As used in line 33, "driving" most nearly means

A) repelling.

B) manipulating.

C) relaying.

D) motivating.

14

As used in lines 45 and 48, "function" most nearly means

A) event.

B) recreation.

C) structure.

D) purpose.

15

The main effect of Tarbell's exclamation in lines 57-58 is to

A) lament a reality that afflicts most women of Tarbell's era.

B) respond to ideas about social reform that Tarbell finds inadvisable.

C) emphasize a shortcoming that is a central topic of Tarbell's analysis.

D) address an apparent weakness of Tarbell's method of explanation.

CONTINUE

16

The final paragraph of Passage 2 provides

A) an exhortation to women to take more active and innovative roles within the home.

B) a broad and admiring overview of women's responsibilities within the home.

C) a synopsis of various ideas about the qualities that distinguish women from men.

D) a description of a specific household that provides a model of effective conduct.

17

Which of the following ideas is present in both passages?

A) Participation in the workforce can have dispiriting effects.

B) Home life should be based on reasonable compromises.

C) Women should be cautious about pursuing social and political reform.

D) Men take little interest in the home-oriented activities of women.

18

One important purpose of each passage is to

A) offer historical commentary on the deteriorating social status of women.

B) describe how women can seek moral improvement despite their disadvantages.

C) explain why few precedents exist for the current situation of women.

D) assess whether women's participation in domestic life is fulfilling and meaningful.

19

Goldman in Passage 1 would argue that the "man" described in line 52 is

A) an intentional caricature that is meant to provoke discussion.

B) a figure of authority who has over-estimated the extent of his power.

C) a symbol of a lifestyle that is quickly vanishing.

D) an accurate embodiment of broad tendencies.

20

Tarbell in Passage 2 would respond to Goldman's central claims in Passage 1 by

A) arguing that Goldman has misinterpreted necessary stages in women's progress as periods of oppression.

B) rejecting Goldman's stance as wrongheaded in its depiction of women as subordinate within their own households.

C) pointing out that Goldman has underestimated the economic importance of home life by focusing mainly on moral failings.

D) expressing doubt about Goldman's contention that men and women both seem resigned to their traditional roles.

21

Which choice provides the best evidence for the answer to the previous question?

A) Lines 45-47 ("If that . . . more!")

B) Lines 58-60 ("They . . . homes")

C) Lines 60-64 ("To insist . . . shell?")

D) Lines 75-77 ("She . . . problems")

CONTINUE

Questions 22-32 are based on the following passage and supplementary material.

This passage is adapted from "Florida's Coral Reefs Provide Window into the Past," an article released* in 2018 by the United States Geological Survey (USGS).

The Florida Keys coral reefs stopped growing or significantly slowed their growth at least 3000 years ago and have been balanced between
Line
5 persistence and erosion ever since, according to a new study by the U.S. Geological Survey. The study, published in the journal Global Change Biology, also points to coral bleaching and disease outbreaks as signs that changing conditions may
10 have recently tipped the 200-mile-long coral reef tract into a state of erosion.

USGS marine scientists based in St. Petersburg, Florida analyzed 46 coral reef cores collected throughout the Keys, reconstructing the reefs' growth from 8000 years ago, when layers
15 of living coral began building up on top of older bedrock, to the present day. Throughout that time, long-lasting climate cycles and associated changes in ocean temperatures have been the most important factors controlling the growth of
20 Florida's reefs, the scientists found. A shift toward cooler water temperatures effectively ended the reefs' development long before the visible declines in coral health and coral cover of the past few decades, they reported.

25 "If you were to test a sample from the top layer of a typical Florida reef, you would most likely find that it's between 3000 and 6000 years old," said Lauren Toth, a USGS research oceanographer and the study's lead author. "Florida's reefs still
30 had living corals after that time, they just weren't building much new reef structure."

The researchers examined reef core samples collected between 1976 and 2017 from Biscayne National Park in Miami-Dade County to Dry
35 Tortugas National Park 70 miles from Key West. The scientists used radiocarbon dating—a standard technique for finding the ages of corals

and other materials—and measured the amount the reef grew between the dates they had identified
40 to create the first comprehensive reconstruction of coral reef growth along the entire Florida reef tract.

Modern coral reefs started growing off the Florida peninsula more than 8000 years ago.
45 Their most rapid growth rate, almost 10 feet every thousand years, peaked about 7000 years ago, when water temperatures were ideal for coral growth, the USGS researchers found. About 6000 years ago, the reefs' growth rate slowed to about 3
50 feet per thousand years.

Corals can be killed by water that is hotter or colder than the narrow band of temperatures in which most species grow best, between about 65 and 85 degrees Fahrenheit. Most reefs are found
55 in the tropics, but the Florida Keys reef tract is unique because it lies in subtropical waters.

About 5000 years ago, a natural cooling cycle made the seas off Florida prone to winter cold snaps. In the colder conditions of the past few
60 thousand years, the reefs became "geologically senescent," meaning that reef growth was negligible and just a veneer of living coral remained, the study found. More than one-third of the reefs have not grown at all in the past 3000
65 years, and the rest have not kept up with rising sea level.

Other factors, such as influxes of estuarine water from shallow Florida Bay, also stressed the Keys reefs, the researchers found. But they were
70 likely not as important as the corals' repeated exposure to cold water in winter.

Even after the Keys reefs stopped growing upward, they supported diverse communities of marine life, protected the island chain from storm
75 waves and erosion, and provided other ecosystem functions for thousands of years. But in the last few decades, warmer water, coral diseases, bleaching and other stresses caused the reefs to begin eroding, the researchers said.

80 "For 3000 years, Florida's reefs have been balanced at a delicate tipping point. Although reefs were no longer growing, there was enough living coral to prevent them from eroding," Toth

*See Page 247 for the citation for this text.

CONTINUE

said. "But with the dramatic declines in living
85 coral in Florida and around the world in recent
decades, we may now be on the verge of losing
reef structures that took thousands of years to
build."

22

Throughout the passage, the author takes the
position of

A) an amateur researcher who intends to contribute
to future projects.

B) an unbiased reporter who possesses specialized
information.

C) an outspoken critic who is unsettled by an
ecological crisis.

D) a thoughtful spectator who hopes to find the
solution to a crisis.

23

The study described in the passage supports the idea
that ocean water temperature changes

A) are difficult to relate to the Earth's climate cycles
in a predictable manner.

B) are one of several important factors that can cause
coral reefs to decrease in size.

C) can compensate for various ways in which human
activity has harmed coral reefs.

D) have become less severe in the past 3000 years.

24

Which choice provides the best evidence for the
answer to the previous question?

A) Lines 1-5 ("The Florida Keys . . . Survey")

B) Lines 16-20 ("Throughout . . . found")

C) Lines 59-63 ("In the colder . . . found")

D) Lines 76-79 ("But . . . eroding")

Statistics: Florida Keys Coral Reef Ecosystem

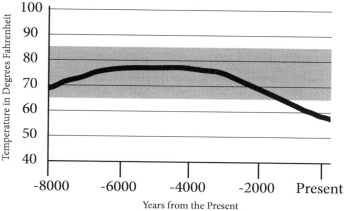

Average Water Temperature Over Time

NOTE: The thick black line represents the average yearly water temperature of the reef ecosystem, while the gray shaded region represents the ideal temperature range for coral reef growth.

Years from Present	Growth Rate (feet per thousand years)
-9000	N/A
-8000	2
-7000	10
-6000	7
-5000	4
-4000	3
-3000	3
-2000	3
-1000	1
0	0

CONTINUE

25

As used in line 7, "points to" most nearly means

A) hints at.

B) singles out.

C) accuses.

D) stigmatizes.

26

Which of the following coral specimens would NOT be present in the reefs of the Florida Keys according to the passage?

A) A 4000 year-old coral specimen that was killed when water temperatures dipped to 60 degrees

B) A 5000 year-old specimen attached to the top layer of the coral reef

C) A 6000 year-old coral specimen that was found at the outer edge of a reef formation

D) A 9000 year-old coral specimen that is directly attached to bedrock

27

Which choice provides the best evidence for the answer to the previous question?

A) Lines 11-16 ("USGS . . . present day")

B) Lines 25-28 ("If . . . Lauren Toth")

C) Lines 29-31 ("Florida's . . . structure")

D) Lines 51-55 ("Corals . . . Fahrenheit")

28

As used in line 46, "peaked" most nearly means

A) reached a maximum.

B) became excessive.

C) was most impressive.

D) defied comparison.

29

The author includes information about conditions "after the Keys reefs stopped growing" (line 72) in order to

A) urge further inquiries that respond to the recent research findings about the role of cold water in reef deterioration.

B) suggest that temperature changes have not prevented the reefs from serving important functions.

C) express optimism that new preservation measures will enable the reef ecosystem to remain robust.

D) argue that a few of the apparent threats to the reefs have been explained on the basis of faulty data.

CONTINUE

30

Together, the graph and the table indicate that

A) the coral reef formation in the Florida Keys reached its largest size 6000 years ago.

B) the erosion of the Florida Keys coral reefs began roughly 3000 years ago.

C) coral reef growth rates can decline even when average temperature remains constant.

D) increases in average water temperature cause consistent increases in coral reef growth rates.

31

On the basis of the passage and the graph, the ideal temperature (in degrees Fahrenheit) for coral growth in the Florida Keys is approximately

A) 65 degrees.

B) 75 degrees.

C) 80 degrees.

D) 85 degrees.

32

Which additional visual, if considered alongside the graph and the table, would be most useful in evaluating Lauren Toth's claims in the final paragraph of the passage?

A) A table indicating the total size of the Florida Keys reef ecosystem in square footage for every thousand years

B) A table recording the rate of reef erosion as measured in feet per thousand years

C) A graph that directly compares growth rate in feet per thousand years to temperature

D) A graph that indicates the mass over time of dead coral in the Florida Keys

CONTINUE

Questions 33-42 are based on the following passage and supplementary material.

This passage is adapted from "Optimism, But Obstacles Abound for the Future of Malaria Control" by Lorenz von Seidlein. Originally published* in Speaking of Medicine, the PLOS medical blog.

On World Malaria Day 2018, there are many things to be hopeful for. The Multilateral Initiative on Malaria hosted the 7th Pan African Malaria
Line conference from April 15th to 20th in Dakar,
5 Senegal, where several drug producers presented information on new anti-malarial candidates. Notably, the Novartis Institute discussed the drug candidates KAF 156 and KAE 609, which could be licensed in the coming years. . . Meanwhile
10 at the Malaria Summit in London, Bill Gates with a number of governments, international organizations, and members of civil society and the private sector pledged investments worth a collective $4 billion in the continued fight against
15 malaria. . .
The future may look bright but the current situation is complex. The 2017 WHO World Malaria Report (WMR) indicated for the first time after many years of steady decreases an increase
20 in the global number of malaria cases from 211 million in 2015 to 216 million in 2016. The report is hampered by the fact that the WHO once more changed its reporting methodology for the 2017 report without giving a clear explanation why
25 and how this was done. As a result the number of cases for previous years has been once more revised in the 2017 report. (Case burden estimates for 2010 have been revised seven times in as many years!) The inconsistency of
30 reporting methodology makes the trends difficult to interpret and adds doubt to the reliability of the findings. The undeniably heterogeneous malaria burden across countries in sub Saharan Africa further complicates the situation. Twenty years
35 ago The Gambia routinely reported a P. falciparum infection prevalence of around 40% at the peak

of the rainy season. Five sub-Saharan countries, including The Gambia, have seen a significant decrease in malaria prevalence, dropping to as low
40 as 0.1% in The Gambia during the 2017 season, whereas 24 high-burden countries saw increases in malaria. Considering the available evidence, it would probably be safer to suggest that trends in malaria burden are mixed.
45 The technologies presented in Dakar and London hold promise, but relying on the potential of new technologies has led to disappointment in the past, as the dashed hope in an ideal malaria vaccine illustrated. The effectiveness
50 of these newer technologies remains unproven; meanwhile, insecticide and antimalarial resistance continue to emerge and spread. . .
Among the few points on which malaria experts working in Africa and Asia can agree
55 is that access to bednets, early diagnosis, and appropriate treatment remain the basic control measures. Uninterrupted, universal access to such basic control measures will over time suppress the transmission of malaria. Supplying every
60 household in malaria endemic regions with access to basic control measures should be a common cause around which all parties can rally. But providing such access to the 3.4 billion people globally at risk for malaria will cost more than
65 even Bill Gates can afford. Only a concerted effort by heads of states of affected malaria-endemic countries as well as high-income countries can address such a challenge.
Meanwhile in the many conflict zones access
70 to basic control measures remains sporadic or permanently absent. In the centre of Africa, Niger, Chad, Central African Republic, and eastern Congo even the most basic reporting of the malaria cases and deaths is unreliable or
75 completely absent. This is a situation which was not discussed, has not been addressed, and will become worse as militarization of these conflict zones increases. Policymakers and intervention forces would be well advised to adopt quickly
80 some of the lessons learned in The Gambia in conflict regions currently neglected by the international malaria programmes.

CONTINUE

There are a number of threats to malaria control, not to mention elimination, including drug
85 and insecticide resistance, disruption of sustained funding, and armed conflicts. But there is also reason for optimism as new antimalarial drugs and vector control technologies could become available. There is a hope that policymakers
90 and the international funders appreciate and can replicate the success in malaria control achieved in a few select countries, like The Gambia.

33

Over the course of the first two paragraphs, the author's focus shifts from

A) praising a long-term solution to suggesting that this approach has unfortunate short-term liabilities.

B) presenting demographic statistics to questioning whether the data in question have been interpreted correctly.

C) citing key figures and organizations in an approving manner to urging them to take greater responsibility.

D) surveying the extent of an endeavor to assessing procedures for documentation.

34

Which choice indicates that the author of the passage is convinced that previous attempts to combat malaria have been deficient?

A) Lines 21-24 ("The report . . . done")

B) Lines 29-32 ("The inconsistency . . . findings")

C) Lines 45-49 ("The technologies . . . illustrated")

D) Lines 57-59 ("Uninterrupted . . . malaria")

35

The primary effect of the parenthetical statement in lines 27-29 is to

A) call attention to one of the central failings of current fundraising practices.

B) present an earlier finding in a more accessible manner.

C) broaden one of the author's critiques to consider a longer period of time.

D) paraphrase a new perspective on a health crisis.

36

Which additional piece of evidence would support the author's argument about malaria trends in sub Saharan Africa for 2017?

A) The number of malaria-related deaths in The Gambia represents a public health crisis to some observers.

B) The Gambia worked with other countries in the region to reduce malaria-related deaths by almost 170,000 from the 2016 figure.

C) Malaria prevalence has risen from under 3% to over 7% in at least half of the countries in this region.

D) Malaria rates in The Gambia were initially projected to mirror those in nations where malaria is most prevalent.

37

As used in lines 58 and 61, "basic" most nearly means

A) indispensable.

B) rough-hewn.

C) natural.

D) formative.

CONTINUE

Test 2

Investment in Efforts to Combat Malaria

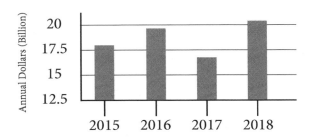

Cases of Malaria Worldwide

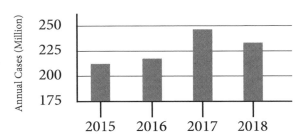

38

As used in line 58, "suppress" most nearly means

A) conceal.

B) inhibit.

C) burden.

D) placate.

39

Within the passage, the author characterizes The Gambia as a nation that

A) has recently resolved a difficult political crisis.

B) experiences severe malaria outbreaks as a result of unique climate and weather conditions.

C) recently improved its official methods for documenting malaria cases.

D) provides a model of malaria prevention that should be imitated by other African countries.

40

Which choice provides the best evidence for the answer to the previous question?

A) Lines 34-37 ("Twenty . . . season")

B) Lines 37-42 ("Five . . . malaria")

C) Lines 71-75 ("In the . . . absent")

D) Lines 78-82 ("Policymakers . . . programmes")

41

On the basis of the two graphs, it can be inferred that increased annual investment in efforts to combat malaria

A) does not correlate to lower numbers of malaria cases worldwide.

B) is a typical response to a worldwide malaria outbreak.

C) has little ability to decrease the number of malaria cases worldwide.

D) is most effective in short-term control of malaria outbreaks.

42

Which of the following statements about Bill Gates best reflects the information provided in the passage and the graphs?

A) His investments have inspired smaller contributions to the campaign against malaria.

B) His contributions to the worldwide campaign against malaria represent a fraction of the total funds dedicated to this cause.

C) His 2018 contribution to the fight against malaria represents the culmination of a long-term initiative.

D) His most recent investment in the campaign against malaria has not been allocated in the most effective manner possible.

CONTINUE

Questions 43-52 are based on the following passage.

This passage is adapted from Amanda Griffin, "Tupperware Takes to Space to Help Improve Astronaut Diets," a 2018 news release* from nasa.gov.

For decades, airtight plastic containers have been synonymous with keeping baked goods and leftovers fresh. Now a manufacturer of iconic,
Line household plasticware is helping provide fresh
5 food in space.

As NASA plans for future missions to deep space destinations, the nutritional boost of fresh food and the psychological benefits of growing plants become more and more paramount. Since
10 2015, NASA astronauts have supplemented their space diet with fresh greens grown in the Vegetable Production System known as "Veggie" on the International Space Station.

One of the challenges with growing plants in
15 space in Veggie has been keeping them properly watered. The Tupperware Brands Corporation has lent its design expertise to help develop a new approach to watering plants in space.

With the Veggie system, astronauts have to
20 push water into each plant pillow with a syringe. In previous crops grown in the Veggie system using pillows, some plants fared better than others because not all the plants received equal amounts of water and oxygen.
25 "The primary goal of this newly developed plant growing system, the Passive Orbital Nutrient Delivery System, or PONDS, is to achieve uniform plant growth," said Nicole Dufour, Veggie project manager at NASA's Kennedy
30 Space Center in Florida.

NASA research scientist Howard Levine initially designed and prototyped PONDS but in early 2017 handed it off to Techshot, a private spaceflight services firm, to further develop and
35 certify the demonstration unit for use on the orbiting laboratory. In turn, Techshot reached out to Tupperware to help create the new system that would provide an alternative to the plant pillows.

"PONDS units have features that are designed
40 to mitigate microgravity effects on water distribution, increase oxygen availability and provide sufficient room for root zone growth," Dufour explained.

The new PONDS system requires less crew
45 maintenance and uses absorbent mats that leverage the basic principles of surface tension and capillary action to send water to seeds and roots through a reservoir system. This approach passively disperses water evenly through each
50 plant cylinder contained within the PONDS reservoirs, facilitating consistent seed germination and seedling development into mature plants.

"It's been great working closely with the talented teams of engineers, designers and
55 scientists at NASA and Tupperware on the project," said Dave Reed, Techshot's PONDS project manager and the company's director of launch operations. "Tupperware brings a wealth of innovative design and knowledge of plastics to
60 this project."

The upcoming SpaceX CRS-14 commercial resupply mission will include seven PONDS modules plus an adapter plate so the modules can be installed in the Veggie system. Included
65 are four black opaque modules that will grow Outredgeous red romaine lettuce—the same lettuce that has been grown previously in the Veggie facility—for about a month. Two shrouded modules each include a clear window and
70 removable cover that allow astronauts to directly observe root growth of the same romaine lettuce plus assess water distribution in the hydroponic reservoir. One clear module will be used to perform testing and videography to characterize
75 the microgravity hydrodynamics of the reservoir.

Six more PONDS modules are slated to launch on an Orbital ATK commercial resupply mission later this year and will be seeded with Mizuna mustard. Both the lettuce and the mustard have
80 already been grown in plant pillows as a part of previous Veggie experiments, so the plant pillow and PONDS growth data will be compared against one another.

*See Page 247 for the citation for this text.

CONTINUE

43

The main purpose of the passage is to

A) describe a nutritional project that represents a decisive improvement.

B) relate the need for new technologies to the emergence of new space missions.

C) explain how a single project promotes a method of cooperation across industries.

D) praise the foresight of researchers who re-purposed everyday items.

44

According to the passage, which statement best describes the problem that the PONDS system was designed to solve?

A) Resources were being dispersed to plants in such a manner that the growth of the plants was not regularized.

B) Arrangements based on the pillow apparatus weakened some plants by causing growing areas to flood.

C) Only plant species that could grow on Earth in conditions of water and oxygen deprivation could be cultivated in space.

D) Microgravity conditions would cause plants that were meant to be kept separate to compete for resources.

45

Which choice provides the best evidence for the answer to the previous question?

A) Lines 19-20 ("With . . . syringe")

B) Lines 21-24 ("In previous . . . oxygen")

C) Lines 36-38 ("In turn . . . pillows")

D) Lines 44-48 ("The new . . . system")

46

Which statement from the passage most effectively supports the claims that the author presents in lines 9-13 ("Since . . . Space Station")?

A) Lines 16-18 ("The Tupperware . . . space")

B) Lines 39-43 ("Ponds . . . explained")

C) Lines 61-64 ("The upcoming . . . system")

D) Lines 64-68 ("Included . . . month")

47

The author of the passage explains that one important feature of the "Veggie" system is

A) module design that intentionally causes plants of different types to grow at different rates.

B) an apparatus that can filter oxygen from other gases when deployed in outer space.

C) manual involvement on the part of the astronauts who will consume the resulting produce.

D) reliance on technologies that were initially developed for household use on Earth.

48

As used in line 33, "handed it off to" most nearly means

A) forced it towards.

B) delegated responsibility to.

C) left it available to.

D) renounced any involvement with.

CONTINUE

49

As used in line 49, "evenly" most nearly means

A) uniformly.

B) calmly.

C) effortlessly.

D) fairly.

50

One advantage of the PONDS system, relative to earlier methods of growing plants in space, is that

A) it is more cost efficient than earlier methods for growing plants in the absence of gravity.

B) it can be operated without any preliminary training on the part of astronauts.

C) it can facilitate robust plant growth in a manner that requires less human supervision.

D) it can grow a more impressive variety of large plants than could be grown under the Veggie system.

51

It can be inferred from Dave Reed's comments in the passage that Reed regards Tupperware's specialists as

A) respected competitors.

B) under-appreciated visionaries.

C) helpful subordinates.

D) insightful collaborators.

52

The final paragraph of the passage functions to

A) underscore a liability of the Veggie system.

B) anticipate a way in which PONDS will build upon earlier growing projects.

C) justify a change in the recommended astronaut diet.

D) signal a future point of collaboration between NASA and Tupperware product engineers.

STOP
If you finish before time is called, you may check your work on this section only.
Do not turn to any other section.

Answer Key: Test 2

Passage 1	Passage 2	Passage 3	Passage 4	Passage 5
1. D	11. C	22. B	33. D	43. A
2. A	12. C	23. B	34. C	44. A
3. B	13. A	24. D	35. C	45. B
4. D	14. D	25. B	36. C	46. D
5. B	15. C	26. D	37. A	47. C
6. B	16. B	27. A	38. B	48. B
7. D	17. A	28. A	39. D	49. A
8. C	18. D	29. B	40. D	50. C
9. D	19. D	30. C	41. A	51. D
10. C	20. B	31. B	42. B	52. B
	21. D	32. B		

Question Types

Major Issue
1-2, 22, 43

Passage Details
3-4, 8, 15-16, 29, 33, 35-36, 47, 50-52

Command of Evidence
5-7, 11-12, 23-24, 26-27, 34, 39-40, 44-46

Word in Context
9-10, 13-14, 25, 28, 37-38, 48-49

Graphics and Visuals
30-32, 41-42

Passage Comparison
17-21

Self-Evaluation
Checklist for Test 2

Passage Types

- Hardest Readings _____ ; _____
- Easiest Readings _____ ; _____

Sources of Difficulty
(Check all that apply.)

_____ Comprehending Main Idea (Passages ___, ___, ___)

_____ Remembering Passage Details (Passages ___, ___, ___)

_____ Working with Style and Vocabulary (Passages ___, ___, ___)

Question Types

- Major Issue: Incorrect _____   Tossup _____   Challenges: _____
- Passage Details: Incorrect _____   Tossup _____   Challenges: _____
- CoE: Incorrect _____   Tossup _____   Challenges: _____
- Word in Context: Incorrect _____   Tossup _____   Challenges: _____

Sources of Difficulty
(Check all that apply.)

_____ Understanding the Question   _____ Locating or Analyzing Evidence

_____ Predicting the Answers   _____ Eliminating False Answers

Vocabulary

- New Words: _____
- Total Questions with Advanced Vocabulary _____   Number Right _____   Number Wrong _____

Overall Strategy

- Time Per Passage (Estimate): 1 _____   2 _____   3 _____   4 _____   5 _____
- Total Time for the Test _____   Time Left Over _____   OR Time Needed Beyond 65 Minutes _____
- Passages with Note-Taking _____   Questions Right for These _____   Questions Wrong for These _____
- Passages with NO Notes _____   Questions Right for These _____   Questions Wrong for These _____

Sources of Difficulty
(Check all that apply.)

_____ Slow Reading or Rereading   _____ Complicated or Time-Consuming Notes

_____ Inaccurate Annotations   _____ Rushed Through Passages or Questions

Answer Explanations
Test 2, Pages 218-233

Passage 1, Pages 218-220

1. D is the correct answer.

The passage focuses on two men meeting one another by chance while sitting on the same train, and the way in which they respond to one another. Choose D, and be careful not to choose C, since it is NOT clear that the two men strike up a friendship, only that they end up speaking to one another. A and B can both be dismissed since there is no evidence that one character has a pessimistic outlook, or that unpleasant events have recently occurred; the fact that Everett is somewhat overshadowed by his brother should not be mistaken for these much stronger negatives.

2. A is the correct answer.

The passage describes some of Everett's memories by noting that "Everett had heard that air on guitars in Old Mexico, on mandolins at college glees, on cottage organs in New England hamlets" (lines 44-46). The narration also includes Everett's reflections, such as when he thinks to himself that "it was the sort of thing that a man of genius outgrows as soon as he can" (lines 57-58). This content hints at Everett's attitude towards the symphony and towards his brother; choose A. Be careful not to choose D, since Everett's background is NOT clearly established in the passage beyond his familial connection to his brother; B can also be eliminated, since not enough information is given for a reader to be able to contrast Everett's past and present. C wrongly indicates that Everett misunderstands *Proserpine*, when in fact he has analyzed the composition and seems to grasp its significance in his brother's career.

3. B is the correct answer.

The train on which Everett travels is known as the High-Line Flyer, which implies energy and dynamism. Instead, the train only has a few passengers and seems to move quite slowly through unexciting locales. In this context, the name of the train can best be understood as ironic; choose answer B. The train does in fact function without inviting disaster (eliminating A) and yet does not inspire affection in any clear way (eliminating C). D can be eliminated because the passage DOES indicate the unusual significance of the train's name rather than attaching a sense of bewilderment or mystery to the train.

4. D is the correct answer.

The landscape the train is passing through is initially described as "bleak, lifeless country" and then the more detailed description in lines 25-30 expands on this impression in a manner that justifies D. It is NOT clear whether or not the landscape is familiar to the travelers, despite the detailed manner in which the landscape is described, so that C can be eliminated. A and B can both be ruled out since it is NOT evident that Everett (who mostly reflects on his brother in an analytic manner) is in a state of discomfort, or what his destination will be like.

5. B is the correct answer.

A focuses on how the man treats Everett in a way that Everett has become accustomed to, while C shows that Everett knows that he is being mistaken for his brother. D describes how, once they begin speaking, the man behaves in a way that Everett has experienced before. B describes how the unknown man responds to Everett's overture of friendliness by introducing himself, which does NOT indicate that this encounter is similar to others that Everett has had before; thus, choose B and dismiss the others.

6. B is the correct answer.

Everett reflects that he was not "exactly ashamed of *Proserpine*; only a man of genius could have written it, but it was the sort of thing that a man of genius outgrows as soon as he can" (lines 55-58); this content suggests that, while Everett has some misgivings, he believes that the symphony is a reflection of his brother's talent. Choose B and be careful not to choose D, since while Everett reflects that he has heard the symphony performed in many different styles, it does NOT follow that he thinks that all of these styles are pleasing. A (which offers a prediction about the future popularity of *Proserpine*) and C (which offers a developed statement about Adriance, who is described mostly in passing) can both be eliminated since they rely on speculation outside of the scope of the passage, which mainly depicts a single scene of interaction.

7. D is the correct answer.

See the previous answer explanation for analysis of the correct line reference. A describes a variety of styles and the different locations where Everett has heard the music performed; B describes how Adriance's career has progressed. C shows how Everett constantly encounters the music, even in unexpected places. None of these other answers reflect Everett's view of his brother's talent, and all should be dismissed.

8. C is the correct answer.

When he learns that he has mistaken Everett for his brother, the traveling man is still very pleased to encounter someone who is associated with a musician whom he admires, as indicated in the final two paragraphs of the passage. Choose C to support this content. Be careful not to choose A, since while the traveling man is still happy to meet Everett, he does NOT respond to him the same way he would have responded to Adriance. B (which mistakes the man's appreciation for Adriance for a more active and involved stance) and D (which mistakes the man's generally positive reaction to *Proserpine* for a more specific desire to appeal to Everett) are both illogical within the scope of the passage.

9. D is the correct answer.

In line 71, "vehemence" refers to the physical force with which the man strikes his hand against his leg; choose D to support this content. A ("unbounded") overstates the strength of the man's action, while B and C both refer to strong positive emotions or to admirable qualities, NOT to a physical movement.

10. C is the correct answer.

In line 81, "concern" refers to the larger entity of which the publishing department forms a part; here, the man is talking about a line of work. Choose C to reflect this content; all of the other answers are illogical within the scope of the passage. A (indicating information), B (indicating an event), and D (indicating a passion or mission) are not effective choices to reflect the straightforward context of employment.

Passage 2, Pages 221-223

11. C is the correct answer.

In lines 28-31, Goldman describes how masculine control over property and domestic life means that wives eventually lose their autonomy and independence. This content best supports C. A can be rejected since Goldman does NOT discuss whether men acknowledge or ignore the impact of societal expectations for women, while B can be rejected because Goldman suggests that the suppression of female agency and curiosity happens organically as a result of domestic life, NOT through deliberate effort on the part of men. D can be rejected since Goldman does not discuss whether men are appreciative or not, and implies that even if a man were to appreciate the domestic labor of his wife, this labor would still be damaging to her.

12. C is the correct answer.

See the previous answer explanation for analysis of the correct line reference. A asks a rhetorical question in order to imply that women grow up with the cultural expectation of eventually becoming wives and mothers, while B notes that if a woman has to both work outside of the home and also handle all of the housework, she is likely to be unsatisfied with her quality of life. D argues that after only a short period of being confined entirely to the domestic world, women become incapable of thriving in the wider world. None of these other answers discuss how men's power over domestic life impacts female independence, and therefore they should all be dismissed.

13. <u>A</u> is the correct answer.

In line 33, "driving" is used in the context of a man reacting to perceived negative qualities in his wife by leaving the house and thus refers to alienating or pushing someone away. Choose A to reflect this meaning. B (inappropriately implying deliberate control and strategy), C (inappropriately referring to transmitting or passing on knowledge), and D (implying encouragement) all introduce improper contexts and should thus be eliminated.

14. <u>D</u> is the correct answer.

In lines 45 and 48, "function" refers to the possible purpose or use of a home and thus indicates the intended goal of something. Choose D to reflect this meaning. A (inappropriately referring to a singular, clearly defined occurrence), B (inappropriately implying leisure or pleasure), and C (implying the way in which something is organized or constructed) all introduce improper contexts and should thus be eliminated.

15. <u>C</u> is the correct answer.

In lines 57-58, Tarbell laments that there are men and women who feel no emotional connection to their family and domestic life, being preoccupied instead with labor and a sense of drudgery. This exclamation shows Tarbell's focus on an area of chief concern in the passage; choose C to support this content. A can be dismissed since Tarbell does NOT believe that this state of emotional disconnection is a reality for many or most women, while B can be rejected since the exclamation identifies a social problem rather than responding to a specific proposal. D can be rejected since the exclamation reflects a topic that Tarbell wants to address, NOT a response to the way in which she addresses it.

16. <u>B</u> is the correct answer.

In the final paragraph of the passage, Tarbell offers a summary of the responsibilities and power involved in running a home, and reflects admiringly on how important women's role as the center of home life is. Choose B to reflect this content. A can be rejected since Tarbell clearly feels that women already occupy a dominant position within the domestic world, while C can be rejected since Tarbell does not discuss male qualities or responsibilities within this portion of the passage. D can be rejected since Tarbell's remarks here are general and relevant to an entire gender, NOT specific and relevant mainly to one household.

17. <u>A</u> is the correct answer.

Both Goldman and Tarbell address the way in which labor can be emotionally and mentally taxing: Goldman compares domestic life to an extension of the oppressive labor involved in working life while Tarbell favorably contrasts the domestic world with the soul-crushing realities of labor. Choose A to reflect this content. B can be eliminated since neither Goldman nor Tarbell spends much time discussing the ideal way to organize domestic life, while C can be rejected since Goldman and Tarbell appear to have sharply divergent views on how women should approach social and political reform. D can also be eliminated since neither passage explores how men feel about domestic labor.

18. <u>D</u> is the correct answer.

Both Goldman and Tarbell seek to answer the question of whether or not women are intellectually and emotionally fulfilled by domestic life, even though these authors arrive at opposite answers. Choose D to support this content. A and C can both be eliminated since neither passage offers a historical perspective or a contrast between past and present (as opposed to analysis mainly of present circumstances), while B must be eliminated since there is not consensus between the passages as to whether or not women are actually disadvantaged.

19. <u>D</u> is the correct answer.

In line 52, Tarbell describes "man" as a figure oppressed by current economic systems and required to focus all his attention on his working life. Goldman, although more interested in describing what happens to women after they marry, also sees current labor conditions as oppressive to both men and women and would therefore likely see Tarbell's description as generally accurate. Choose D to reflect this content. A can be rejected since both Tarbell and Goldman take the oppression created by current labor conditions quite seriously, while B can be eliminated since Tarbell's description reveals someone who is victimized, not someone who is in a position of power or authority. C can also be rejected since Goldman does not present a perspective that construes current labor conditions as in the process of rapid change, despite her overall interest in labor-related problems.

20. <u>B</u> is the correct answer.

In lines 75-77, Tarbell argues that women hold a significant degree of authority and autonomy within domestic life, functioning as the primary decision makers about questions related to the home. This content suggests that she would disagree with Goldman's premise that women lack authority within the domestic sphere; choose B to reflect this content. A can be rejected since neither passage gives a chronological explanation of social progress, while C can be eliminated since Tarbell does NOT discuss in detail the economic implications of domestic life. D can also be ruled out since Goldman does NOT necessarily assume that women are resigned to their roles, and Tarbell does not contradict this assumption directly.

21. <u>D</u> is the correct answer.

See the previous answer explanation for analysis of the correct line reference. A contrasts the moral and emotional purpose of a home with a strictly materialist view, while B laments how some types of men and women misunderstand the purpose and function of a home. C underscores Tarbell's view of how destructive it would be to give in to a viewpoint that does not celebrate the significance of domestic life. None of these other line references challenge Goldman's view that women lack authority within the domestic world, and therefore they can all be dismissed.

Passage 3, Pages 224-227

22. B is the correct answer.

In lines 4-5, the author refers to "a new study by the U.S. Geological Survey," indicating access to specialized knowledge. Throughout the passage, the author maintains an objective and factual tone, indicating an unbiased perspective; choose B to support this content. A can be eliminated since the author never refers to having personally conducted any research; C and D can also be eliminated, since while the author quotes a researcher who expresses concern about "losing reef structures that took thousands of years to build" (lines 86-88), it does NOT necessarily follow that the author is personally unsettled by the crisis or seeking a solution to it.

23. B is the correct answer.

Lines 76-79 explain that "warmer water, coral diseases, bleaching, and other stresses caused the reefs to begin eroding." This information indicates that a change in water temperature is one of several factors that can decrease reef size; choose B to support this content. C can be dismissed as illogical, since the passage indicates that changes in water temperature contribute to reef erosion, NOT that they counteract it. A and D can also be eliminated as outside of the scope of the passage, since these answers do not reflect that the passage considers temperature changes in the context of coral reef growth and AVOIDS discussion of temperature change on its own.

24. D is the correct answer.

See the previous answer explanation for analysis of the correct line reference. A summarizes the finding of a study indicating that the Florida Keys Reef is no longer growing, while B describes the relationship between changing water temperatures and the growth of the reef. C gives a more detailed description of how colder water temperatures impacted reef growth. While some of these other answers discuss a connection between water temperature and a lack of growth, none of these answers address the connection between water temperature and an existing reef decreasing in size. Therefore, all other answers should be eliminated.

25. B is the correct answer.

In line 7, "points to" refers to how specific occurrences (bleaching and disease outbreaks) signify a larger condition (a state of erosion). Choose B to reflect this meaning. A (inappropriately implying a subtle or unstated connection), C (inappropriately implying a personalized statement of blame), and D (inappropriately implying the introduction of prejudice or shame) all introduce improper contexts and should thus be eliminated.

26. D is the correct answer.

The passage indicates that "marine scientists based in St. Petersburg, Florida analyzed 46 coral reef cores collected throughout the Keys, reconstructing the reefs' growth from 8000 years ago, when layers of living coral began building up on top of older bedrock, to the present day" (lines 11-16). A 9000 year-old coral specimen falls outside this range and would be unlikely to be present; choose D to support this content. A, B, and C all describe specimens that fall within a range in which coral specimens were known to exist.

27. <u>A</u> is the correct answer.

See the previous answer explanation for analysis of the correct line reference. B describes the likely age of a coral specimen from the reef's top layer, while C describes a shift in the reef's growth and expansion. D describes the ideal water temperature in which coral can thrive. None of these other answers identify why a 9000 year-old specimen would NOT be found in the reef, and all should be dismissed.

28. <u>A</u> is the correct answer.

In line 46, "peaked" refers to the moment at which the growth rate reached its maximum pace, after which it started to decline. Choose A to reflect this meaning. B (inappropriately implying negative connotations associated with the rate of growth), C (inappropriately implying a personal reaction to the rate), and D (inappropriately implying that certain types of measurement were not possible) all introduce improper contexts and should thus be eliminated.

29. <u>B</u> is the correct answer.

While some might assume that a coral reef stops thriving after it stops growing, the passage describes how "Even after the Keys reefs stopped growing upward, they supported diverse communities of marine life, protected the island chain from storm waves and erosion, and provided other ecosystem functions for thousands of years" (lines 72-76). The reef made valuable ecological contributions even while no longer growing; choose B to reflect this content. Since the focus here is on the period of reef non-growth, NOT reef deterioration, A can be eliminated. C and D can be eliminated since the focus here is on factual description, not expressions of rhetoric or emotion that involve strong and critical negative tones.

30. <u>C</u> is the correct answer.

The table indicates that the growth rate of the coral reef declined steadily beginning 7000 years ago, while the chart indicates that in the period between 6000 and 3000 years ago, water temperatures remained fairly stable. The combination of this data indicates that reef growth can decline even when water temperature remains steady; choose C to support this content. D can be eliminated as illogical, since the table indicates decline in growth rates rather than increase. A and B can also be eliminated since the additional data sources do NOT offer details of erosion rates or overall reef size.

31. <u>B</u> is the correct answer.

The passage indicates that the reef's "growth rate . . . peaked about 7000 years ago, when water temperatures were ideal for coral growth" (lines 45-48), while the chart indicates that 7000 years ago, the average water temperature was around 75 degrees. Choose B to support this content. While A, C, and D all indicate temperatures that fall within a range of ideal temperatures for coral growth, none of these other answers reflect temperatures aligned with the average temperature 7000 years ago.

32. <u>B</u> is the correct answer.

In the final paragraph, Toth refers to "dramatic declines in living coral," and this claim could best be evaluated if data were provided to show rates of reef erosion over time. Choose B to support this content. Be careful not to choose A since changes in reef size are not only attributable to erosion and decline. C and D can be eliminated since growth rates and measurements of dead coral do NOT help to measure declines.

Passage 4, Pages 228-230

33. <u>D</u> is the correct answer.

The author begins the passage by describing "many things to be hopeful for" (lines 1-2) and listing the extent of endeavors to control malaria, but then shifts to acknowledging that "the current situation is complex" (lines 16-17) and assessing the WHO World Malaria Report. Choose D to support this content. B can be eliminated since the passage begins with content that emphasizes events, NOT statistics, and C can be eliminated since the author does not encourage the initial figures and organizations to take more responsibility (as opposed to recording results). Be careful not to choose A, since the opening section describes potentially useful interventions but NOT long-term solutions.

34. <u>C</u> is the correct answer.

In lines 45-49, the author refers to how "relying on the potential of new technologies has led to disappointment in the past," a statement which indicates that previous attempts at malaria control have apparently been inadequate. Choose C to support this content. A offers a critique of report methodology while B expands on this critique to explain the problems created by inconsistent methodology. D articulates an argument about which measures will actually effectively combat malaria. None of these other answers give the author's perspective on previous malaria control attempts, and they should all be eliminated.

35. <u>C</u> is the correct answer.

In lines 27-29, the author uses a parenthetical statement to expand an initial critique. The initial critique notes that the 2017 case burden estimate has been revised while the expanded critique refers to the case burden estimate for 2010 having now been revised seven times. Choose C to support this content. A and B can be eliminated since the critique is related to reporting, NOT related to fundraising, and the parenthetical statement communicates new information, NOT the same information in a new way. D can be eliminated since the statement does not involve paraphrase and in fact presents new information.

36. <u>C</u> is the correct answer.

In lines 37-42, the author explains that "Five sub-Saharan countries . . . have seen a significant decrease in malaria prevalence . . . during the 2017 season, whereas 24 high-burden countries saw increases in malaria."

Evidence indicating that rates have risen in some countries would support this claim; choose C to support this content. A, B, and D present specific data related to The Gambia, and therefore would not support arguments about BROADER malarial trends.

37. <u>A</u> is the correct answer.

In lines 58 and 61, "basic" refers to malarial control measures that are essential and highly functional. Choose A to reflect this meaning. B (inappropriately implying a lack of sophistication or refinement), C (inappropriately implying a lack of artificial intervention), and D (inappropriately implying that these measures contribute to further development) all introduce improper contexts and should thus be eliminated.

38. <u>B</u> is the correct answer.

In line 58, "suppress" refers to control measures for preventing malaria transmission. Choose B to reflect this meaning. A (inappropriately implying hiding or lying), C (inappropriately implying inconvenience), and D (inappropriately implying soothing action) all introduce improper contexts and should thus be eliminated.

39. <u>D</u> is the correct answer.

In lines 78-82, the author argues that "Policymakers and intervention forces would be well advised to adopt quickly some of the lessons learned in The Gambia," implying that the author views The Gambia as a country whose model of malaria prevention should be adopted by other countries. Choose D to support this content. A and B can both be eliminated since there is no discussion of political circumstances, weather, or climate conditions in The Gambia. C can be eliminated since the focus is on prevention, NOT documentation.

40. <u>D</u> is the correct answer.

See the previous answer explanation for analysis of the correct line reference. A reports a malaria rate in The Gambia at a previous point in time, while B summarizes the range of shifts in malaria rates in different countries and C describes how some countries are noted for their severely limited reporting mechanisms. None of these other answers DIRECTLY reflect how the author characterizes The Gambia, and therefore all should be eliminated.

41. <u>A</u> is the correct answer.

The two graphs show that, between 2015 and 2016, investments in efforts to combat malaria increased, but that during the same period the number of worldwide cases increased. This situation indicates that increased annual investment does not necessarily correlate to a decreasing number of cases; choose A to support this content. B and D can be eliminated since the graphs do not provide data related to specific outbreaks, only to overall annual case numbers. Be careful not to choose C since in most, but not ALL, years increased investment was associated with a lower number of cases.

42. <u>B</u> is the correct answer.

In lines 63-65, the author explains that "providing such access to the 3.4 billion people globally at risk for malaria will cost more than even Bill Gates can afford." This statement indicates that personal contributions by Gates represent only a percentage of the total budget for intervention; choose B to support this content. A, C, and D can all be eliminated since the graph does not provide information about Gates's interventions as inspirations for other contributions, about long-term initiatives, or about the allocation of his contributions; however, raw funding numbers ARE addressed in both the passage and the graph.

Passage 5, Pages 231-223

43. <u>A</u> is the correct answer.

The passage focuses on describing how "a manufacturer of iconic, household plasticware is helping provide fresh food in space" (lines 3-5). Choose A to support this content. B can be dismissed since there is no discussion of new space missions in the passage, and C can be eliminated since the initiative was led by a single company, not a cross-industry collaboration. D can also be eliminated, since the project did not involve re-purposing specific existing items, as opposed to ADAPTING a signature technology.

44. <u>A</u> is the correct answer.

In lines 21-24, the author describes how "In previous crops grown in the Veggie system using pillows, some plants fared better than others because not all the plants received equal amounts of water and oxygen." This information indicates that plants were receiving inconsistent levels of nutrients and did not flourish equally; choose A to support this content. B and C can be dismissed since the passage does not discuss issues with flooding, or choosing specific plant species. Be careful not to choose D, since while the passage does discuss unequal distribution of resources, it does NOT discuss microgravity as a source of this inequality.

45. <u>B</u> is the correct answer.

See the previous answer explanation for analysis of the correct line reference. A describes a previously existing growing system, while C describes how Tupperware came to be tasked with developing a replacement technology and D describes how the new PONDS system functions. None of these other answers describe the problems that PONDS was designed to solve, and therefore all should be eliminated.

46. <u>D</u> is the correct answer.

In lines 9-13, the passage indicates that the Veggie system has allowed astronauts to eat fresh vegetables. Lines 64-68 describe a specific vegetable product produced by the PONDS system that will be available to astronauts; choose D to support this content. A names the corporation that collaborated on the project, while

B features an expert explaining the benefits of the PONDS system. C describes the outcome of the project. None of these other answers support the claim about the benefits of eating fresh vegetables in space, and all should be eliminated.

47. C is the correct answer.

In addition to indicating the health benefits of eating fresh vegetables, the passage examines "the psychological benefits of growing plants" (lines 8-9). Choose C to support this content. A and B can be eliminated since there is no discussion of plants growing at different rates, or of filtering oxygen from other gases. D can also be eliminated since the passage addresses technologies that were designed specifically for outer-space use.

48. B is the correct answer.

In line 33, "handed it off" refers to how a NASA research scientist transferred responsibility for a project to someone else. Choose B to reflect this meaning. A (inappropriately implying that the other party did not want to accept the project), C (inappropriately implying giving the other party a choice about whether to accept the project), and D (inappropriately implying abandoning responsibility) all introduce improper contexts and should thus be eliminated.

49. A is the correct answer.

In line 49, "evenly" refers to water being distributed at a steady and uniform rate. Choose A to reflect this meaning. B (inappropriately implying a particular emotional state), C (inappropriately implying personal effort), and D (inappropriately implying justice and equity) all introduce improper contexts and should thus be eliminated.

50. C is the correct answer.

The passage describes how the PONDS system "requires less crew maintenance" (lines 44-45) and facilitates "consistent seed germination and seedling development into mature plants" (lines 51-52). Choose C to support this content. A and B can be eliminated since there is no discussion of cost or required training in the passage, while D can be eliminated since the passage suggests that the same plants will be grown in the new system, NOT that new, larger plants will be grown.

51. D is the correct answer.

In lines 58-60, Reed is quoted as saying that "Tupperware brings a wealth of innovative design and knowledge of plastics to this project." This statement implies that Reed sees the specialists at Tupperware as insightful collaborators; choose D to support this content. A and C can be eliminated since Tupperware is presented as working equally towards shared goals, not as competing with or being subordinate to Techshot. Be careful not to choose B, since Reed's recognition of the Tupperware team members does NOT necessarily imply that they are under-appreciated and thus need more recognition for their work.

52. <u>B</u> is the correct answer.

The final paragraph describes future plans for how "the plant pillow and PONDS growth data will be compared against one another" (lines 81-83). This information indicates that PONDS will be used to build upon existing plant growth technologies; choose B to support this content. A and C can be eliminated since the final paragraph does not offer any risks associated with the Veggie system or recommended changes to astronaut diet. D can also be eliminated since there is no discussion of plans for future collaborations, as opposed to future launches and observations.

NOTES

- Passage 3 on Pages 224-225, "Florida's Coral Reefs Provide Window into the Past," is adapted from the article of the same name published by the United States Geological Survey. 23 October 2018, USGS. https://www.usgs.gov/news/floridas-coral-reefs-provide-window-past. Accessed 7 January 2019.

- Passage 4 on Pages 228-229, "Optimism, But Obstacles Abound for the Future of Malaria Control," is adapted from the article of the same name published by Speaking of Medicine, a PLOS community blog. 26 April 2018, the PLOS Blogs Network. https://blogs.plos.org/speakingofmedicine/2018/04/25/optimism-but-obstacles-abound-for-the-future-of-malaria-control/. Accessed 7 January 2019.

- Passage 5 on Page 231, "Tupperware Takes to Space to Help Improve Astronaut Diets," is adapted from the article of the same name published by NASA. 29 March 2018, NASA.gov. https://www.nasa.gov/feature/tupperware-takes-to-space-to-help-improve-astronaut-diets. Accessed 7 January 2019.

Additional Content
Checklists and Citations

Fiction Checklist
Main Issue Strategy

Can you identify the following elements as they appear in the passage?

Important Characters

Character 1: _____ ; Role/Traits: _____
_____

Character 2: _____ ; Role/Traits: _____
_____

Character 3: _____ ; Role/Traits: _____
_____

Character 4: _____ ; Role/Traits: _____
_____

Overall Issues

Setting: _____

Shifts in Tone or Topic: 1: _____ ➡ _____

2: _____ ➡ _____

Structure: _____

Themes: 1. _____ 2. _____

3. _____ 4. _____

Social Studies Checklist
Main Issue Strategy

Can you identify the following elements as they appear in the passage?

Overall Content

Core Topic or Question: _____

Source/Study 1: _____; Position: _____
Evidence/Support: _____

Source/Study 2: _____; Position: _____
Evidence/Support: _____

Source/Study 3: _____; Position: _____
Evidence/Support: _____

Author: _____; Position: _____
Evidence/Support: _____

Overall Issues

Thesis: _____

Conclusive: ___ or Inconclusive: ___ and WHY: _____

Shifts in Tone or Topic: 1: _____ ➡ _____

2: _____ ➡ _____

Structure: _____

Visuals Summary: _____

Visuals Related to Passage: _____

Science Checklist
Main Issue Strategy

Can you identify the following elements as they appear in the passage?

Inquiry or Issue

Core Topic: _____ Core Question: _____

Source 1: _____; Hypothesis: _____

Source 2: _____; Hypothesis: _____

Other Hypotheses: _____

Research and Experiments

Method 1: _____

Outcome 1: _____ Conclusion 1: _____

Method 2: _____

Outcome 2: _____ Conclusion 2: _____

Broad Outcomes: _____

Overall Issues

Shifts in Tone or Topic: 1: _____ ➡ _____

2: _____ ➡ _____

Structure: _____

Visuals Summary: _____

Visuals Related to Passage: _____

History Checklist
Main Issue Strategy

Can you identify the following elements as they appear in the passage?

Main Idea

Core Topic: _____

Author's Position: _____

Author's Purpose: _____

....

Author's Argument

Reason 1: _____ Tone: _____

Reason 2: _____ Tone: _____

Reason 3: _____ Tone: _____

Opponent 1: _____ Idea: _____ Flaw: _____

Opponent 2: _____ Idea: _____ Flaw: _____

....

Passage Organization

Shifts in Tone or Topic: 1: _____ ➡ _____

2: _____ ➡ _____

3: _____ ➡ _____

Structure: _____

Main Writing Techniques: _____

Science Pairing
Passage Strategy

Can you identify and compare the main elements of the two passages?

Passage 1

Inquiry/Issue: _____
_____

Hypothesis 1: _____
_____

Hypothesis 2: _____
_____

Method 1: _____
Outcome 1: _____

Method 2: _____
Outcome 2: _____

Shifts: _____ ➡ _____

Final Outcomes: _____
_____

Passage 2

Inquiry/Issue: _____
_____

Hypothesis 1: _____
_____

Hypothesis 2: _____
_____

Method 1: _____
Outcome 1: _____

Method 2: _____
Outcome 2: _____

Shifts: _____ ➡ _____

Final Outcomes: _____
_____

Passage Comparison

Core Relationship: _____

Points of Similarity: _____

Present ONLY in Passage 1: _____

Present ONLY in Passage 2: _____

History Pairing
Passage Strategy

Can you identify and compare the main elements of the two passages?

Passage 1

Core Topic: _____

_____

Author's Position: _____

_____

Reason 1: _____

_____

Reason 2: _____

_____

Opponents: _____

_____

Shifts: _____ ➡ _____

Techniques: _____

Passage 2

Core Topic: _____

_____

Author's Position: _____

_____

Reason 1: _____

_____

Reason 2: _____

_____

Opponents: _____

_____

Shifts: _____ ➡ _____

Techniques: _____

Passage Comparison

Core Relationship: _____

Points of Similarity: _____

Present ONLY in Passage 1: _____

Present ONLY in Passage 2: _____

Fiction Checklist
Main Issue Strategy

Can you identify the following elements as they appear in the passage?

Important Characters

Character 1: _____ ; Role/Traits: _____
_____

Character 2: _____ ; Role/Traits: _____
_____

Character 3: _____ ; Role/Traits: _____
_____

Character 4: _____ ; Role/Traits: _____
_____

Overall Issues

Setting: _____

Shifts in Tone or Topic: 1: _____ ➤ _____

2: _____ ➤ _____

Structure: _____

Themes: 1. _____ 2. _____

3. _____ 4. _____

Social Studies Checklist
Main Issue Strategy

Can you identify the following elements as they appear in the passage?

Overall Content

Core Topic or Question: _____

Source/Study 1: _____; Position: _____
Evidence/Support: _____

Source/Study 2: _____; Position: _____
Evidence/Support: _____

Source/Study 3: _____; Position: _____
Evidence/Support: _____

Author: _____; Position: _____
Evidence/Support: _____

Overall Issues

Thesis: _____

Conclusive: ___ or Inconclusive: ___ and WHY: _____

Shifts in Tone or Topic: 1: _____ ➡ _____

2: _____ ➡ _____

Structure: _____

Visuals Summary: _____

Visuals Related to Passage: _____

Science Checklist
Main Issue Strategy

Can you identify the following elements as they appear in the passage?

Inquiry or Issue

Core Topic: _____ Core Question: _____

Source 1: _____ ; Hypothesis: _____

Source 2: _____ ; Hypothesis: _____

Other Hypotheses: _____

. . . .

Research and Experiments

Method 1: _____

Outcome 1: _____ Conclusion 1: _____

Method 2: _____

Outcome 2: _____ Conclusion 2: _____

Broad Outcomes: _____

Overall Issues

Shifts in Tone or Topic: 1: _____ ⟹ _____

2: _____ ⟹ _____

Structure: _____

Visuals Summary: _____

Visuals Related to Passage: _____

History Checklist
Main Issue Strategy

Can you identify the following elements as they appear in the passage?

Main Idea

Core Topic: _____

Author's Position: _____

Author's Purpose: _____

Author's Argument

Reason 1: _____ Tone: _____

Reason 2: _____ Tone: _____

Reason 3: _____ Tone: _____

Opponent 1: _____ Idea: _____ Flaw: _____

Opponent 2: _____ Idea: _____ Flaw: _____

Passage Organization

Shifts in Tone or Topic: 1: _____➡_____

2: _____➡_____

3: _____➡_____

Structure: _____

Main Writing Techniques: _____

Science Pairing
Passage Strategy

Can you identify and compare the main elements of the two passages?

Passage 1

Inquiry/Issue: _____

_____

Hypothesis 1: _____

_____

Hypothesis 2: _____

_____

Method 1: _____
Outcome 1: _____

Method 2: _____
Outcome 2: _____

Shifts: _____ ➡ _____

Final Outcomes: _____

_____

Passage 2

Inquiry/Issue: _____

_____

Hypothesis 1: _____

_____

Hypothesis 2: _____

_____

Method 1: _____
Outcome 1: _____

Method 2: _____
Outcome 2: _____

Shifts: _____ ➡ _____

Final Outcomes: _____

_____

Passage Comparison

Core Relationship: _____

Points of Similarity: _____

Present ONLY in Passage 1: _____

Present ONLY in Passage 2: _____

History Pairing
Passage Strategy

Can you identify and compare the main elements of the two passages?

Passage 1

Core Topic: _____
_____

Author's Position: _____
_____

Reason 1: _____
_____

Reason 2: _____
_____

Opponents: _____
_____

Shifts: _____ ➡ _____

Techniques: _____

Passage 2

Core Topic: _____
_____

Author's Position: _____
_____

Reason 1: _____
_____

Reason 2: _____
_____

Opponents: _____
_____

Shifts: _____ ➡ _____

Techniques: _____

Passage Comparison

Core Relationship: _____

Points of Similarity: _____

Present ONLY in Passage 1: _____

Present ONLY in Passage 2: _____

Appendix B: Passage Citations

Readings: Main Issue and Passage Details

Citations

- Passage 2 on Pages 49, 86, and 174 (in the Visuals section), "Game Corrects Children's Misreading of Emotional Faces to Tame Irritability," is adapted from the article of the same name published by the National Institute of Mental Health. 22 June 2016, NIMH. https://www.nimh.nih.gov/news/science-news/2016/game-corrects-childrens-misreading-of-emotional-faces-to-tame-irritability.shtml. Accessed 7 January 2019.

- Passage 3 on Pages 55 and 88, "A New Fossil Lace Bug with Unusual Antennae Joins the 'Big' Club," is adapted from the article of the same name published by EveryOne, the PLOS One community blog. 18 December 2015, PLOS Blogs Network. https://blogs.plos.org/everyone/2015/12/18/a-new-fossil-lace-bug-with-unusual-antennae-joins-the-big-club/. Accessed 7 January 2019.

- Passage 6 on Pages 66-67 and 94-95, "The Dreams Ideas Are Made Of," is adapted from the article of the same name published by Inventors Eye. August 2014, United States Patent and Trademark Office. https://www.uspto.gov/inventors/independent/eye/201408/index.jsp#ieye-article1. Accessed 7 January 2019.

- Passage 7 on Pages 68-69, 96-97, and 176-177 (in the Visuals section), "NIH researchers discover highly infectious vehicle for transmission of viruses among humans," is adapted from the article of the same name published by the National Institutes of Health. 8 August 2018, NIH. https://www.nih.gov/news-events/news-releases/nih-researchers-discover-highly-infectious-vehicle-transmission-viruses-among-humans. Accessed 7 January 2019.

Readings: Command of Evidence and Word in Context

Citations

- Passage 2 on Pages 112-113 and 134-135, "Creativity Connects: Trends and Conditions Affecting U.S. Artists," is adapted from the article of the same name published by the Center for Cultural Innovation, National Endowment for the Arts. September 2016, NEA. https://www.arts.gov/sites/default/files/Creativity-Connects-Final-Report.pdf. Accessed 7 January 2019.

- Passage 4 on Pages 116-117 and 138-139, "What in the World Is an Exoplanet?," is adapted from the article of the same name published by NASA. 12 April 2018, NASA.gov. https://www.nasa.gov/feature/jpl/what-in-the-world-is-an-exoplanet. Accessed 7 January 2019.

- Passage 6 on Pages 120-121, 142-143, and 178-179 (in the Visuals section), "Linking Isolated Languages: Linguistic Relationships of the Carabayo," is adapted from the article of the same name published by EveryOne, the PLOS One community blog. 28 April 2014, PLOS Blogs Network. https://blogs.plos.org/everyone/2014/04/28/linking-isolated-languages-linguistic-relationships-carabayo/. Accessed 7 January 2019.

- Passage 7 on Pages 122-123 and 144-145, "Fruit Fly Mating Driven by a Tweak in a Specific Brain Circuit," is adapted from the article of the same name published by the National Institutes of Health. 16 July 2018, NIH.https://www.nih.gov/news-events/news-releases/fruit-fly-mating-driven-tweak-specific-brain-circuit. Accessed 7 January 2019.

Readings: Paired Passages

Citations

- Reading 1, Passage 1 on Pages 156 and 181 (in the Visuals section), "New 3D Measurements Improve Understanding of Geomagnetic Storm Hazards," is adapted from the article of the same name published by the United States Geological Survey. 8 March 2018, USGS. https://www.usgs.gov/news/new-3d-measurements-improve-understanding-geomagnetic-storm-hazards. Accessed 7 January 2019.

- Reading 1, Passage 2 on Pages 156 and 181 (in the Visuals section), "Preparing the Nation for Intense Space Weather," is adapted from the article of the same name published by the United States Geological Survey. 1 May 2017, USGS. https://www.usgs.gov/news/preparing-nation-intense-space-weather. Accessed 7 January 2019.

- Reading 3, Passage 1 on Page 161, "Could sleepless nights of terror be good for you?," is adapted from the article of the same name published by EveryOne, the PLOS One community blog. 24 October 2012, PLOS Blogs Network. https://blogs.plos.org/everyone/2012/10/24/could-sleepless-nights-of-terror-be-good-for-you/. Accessed 7 January 2019.

- Reading 3, Passage 2 on Pages 161-162, "Does poor sleep raise risk for Alzheimer's disease?," is adapted from the article of the same name published by the National Institute on Aging. 29 February 2016, NIH. https://www.nia.nih.gov/news/does-poor-sleep-raise-risk-alzheimers-disease. Accessed 7 January 2019.

Please note that the visual evidence designed to accompany these passages and others in this book is designed to test critical thinking skills and may not reflect historical data as a consequence of this intent.

For additional readings and relevant practice exercises please visit **prepvantagetutoring.com/reading**.

Made in the USA
San Bernardino, CA
04 January 2020